BOSTON UNIVERSITY
African Research Studies
Number Five

THE FAMILY ESTATE IN AFRICA

Contributors:

ROBERT F. GRAY

E. V. WINANS

ROBERT A. LeVINE

IGOR KOPYTOFF

ALFRED AND GRACE HARRIS

EILEEN JENSEN KRIGE

P. H. GULLIVER

THE FAMILY ESTATE IN AFRICA

Studies in the Role of Property in Family Structure and Lineage Continuity

Edited by
Robert F. Gray and P. H. Gulliver

African Studies Program
Boston University

BOSTON UNIVERSITY PRESS
1964

© Robert F. Gray and P. H. Gulliver 1964

Published in Great Britain by
Routledge and Kegan Paul Ltd, London

Printed in Great Britain

Library of Congress Catalog Card Number: 64-19442

Distributed by
New York University Press
Washington Square
New York, New York 10003

CONTENTS

INTRODUCTION Robert F. Gray	page 1
THE SHAMBALA FAMILY E. V. Winans, *Ph.D. (California)*	35
THE GUSII FAMILY Robert A. LeVine, *Ph.D.(Harvard)*	63
FAMILY AND LINEAGE AMONG THE SUKU OF THE CONGO Igor Kopytoff, *Ph.D. (Northwestern)*	83
PROPERTY AND THE CYCLE OF DOMESTIC GROUPS IN TAITA Alfred Harris, *Ph.D. (Cantab)* and Grace Harris *Ph.D. (Cantab)*	117
PROPERTY, CROSS-COUSIN MARRIAGE, AND THE FAMILY CYCLE AMONG THE LOBEDU Eileen Jensen Krige, *D.Litt. (Witwatersrand)*	155
THE ARUSHA FAMILY P. H. Gulliver, *Ph.D. (London)*	197
SONJO LINEAGE STRUCTURE AND PROPERTY Robert F. Gray, *Ph.D.(Chicago)*	231
INDEX	263

v

INTRODUCTION

Robert F. Gray

THE essays in this book deal with certain aspects of family life in seven societies of eastern and central Africa. In planning the symposium the writers came to an agreement to analyse and present their material from a viewpoint which would stress these two aspects of the family: (1) the attachment of the family to property and resources, and (2) the developmental aspect or the time dimension.

The study of these aspects is not new in anthropology, and we do not claim to be introducing original concepts or methods. On the contrary, we agreed to recognize as specific prototypes of our symposium two works previously published. The first is an analysis by P. H. Gulliver of two societies of East Africa, the Jie of Uganda and the Turkana of Kenya.[1] The author traces in detail the social transactions concerning livestock, demonstrating clearly that domestic animals serve as foci of social rights and obligations, as indices of social relationships. This pioneer study provided us with a working hypothesis. These two societies are predominantly pastoral, the Turkana almost exclusively so, while the seven societies described in the present book are predominantly agricultural, though livestock are also quite important in some of them. The hypothesis is that in these societies other forms of property are foci of social rights and obligations just as livestock are for the Jie and Turkana. Our task, then, was to test this hypothesis and determine in each case the social role of different forms of property.

Gulliver in his book also analyses the process of family development, giving emphasis to the temporal aspect, which is our second special concern. He recognizes that social and

[1] Gulliver, 1955.

property relationships and the interaction between them are not static but are in constant change. 'Where kinship relations are also, and importantly, property relations, a change in the former necessarily causes a redistribution and redefinition of the latter. This is a constant process in both societies.'[1]

There appeared subsequently a volume of Cambridge studies, edited by Jack Goody,[2] devoted to the analysis of the time factor in the life of domestic groups. We are all greatly indebted to this thoughtful book, particularly the essays dealing with African societies, in which the material is more comparable to our own material, and the introduction by Meyer Fortes. Our book, however, does not cover exactly the same ground. It lays greater stress on property than the Cambridge volume, while on the other hand it neglects one of the major theoretical problems dealt with by the latter: namely, the relation between the family group and society at large, or, as Fortes phrases it, the 'domestic domain' and the 'politico-jural domain'.[3]

Thus the unity of this book derives from a common subject matter and background of ideas and an agreement to narrow our treatment to the two aspects of society stated above. By consciously focusing on these two aspects in combination, we believe that our understanding of family processes in general, and more specifically the African family, will be furthered. In the rest of this introductory chapter I shall discuss these guiding ideas and some of their implications, and indicate some of the results of their application.

The Family

Nearly all students agree that the family—the principal focus of the studies in this book—is in some way or other a fundamental unit of society. At first glance, the natural existence of the family, apparently derived from the biology of human reproduction, seems to be self-evident. But when the family is examined critically by anthropologists as a social institution, doubts arise as to its nature and composition, and even its universal existence. Thus, according to Evans-Pritchard, the family should not be considered a 'structural

[1] *Ibid.*, p. 4.   [2] Goody, 1958.   [3] Fortes, 1958, p. 6.

INTRODUCTION

group'. Referring to his own definition of social structure, he states:

> In this definition of structure the family is not considered a structural group, because families have no consistent and constant interrelations as groups and they disappear at the deaths of their members.[1]

The general concept of 'social structure' will be discussed later. Here I only wish to call attention to Evans-Pritchard's view of the family as something that is not static or permanent.

Meyer Fortes, in his introduction to the Cambridge studies, mentioned above, avoids dealing directly with the 'family' as such, but merges it into a new concept which he calls the 'domestic domain' of society, and which he differentiates from the 'politico-jural domain'. The domestic domain is defined as 'the system of social relations through which the reproductive nucleus is integrated with the environment and with the structure of the total society'.[2]

In his book *Social Structure*, G. P. Murdock characterizes the nuclear family as 'a universal human grouping'.[3] Since the reasons for the universality of the family may not be readily apparent, he explains that:

> Only when it is analysed into its constituent relationships, and these are examined individually as well as collectively, does one gain an adequate conception of the family's many-sided utility and thus its inevitability.[4]

In an article published ten years later, Murdock concedes that the nuclear family appears to be lacking in several societies.[5]

The conventional conception of 'the family' is severely criticized by Levy and Fallers on somewhat different grounds: they feel that 'the concept as it is most often used is ill-adapted to comparative analysis'.[6] In their view, the most significant attributes of what is commonly thought of as the 'family' are certain social functions of which the most important is the socialization function.

---

[1] Evans-Pritchard, 1940, p. 262. [2] Fortes, 1958, p. 9.
[3] Murdock, 1949, p. 2. [4] *Ibid.*, p. 3.
[5] Murdock, 1959, p. 140. [6] Levy and Fallers, 1959, p. 647.

This being so, we suggest that the concept 'family', to be useful for general comparative purposes, should be used to refer not to a single social unit in each society, but rather to any small, kinship-structured unit which carries out aspects of the relevant functions.[1]

And so we could go on; but this, I think, is a fair sampling of current anthropological views of the family. If these views are combined, the composite picture of the family that we come out with is something like this: an ephemeral, non-structural group; located in the domestic domain of society, which comprises a system of integrating relations; almost universal by virtue of the utility of its constituent relationships; variable in composition, and defined by aspects of certain functions which it serves. As a working definition, this is a rather unwieldy formulation upon which to base systematic analysis. It does reflect a general dissatisfaction with older conceptions and a veering away from the idea of a single institution or a static structure. Evidently the concept of 'family', as now employed in social anthropology, cannot be encompassed in a simple definition. In that case it might be approached in some other way, perhaps as a nexus of certain processes. Such a conception, vague though it may seem, provides a point of departure for the studies in this book. But before going on to indicate the special characteristics of the 'families' which are dealt with, I wish to explain something about the particular processes to be analysed.

The Family Estate

Those parts of the physical environment which people manipulate and consume for their needs and comforts are generally known as natural resources. Rights to the use of these resources and the products derived from them—and also rights to other, non-material, goods—are governed in every society by rules which are more or less definitely formulated. The processes involved in exploiting resources, and those resulting from the application of the rules which govern rights to them, constitute the subject matter of the science of economics; this is the case when our concern is with a whole society, or perhaps the whole world. When our focus is narrowed to encompass only the

[1] *Ibid.*, p. 650.

INTRODUCTION

members of the family group these economic rights are usually found to be different in character. For example, the rules may be less strict and they are not commonly sanctioned, as in the case of society at large, by the full political authority of the society. Thus, young children obtain their just share of goods not, as a rule, by demanding enforceable rights but mainly through the largesse of their parents. As members of a family become older their economic rights become more definite. In later generations, as the relationships between their descendants become attenuated, depending on the kinship and lineage system of the particular society, these descendants tend to come more and more under the general economic laws of the society. As the economic processes of society at large are studied by economists, so, by the present division of scientific labour, those within the family situation are usually studied by anthropologists or sociologists.

In the small tribal societies which are the traditional subject of anthropological research, direct exploitation of natural resources is usually carried out for the most part by families, and the economic processes of distribution, use, and consumption of goods occur largely within the family context. Thus in most African societies a family group of some kind produces food by cultivating its own land or herding its own cattle and consumes most of this food at its own homestead. Natural resources are major points of ecological contact between human communities and their physical environment, and in tribal societies the ecological processes of exploitation occur mainly in a family milieu. The labour and skills necessary for exploiting the natural resources are funnelled through the family in actual application, while the goods consumed are distributed through family channels. Individuals obtain their vital sustenance largely through the mediation of the family structure. Thus the family is a principal locus of ecological processes.

This complex of processes, involving on the one hand natural resources and products derived from them and on the other hand the family groups which exploit them, centres on what can conveniently be called the *family estate*. It is the principal subject matter dealt with in the chapters which follow. We chose this subject, among other reasons, because it obliges the investigator to give due consideration to the basic ecology of the community he studies, and this aspect of African communities has been relatively neglected. The tendency in social anthropology has been to study societies as if they were isolated, self-sufficient systems, subsisting on thin air, with no visible roots in the soil. The guiding principle, derived in large part from Durkheim and more explicitly from Radcliffe-Brown, has been that social facts require sociological explanations.

This approach certainly cannot be considered 'wrong', for it has resulted in a series of superb monographs and has greatly increased our understanding of African societies. However, it imposes limitations which have left certain problems unsolved. For instance, inheritance has usually been dealt with in an overly-legalistic manner. Our agreed aim was to treat inheritance as an ongoing process by means of which individual members of the family are allocated definite rights and obligations with respect to control, ownership, and exploitation of resources and goods; and in such a manner that as the position of an individual in the family changes concurrently with events such as births, marriages, and deaths, his mode of attachment to the family estate shifts accordingly; the element in this process which is relatively constant being a firm and continuous attachment of the whole family group to the natural resources which sustain it.

The processes by which lineage groups maintain continuity over generations and yet periodically undergo fission have by no means been fully explained, possibly because of limitations of the purely sociological approach. Although this problem falls somewhat outside the scope of the present book, it is not altogether unrelated. For when the family is conceived of as a nexus of processes rather than as a discrete thing there is considerable overlap in the concepts of family and lineage. In unilineal societies (such as the seven societies described here) the major property rights within the family are usually vested in individuals who also constitute a local segment of the lineage system. The cast of principal characters is the same in both groups. A lineage segment of this kind, at least in patrilineal societies, has one characteristic that is generally overlooked: all its members, including the founder—the man who will become the 'apical ancestor' when he dies—are normally

INTRODUCTION

living. These men represent the growing point of the lineage system, and the process of growth inevitably involves the shifts in family property rights with which we are specially concerned. Family development and lineage growth are really aspects of the same set of processes. The family estate serves to sustain the individuals who perpetuate their lineage.

Another aspect of communities which specially concerns us is the pattern of settlement. Settlement patterns are too often taken for granted as basic, irreducible data which are of scientific interest mainly as determinants of kinship systems or 'rules of residence', whereas a more realistic understanding should result from considering in detail the ecological processes by which a people adjusts itself to the environment in establishing its pattern of settlement. In studying the spatial aspect of the family estate, as we shall note later, certain inherent tendencies towards social change can be discerned.

The Time Factor

Since our intention in this book is to stress the time factor in analysing our material, let us pause for a moment and consider in more general terms what this means. Fortes, in his introduction to the Cambridge volume, writes:

> The most promising advance in recent research on the social structures of homogeneous societies has been the endeavour to isolate and conceptualize the time factor. By this I do not mean the amorphous subject matter usually labelled 'culture change' or 'social change'.[1]

He then explains that he is concerned with the 'processes' by which 'a social system or a social structure' and its components are 'maintained' and 'replaced'.[2]

This is getting close to the problems of the present book. However, the terms 'structure' and 'process' raise some difficult philosophical problems, and I wish to comment on them though without attempting a final solution. The concept of social structure has been dominant in social anthropology for the last generation. Radcliffe-Brown was influential in establishing the concept; for him the structure of a society was a

[1] Fortes, 1958, p. 1. [2] *Ibid.*

very definite thing, the main object of scientific research. Since it is very hard to explain a pure social structure and convey any sense of its reality, he sometimes used analogies. Thus in one of his papers he compares a society with a biological organism.

> As the terms are used here the organism is *not* itself the structure; it is a collection of units (cells or molecules) arranged in a structure, *i.e.* in a set of relations; the organism *has* a structure.[1]

Analogously, a society and its structure are two different things, and Radcliffe-Brown sometimes wrote as if the structure has more reality than the society.

Nearly every social anthropologist for the last two decades or so has used social structure as a major conceptual tool. The concept has obvious value, for it has produced a series of monographs which are far superior to previous accounts of primitive societies. No one, of course, really thinks that a social structure is a concrete thing existing independently in nature; it is an abstraction of some kind. But there has seemed to be no harm in treating it *as if* it were a concrete reality, as in the case of a scientific fiction with considerable heuristic value. The nature of the concept was rarely examined critically, or its value questioned, because it seemed to work so well. Leach, at the beginning of his book on Kachin society, suggests an explicit definition of the concept which is quite different from Radcliffe-Brown's representation. He writes that 'The structures which the anthropologist describes are models which exist only as logical constructions in his own mind.'[2] Nadel, in his book *The Theory of Social Structure* goes further in divesting the concept of its reality as something existing 'out there'. He tells us what, in his opinion, the uses of these mental constructions are. They 'enable us to sum up and visualize complex situations in the form of schemata, diagrams, and formulae'.[3] He is perhaps the first to express serious doubts about the value of the concept as an analytical tool. 'In the final analysis, its weaknesses seem greatly to outweigh its strength.'[4]

Not all anthropologists would agree with these views, but I think they indicate a growing suspicion that the concept of

[1] Radcliffe-Brown, 1952, p. 179.   [2] Leach, 1954, p. 5.
[3] Nadel, 1952, p. 154.   [4] *Ibid.*, p. 155.

INTRODUCTION

'social structure' may not be as definite and reliable as we once thought. The present trend seems to be to study social 'processes', and that is the approach we have attempted to follow in our symposium. This does not necessarily mean discarding the concept 'structure'. Fortes, in the passage referred to above, combines both concepts when he speaks of the 'processes' which maintain the 'structure'. However, Leach, on the same page that he defines structure, states that 'Every real society *is* a process in time.'[1] If this were a true and full statement, it might conceivably be possible to give an account of a society solely in terms of processes without any reference to its structure, or by reducing structure to the status of research devices—diagrams and so forth—as Nadel suggests. There would be no point in doing this, though, unless it could be shown that the concept 'structure' somehow hindered our understanding.

At the same time that the structural approach was dominant in social anthropology the opinion was widely held that African societies were relatively static or changeless; that they had no histories, or at least that it was not the proper business of social anthropology to study their histories. I think it is legitimate to inquire whether there might be some causal relation between the structural approach and the historical attitude that accompanied it. Applying the test of linguistic usage to this question, we note that while it is perfectly natural to speak of the history of a society, it is rather awkward to speak of the history of a social structure, as if there were something incompatible about these two terms. If structure is really an abstract mental construction as Leach maintains, perhaps by hypostatizing the concept too definitely we have been inhibited from understanding the historical aspects of societies.

For our opinions about the history of Africa are changing. It is now generally accepted that African societies do have histories, and scholars are everywhere busy investigating these histories; books and journals are appearing with African History in their titles. Social anthropology surely has a valuable contribution to make to this endeavour. This seems to be what Evans-Pritchard recommends. In his recent Manchester lecture

[1] Leach, 1954, p. 5. (My italics)

he endorses Maitland's opinion that 'anthropology must choose between being history and being nothing', but with the proviso that 'history must choose between being social anthropology or being nothing'.[1] But in order to become historians we may have to overhaul some of our favourite concepts, and of these I think the concept of social structure is most suspect.

These problems were recently discussed in a thoughtful article by Vogt.[2] He starts by contrasting 'structure' and 'process' as if at present they were mutually exclusive concepts, and then suggests that their integration 'poses one of the *key* methodological and theoretical problems of our generation'.[3] If structure is understood as a mental construction rather than an objective thing, this hard separation between the two concepts should not be necessary. Vogt then goes on, as others have done, to distinguish between 'recurrent' processes and 'directional' processes and discusses the relation between them. Although he deals with this problem mainly in the context of 'culture', the same problem exists when our subject is 'society'. It is easy enough to assimilate the idea of recurrent processes to our conventional set of concepts. These are the processes that Fortes had in mind. They maintain the social structure and preserve the identity of a society over time. Assuming, however, that societies do undergo historical changes, there must be processes which produce these changes, and these are what Vogt calls directional processes. They must be different from recurrent processes, for the latter leave things unchanged in the long run and could not account for historical change. Vogt postulates the existence of these directional processes but does not really explain their nature or how they are related to recurrent processes. To my mind, this is the most difficult of all our problems, and frankly I cannot see a solution to the problem stated in this way. Vogt makes the hopeful, though perhaps impracticable, suggestion that if a society were constantly observed for a period of twenty years we might get adequate data for understanding directional processes.

If we turn for help to the older science of biology, we find that research workers are occupied for the most part with

[1] Evans-Pritchard, 1961, p. 20.   [2] Vogt, 1960.   [3] *Ibid.*, p. 18.

INTRODUCTION

studying processes, such as the genetic processes of gene reproduction and mutation, metabolic processes, or the ecological processes of adaptation and selection. The concept of structure is not much in evidence; there is little need to bring it in for solving the problems of current interest. Structure in the sense of the anatomical construction of an organism must, of course, be studied and understood, but this tends to be taken for granted, or regarded as a preliminary to the main scientific task of studying processes. No clear distinction seems to be made between recurrent and directional processes. It is just that some are more obviously recurrent than others: reproductive processes, for example, seem to repeat themselves almost perfectly. Concepts which are purely directional, such as orthogenesis or *élan vital* are not in very good repute. 'Direction' enters the picture as a synonym for evolutionary trend rather than as a distinctive feature of certain processes.

If an analogy with biology is legitimate, perhaps anthropology is just leaving the anatomical stage of its development as a science, and in that case we should henceforth apply ourselves more and more to the study of processes. The concept of structure may be serving the purpose of a crutch to help us through the transition, later to be discarded or relegated to the status of a preliminary discipline in the training of anthropologists. Should this happen, the distinction between recurrent and directional processes which now puzzles us may simply disappear. With our minds unhampered by social structures, which are hard to conceive of as changing, perhaps we would not be so predisposed to assume that social processes are perfectly recurrent or cyclical in character. It may turn out that processes which are cyclical in the short run have an inherent tendency to produce the conditions for their own evolution or for historical changes. At any rate the time has come when we should be alert to detect any historical trends which result from ordinary social processes.

One result of removing structure from the centre of focus might be that we could no longer expect to apprehend a society as a whole. The loss would not be great, for our success in achieving this with the structural approach has been largely illusory. Even while recognizing that process is the main subject of our research there is still danger of overreaching ourselves by trying to encompass a whole society in one concept. When Leach characterizes a real society as 'a process in time' he is overstretching the concept. It would be safer to use the term in the plural, speaking of a 'set' or 'system' of processes, or something like that. Turner, in a study of social processes among the Ndembu, which in many respects is exemplary, delimits his field to the village group. However, he attempts to visualize this whole complex unit as a single process.

> My aim was to show how the general and the particular, the cyclical and the exceptional, the regular and the irregular, the normal and the deviant, are interrelated in a single social process.[1]

The things he enumerates seem to be adjectives describing a variety of different processes. In that case it would be more intelligible to consider the village as the field or locus of their operation and interaction rather than as a single, magnified process. Nevertheless this is an important book, moving boldly in the new direction which social anthropology seems to be taking.

The field of investigation in the present book is smaller than Turner's village. We have not formally defined our subject at all, but try to regard it as a nexus of certain processes which are closely interconnected and in which we are specially interested for the time being. We have not been entirely successful in our aim, for every essay contains at least vestiges of the structural approach, but we have tried to give priority to the processes. Ingrained habits of thought are not easily changed, and if static structure is expelled from one place it tends to pop up in another. For example, Middleton in his book *Lugbara Religion* presents a study of the processes centring on the ritual activities of these people. His method is illustrated by this statement about the cult of the dead: 'The rites of the cult of the dead are performed at points of crisis in the perpetual process of realignment in relations of authority within the lineage.'[2] The anthropologist is here thinking in terms of processes and has freed himself from the idea of an unchanging, static structure, but the latter immediately reappears in the minds of the natives. The author tells us that the 'Lugbara idea about their

[1] Turner, 1957, p. 328.   [2] Middleton, 1960, p. 264.

INTRODUCTION

society ... is of a social order that is unchanging. It is one of a static system of authority relations.'[1] To determine what is in the minds of other people is not easy, even people whom you know intimately. Evans-Pritchard wrote that to base social anthropology on psychology is 'to build a house on shifting sands'.[2] However, this is only a minor deviation in a method which deals in the main with dynamic social processes. The lapses from our professed aim in this symposium are no doubt equally great.

Populations and Land

The problem posed by Malthus has not yet been squarely faced by anthropology. If populations increase at a substantially greater rate than their means of subsistence this unbalance must produce social changes, set in motion processes, which in given circumstances follow a regular pattern. Durkheim, in *The Division of Labor in Society*, proposed one solution to the problem. Having established to his satisfaction that one great trend in social evolution was for 'segmental' societies with 'mechanical solidarity' to develop into 'organized' societies based on 'organic solidarity', he then sought for causes which might bring about this transformation. The principal cause, he decided, was population increase.

> The division of labour varies in direct ratio with the volume and density of societies, and, if it progresses in a continuous manner in the course of social development, it is because societies become regularly denser and generally more voluminous.[3]

This statement, of course, would require considerable qualification to give it even *prima facie* validity.[4] As a hypothesis, it will not be tested here, for the question of social differentiation falls outside the scope of the essays. However, one of our societies fulfils Durkheim's population generalization in a striking manner.

The Arusha first settled as a small group of immigrants on

---

[1] *Ibid.*, p. 264–5. [2] Evans-Pritchard, 1951, p. 44.
[3] Durkheim, 1947, p. 262.
[4] Fortes and Evans-Pritchard (1940, p. 7) found a negative correlation between population density and the presence of centralized political institutions in their sample of African societies.

the slopes of Mt. Meru little more than a century ago, and their population is now 63,000. Thus they have very rapidly become 'denser and more voluminous', and from the information given by Gulliver we can deduce certain social consequences. We note variations in the inheritance and authority pattern within the family which seem to be connected with this population expansion. The 'ideal' Arusha pattern is for sons to be allotted portions of the family estate as they acquire families of their own and require resources to support them. These allocations are made by the father, and he has the power to alter or even revoke the rights to property that he confers upon his sons. He also exercises considerable authority over his sons in other matters. As Gulliver puts it, 'Because a guardian controls the property he controls the people associated with it.'

When a society fills in its territory and continues to expand, the family estate in some cases become fragmented to the point where the resources are not sufficient for all the sons, and some new adjustment must then be made. The Arusha met this situation by the pioneering of new land by sons whose needs could not be satisfied from the family estate—first the choice mountain land and later the less desirable land of the plains.[1] In theory, the father's control over his sons' property extends to this pioneered land; that is, the new land was regarded as part of the family estate so that the ideal pattern of authority and inheritance would be preserved. However, as Gulliver makes clear, the father's control of land acquired independently by sons is illusory. In this situation, the ideal pattern of authority competes with ecological reality, and as a result 'the Arusha are equivocal concerning the locus of authority over pioneered land'. Among the Sonjo, where land must be irrigated, there is no opportunity for pioneering new land; as a result, the father's control over the family estate remains unchallenged as long as he lives.

Where the subsistence processes operate almost exclusively within the context of the family estate, the organization of the family group may be almost sufficient for the cohesion of a small society. But when the family estate is enlarged and dispersed as a result of population growth, extra-familial groupings and

[1] These consequences of land shortage are explained more fully in another paper (Gulliver, 1963) which traces the history of Arusha land usage.

INTRODUCTION

alignments would become necessary to maintain social cohesion. In the case of the Arusha, and in several of the other societies of similar situation (e.g. Taita, Gusii, and Shambala) these wider alignments are found in a segmentary lineage system. The Sonjo, however, do not have these systematically segmented lineages. One reason for this is that the family estate tends to remain intact and cannot be enlarged through the efforts of sons; control of property and personal authority coincide, so that the family group, or minimal lineage, remains tightly organized.

I should like to comment on one more contrast between the Arusha and Sonjo. When a father's control over his son's property is weakened, as with the Arusha, the unity of the family group might be seriously endangered unless the bonds were reinforced in some other manner. For the Arusha, this reinforcement is provided by the ancestral cult, for only a father has 'ritual competence' in this cult: the sons depend upon their father for ritual services, and this constitutes a supplementary sanction for his authority. A Sonjo father has such firm control over his sons' property that he has no need for additional authority, and perhaps partly for this reason the ancestral cult plays an insignificant role in family organization.

These findings, I think, offer us important clues for understanding some of the historical processes of Africa. From the evidence of their present distribution, their linguistic and cultural affiliations, and from their historical traditions, we know that the Bantu-speaking peoples have migrated widely and frequently. The impelling force behind these migrations in many cases must have been population growth outstripping local resources. When bands of immigrants, such as the forefathers of the Arusha or Shambala, settled in a new location, the immediate problems of economic co-operation and social cohesion could be solved within the homestead groups, consisting of a family or small lineage with dependents. As the new society grew in size and density with natural increase and the accretion of fresh immigrants, the family structure would tend to weaken, and the discrete family groups would require integration by means of political institutions of wider scale.

In the past it has been difficult to conceive of these migrations which we know took place. The concept of social structure as something durable and unchanging which permeates a society inclines us to imagine migrations as involving whole societies moving as a body from one place to another. This is highly unlikely except in very unusual circumstances. It is probable that in most cases the pioneer immigrants were small bands of family groups, as in the attested case of the Arusha. At any rate, by focusing on the social processes of ecological adaptation we should gain a more realistic understanding of the historical processes in the Bantu migrations.

It may sometimes happen that the family estate exceeds immediate needs, as in families with few sons, or perhaps none. This situation is discussed in several of the essays. One type of adjustment, described, for example, for the Lobedu and Taita, is for the father to transfer temporary rights to this excess land to relatives who are not members of the family lineage. Among the Taita it is customary for a daughter to be given some spare land if available; it then comes under the effective control of her husband, the owner's son-in-law. This custom is so preferred that the Harrises describe it as the satisfaction of definite rights of a daughter—rights *qua filia*. Ultimate rights to this land, however, remain with the patrilineal descendants of the original owner, but these rights may not be pressed for a long time, or until the land is actually needed. Among both the Taita and Gusii we are told that a young man needing land applies first to relatives of collateral patrilineages and is given preference. In this way the larger lineage segments enter into the system of property ownership and family substance. The Sonjo achieve the necessary flexibility in land distribution in a different way. Idle land can be leased or sold for a definite price to another family that needs it, but with the provision that it may be reclaimed if required later for an adult son upon repaying the original price. This option to recover land expires with the death of the original owner, so that title to the land does not become hopelessly complicated in later generations.

Livestock

In most of our societies, livestock is dealt with in much the same way as land, up to a certain point. A husband–father allocates portions of his herd, first to his wives, if he has more

INTRODUCTION

than one, and then to his adult sons when they grow up and have families of their own. Usually he retains at least nominal control or ownership of all the livestock possessed by his family, and when he dies the sons inherit the animals in their possession, with their father's residual herd then being divided among them. Beyond this point the two forms of property are treated quite differently. Among the Sonjo, meat and milk—the principal products derived from livestock—tend to be distributed and consumed communally rather than by discrete families. This is partly because goats—the only livestock kept by the Sonjo—are rarely slaughtered except for sacrifices or at some ceremonial occasion. Although the Sonjo know how to preserve meat by drying it in thin strips, this is seldom done. The carcass of an animal is too much for a single family to consume immediately, and therefore it is distributed among friends and neighbours according to circumstances. In tribes where cattle are kept as the chief form of livestock, the amount of meat available for consumption when an animal is killed is much greater than in the case of goats. Thus, as a source of meat, livestock comes in units which are too large to be consumed by the members of a single homestead. However, although meat, as compared to food crops, tends to be distributed outside the family group, the ownership of livestock is nearly always vested in an individual or a family, rather than a larger communal group. One reason for this is that livestock exist in the form of indivisible, equivalent units which provide a natural standard of value and thus they are used in various kinds of exchange. The most significant exchange transaction, in the context of the present study, is the exchange of livestock as bride-price for wives, and this use of livestock is stressed in most of the papers.

Krige writes that among the Lobedu (the only group for which we are given a quantitative statement on the question) bride-price transactions accounted for 95 per cent of all transfers of cattle in the tribe. This is perhaps an extreme case, but certainly in most cattle-keeping tribes bride-price accounts for a large proportion of livestock transactions. I have argued elsewhere[1] that bride-price can best be understood as a system of economic exchange rather than merely as a complex of

[1] Gray, 1960.

customs which have the social functions of stabilizing marriage, legitimizing offspring, and so forth. In a more recent paper, Burling presents a persuasive case for considering an entire society as an economic exchange system in which behaviour is regulated by the principle of maximization of satisfaction. His theory is based on the assumption that 'economics deals not with a type but rather with an aspect of behavior'.[1] From an economic viewpoint a society is seen as an exchange system; economics provides one distinctive model for analysing societies.

Lobedu society, as described in this book, has a surprising resemblance to a complex exchange system. Whether this is because the Lobedu are unusually amenable to analysis by Burling's method, or because the author's viewpoint is more economically oriented than in the case of the other writers, I shall not attempt to decide. At any rate, the result is a very coherent picture of family processes in which livestock plays a leading role. Krige describes the exchange of cattle and women as 'quasi-economic transactions', and the consequences of these transactions ramify widely through the society. The basic rule is that a brother has a right to the bride-price paid for his sister to obtain a wife for himself; in return for the use of his sister's bride-price, the brother must provide a daughter as a wife for her son. This normally results in matri-lateral cross-cousin marriage. Fresh bride-price is transferred at every marriage, and thus two distinct but related sets of economic obligations must be satisfied at a marriage: one family is obliged to offer a daughter, and the other family must pay a bride-price. The actual situations in many families as regards available daughters and sons often make it impossible to immediately fulfil these obligations, and thus there are innumerable variations in marriage arrangements, which yet in the long run tend to preserve the exchange pattern. For example, if a woman has no son to claim a wife to whom he would have been entitled, the woman herself may 'marry' a 'wife' in the name of her fictitious son; the offspring of this 'marriage' are regarded as the woman's grandchildren and they perpetuate her husband's lineage.

The Gusii system is equally comprehensive, but has a different emphasis and pattern. Again a brother has a right to use

[1] Burling, 1962, p. 817.

INTRODUCTION

his sister's bride-price, but he must be a full brother. If the bride-price is used by the girl's half-brother, or her father, then a debt is incurred by the matri-centric group using the cattle for a new wife. The obligations and rights involved in a debt of this kind are inherited by the patrilineal descendants of the 'houses' concerned, and must eventually be satisfied, though several generations may pass before the final settlement. As in the case of the Lobedu, the basic principle or pattern is exemplified in many variations.

Widows and Orphans

In all our societies except the Suku, the crucial events which bring about changes in the mode of attachment of individuals to the family estate are similar in character and tend to follow a standard sequence. The common denominators appear clearly when we consider the family group, with its time dimension, in the simplest form. As a starting point we may take a married couple with an equal number of sons and daughters; the daughters fetch bride-price which is used in obtaining wives for the sons; the sons establish nuclear families of their own and are allocated portions of the family estate for their support; then the parents die and each son becomes an independent proprietor of his own estate. If land is at all scarce we might have to postulate a single son and daughter for the original couple to avoid complications in this simple sequence, for we have already noted that an expanding population, in which the family estate is insufficient for the sons, produces changes in the simplest pattern of settlement, authority, and property control.

Two possible variations on this simple form are related to the length of the father's life. If he lives unusually long his grandsons may have already established nuclear families of their own and acquired the property necessary for subsistence while the family estate was still under the control of the grandfather. In this case, the middle generation of men—the owner's sons— would not have opportunity to exercise the normal prerogative of a father to allocate property to his sons. Although this situation must occur occasionally, it is not analysed systematically in any of the papers. A much more common contingency is for a father to die while his sons are immature and the family estate is still operated as an undivided unit. When this happens a number of adjustments must be made with respect to property rights and personal authority. Perhaps no two societies deal with this situation in exactly the same way; although certain common results are aimed at in every case, these results are achieved through processes that are different in some respects, though alike in other respects.

The analysis of this problem can be approached in different ways, which are exemplified in some of the papers in the book. In the preceding paragraphs I spoke of the 'simplest' pattern of continuity processes and then mentioned some of the variations and complications. In his analysis of the Arusha family, Gulliver starts with the concept of the 'ideal' pattern, and quotes from a native text to show that this idea exists in the minds of the people. He then goes on to demonstrate and analyse some of the deviations from this ideal. In my own paper on the Sonjo I describe several different family patterns without designating any one of them as 'ideal' or 'normal', calling them 'allomorphic' forms. Both approaches lead to similar analytical results and insights, and the choice of method is largely a matter of convenience with respect to the nature of the data and the aim of the research. It should be advantageous to experiment with different methods and concepts in studying questions of this kind.

When a young father dies, it leaves a young widow (or widows) who needs a new husband if she is to play her proper role in society; orphans who need the support and protection of a father; and it leaves an ambiguous situation as regards property rights and personal authority within the family group which is now without a head. These problems are solved in different societies by various shifts in social relations and positions, with the family estate providing the stage for these moves. It seems to me that this is the best approach for studying the consequences of a father's premature death. It has been more common in the past to approach the question from the viewpoint of the father's generation, determining the respective rights of the surviving brothers to inherit the widow and orphans and the disposal of the dead man's property. This assumes that other societies deal with such a crisis in a legalistic manner, as

INTRODUCTION

is the case in our society when a man dies and his estate is probated. This may be useful for the purpose of codifying 'native law', but it fails to reveal the ongoing processes of family continuity in a contingency that frequently arises.

In general, this situation is dealt with in one of two ways. Either the estate remains intact, with the surviving family members retaining their attachment to it, and some outsider (usually the deceased's brother) steps in to replace the dead husband and father; or else the survivors and their estate are merged with another family group. Among the Sonjo this decision is usually determined automatically by considering the status of the family estate at the time of death. If the dead man's father was still alive, the estate of the bereaved family could not yet have been fully sequestered, but would still belong to the grandfather's estate; therefore this property would be re-allocated among the brothers, and one of them would inherit the widow and adopt the orphans. In effect, the incipient family and estate would lose its identity and become assimilated to another family and estate. However, if the dead man had already come into full title of his estate through the prior death of his father, then the estate is preserved as a unit until the orphan sons are old enough to claim their shares; the widow is married by one of her brothers-in-law, who acts as head of the family and manager of the estate. In his relation to the orphans he has more the character of a stepfather and trustee than a foster father.

Three of our societies are reported as practising the levirate —Lobedu, Gusii, and Shambala. The levirate is usually defined as a custom by which a man marries his brother's widow and then 'raises seed' to the dead man. It is distinguished from 'widow inheritance' by this mystical idea of raising seed. The leviratic husband is, in a sense, acting as a substitute for the dead man. I suggest that it might be more enlightening to distinguish between processes which maintain the discrete unity of the bereaved family group, so that the members retain exclusive rights to their own estate, and processes which merge these people and their property with another family. In the first case the arrangements for the widow could be termed 'husband succession', and in the second case 'widow inheritance'. Husband succession might or might not involve the mystical notion that future children borne by the widow 'belonged' to the dead man. The Sonjo practise husband succession in the circumstances explained above but do not have the idea of the levirate. However, wherever the levirate exists we should expect to find the husband-succession complex of rules.

Each of these two general ways of dealing with widows and orphans permit wide variations in meeting special contingencies, depending on the customs and rules prevailing in different societies. The age of the surviving children is an important variable. If there is an adult son with a stable home of his own, he may temporarily act as head of the family and manage the estate, with no need for an outsider to step in. The problem of who should receive bride-price for daughters and provide it for sons is handled in different ways in different societies. It is possible, of course, for property rights to be treated separately from personal authority and affiliation, though this probably only happens when inheritance and descent follow different lines. Among the Wambugwe of Tanganyika, as an example, husband succession is practised very strictly. However, the successor to the dead husband is a matrilineal kinsman, not a brother, and has little control over the property of the orphans. The reason for this is that inheritance of property is mainly in the male line, while organized descent groups are matrilineal.[1]

Descent

Six of our societies are described by the authors as patrilineal, while the seventh society, the Suku, is matrilineal. Let us consider first several aspects of descent in the patrilineal societies and then the matrilineal Suku, who have been neglected up to this point.

Under the influence of the prevailing concept of social structure, it has been the usual thing to treat the lineage system as a primary determinant of marriage arrangements, lines of authority, property rights, and so forth. If we are attempting to make a 'synchronic' study this is perhaps the only possible method. At any given time we find a unilineal society seg-

[1] Gray, 1953.

INTRODUCTION

mented into certain clans and lineages; and if the lineage groups are localized, as is the case to some extent with our present patrilineal societies, we find individuals residing and tilling the land where they do apparently because they are members of the lineage occupying that territory. Disputes and unlawful behaviour are dealt with by lineage leaders, or if there is a dispute with a member of a different lineage one's lineage mates come to one's support and this may lead to a feud between lineages. Wives must be obtained outside the lineage of that level of segmentation at which exogamy is required. The lineage claims the children of its male members. All these customs and rules seem to have the function of maintaining the structure of the lineage, when it is conceived of as a primary unchanging thing.

This structural conception, however, is not very helpful when we study a society at (literally) the grass-roots level of the family estate. What we see then are individuals and small family groups trying to sustain and propagate themselves by exploiting natural resources, which are usually scarce so that their use must be governed by agreed rules in order to avoid disastrous competition and conflict between individuals and families. From this viewpoint, the larger lineages and clans appear to be the natural outgrowth of family processes—fundamentally, ecological adaptations—and to have the functions of supporting the family groups and facilitating the ecological processes.

The male members of a family group themselves constitute the smallest segment of a lineage system—in this case a perfect lineage with all members living. When the head of this lineage dies and his sons become proprietors of their own estates and heads of their own living lineages, these sons then constitute a lineage of the next higher order having as component parts the new living lineages. In time, the grandsons of the original head become heads of family lineages and together form a third order lineage which is subdivided into several second order lineages descended from the different sons of the man with whom we started. This process goes on over the generations to produce, in theory, an additional level of lineage segmentation with every generation. However, formal recognition is never given to every potential level of lineage segmentation, as we know from empirical investigation. Moreover, my description contradicts reality in at least two respects. It assumes (1) that generations stay even with one another through time, implying a synchronization of marriages and births which does not actually occur; and (2) that every father has at least two sons, which again is an untrue assumption.

Even if a society deliberately planned a lineage system in which segments at every generation were to be given recognition, the plan would be inoperable because of the tendency for generations in different descent lines to get out of phase. This is probably one negative reason why in actual systems lineage groups are recognized at only a limited number of levels, usually with several generations between segment levels. If a family has only one son, then when his generation reaches the second order of segmentation, he, as an individual, cannot constitute a lineage group. If there are single sons for several generations—not an unlikely situation in real life—these descendants would become unattached individuals falling outside the lineage system. This does not seem to happen in actual fact; somehow or other they merge with collateral lineages which are going concerns. Where genealogical connections are required to validate membership in a lineage, the genealogies may be manipulated, as Winter, for example, has demonstrated for the Bwamba.[1] More often—at least among the societies described in this book—precise genealogical relations are not important: a collateral relative is merged into a lineage because it is mutually advantageous for him to join.

Granting that a segmented lineage system is the natural result of processes of family continuity, though not genealogically accurate, why would these lineages crystallize out at certain generational levels as definite groups which often have corporate characteristics? In the kind of societies with which we are here concerned, population growth and the proliferation of family groups takes place as a rule in a limited continuous area. Thus the more numerous descendants of the original settlers are neighbours as well as kinsmen and in any case would acquire territorial solidarity which is superimposed upon the original kinship solidarity, the result being a larger group having the need and will to organize itself for peaceful com-

[1] Winter, 1956, p. 214.

INTRODUCTION

munity living. A family group alone would have great difficulty defending its property rights, especially when land shortage arises through population growth. If these rights are accepted by the local community, then it is only against outsiders that the property must be defended. In time a community normally outgrows its original territory and must expand or hive off to start new centres. The people of different settlements, though more distantly related than those of the same settlement, still find it advantageous to recognize some commonalty, and may form a corporate lineage of a higher order, almost certainly with less correspondence to the putative genealogical group than in the case of lower order lineages. It would be useless to pursue this hypothetical process further, because conditions and groupings of actual societies differ so widely.

LeVine and the Harrises state expressly in their papers that when a young man seeks new land because there is none left for him at his family estate, he applies to someone of his own lineage with spare land. The idea of buying and selling land does not seem to be indigenous to any of these societies, with the partial exception of the Arusha and Sonjo. Land rights are obtained by an individual in the first instance through his attachment to the family estate, and if this is insufficient additional land is usually sought in the larger lineage community that is derived from family processes. Outsiders, who have no connection with these family and lineage processes, are excluded from lineage land, or if they are granted land it is usually by assimilating them to the lineage system, either as adopted members or recognized dependents or clients. Thus the family needs the protection and support of the larger lineage to which it belongs, and the lineage as a corporate group needs the loyalty of its constituent families and depends on them to provide a constant supply of new members.

Lineage communities, of course, serve other public functions besides providing security for family groups. Thus every society has a ritual life of some kind, if little more than the celebration of *rites de passage* marking births, marriages, deaths, and so forth. In order to be psychologically effective, and to have the uniformity characteristic of ritual, these rites are enacted in the context of a larger community than the family group. The form of ritual most commonly found in segmentary societies is associated with a cult of ancestral spirits; the central figure is an apical ancestor who may be interpreted in some respects as a magnified family head. In comparing families and larger lineages it is easy to forget that the people of the society are simultaneously members of both types of groupings: it is not a matter of contrast or opposition between different sets of people. Opposition, as Evans-Pritchard has so clearly demonstrated for the Nuer, is found usually between families and between lineage segments of the same order. Higher order segments provide the matrix in which oppositions are resolved. At the highest level of segmentation it may be that no resolution is possible short of genuine warfare, that is, unless there is a centralized political power standing outside the lineage system.

Two of our patrilineal societies, the Lobedu and Shambala, are organized as kingdoms. There is not space here to discuss the special features of these systems, and in any case the effects at the family level are relatively small. These are indicated in the respective papers. The Sonjo also have a political institution—the village council—with considerable power, and this is separate from the lineage system, though it is not focused on an individual as in a kingdom. The Sonjo practise irrigation, and this means that the family groups are competing for an additional resource, water, which demands closer co-ordination and regulation than is the case with rain-crop farming. Therefore I have interpreted the village governing councils as a necessary social development for this kind of ecological adaptation. The Arusha and Sonjo have age-group systems which cut across the lineage system and provide an additional means of integration for the whole society.

So far we have not specifically considered the question of polygyny, which is practised in all seven societies. An obvious consequence of polygyny is that it produces more offspring for the head of the family. In nearly every report of an African society, we are told that individuals desire as many offspring as possible. While this is not the only reason for desiring offspring, a father certainly wants his estate to be fully occupied and eventually transferred to his own offspring. With only one wife there is greater danger that he will have no heir, or only one, and in that case his property, or part of it, might fall into the hands of outsiders. If the family estate should go out of

INTRODUCTION

existence the family itself would most likely have no further continuity. With polygyny the family and its estate are less liable to become extinct. With polygyny, however, a father is likely to overshoot the mark and end up with more heirs than the estate can accommodate. This results in the processes which were mentioned earlier in discussing problems of land and population, where we noted that the tendency towards overcrowding of the family estate is one of the dynamic forces in the growth and differentiation of a society. A family group must not only continue to occupy its estate effectively, but must also defend it against encroachment. The sanctions which societies like these give to a family's land rights are not nearly as definite as in our society with registered deeds and the like. LeVine states that among the Gusii the men of a family group traditionally would organize themselves as a military unit, and in almost any society the larger the family group the more confidently could they defend their estate against intruders.

A polygynist normally allocates portions of his estate to his several wives, in the first instance, and in time each portion is distributed among the sons of the wife who received it. Thus the family estate is subdivided at two levels—first among the wives (with the head usually retaining a portion for himself), and then the sons. At the same time, the living lineage becomes internally segmented into sets of full-brothers. It is customary to refer to these sub-units consisting of a wife, her children, and their allocated portion of the property as a 'house'. A house has the potentiality of becoming a separate lineage group if its unity and solidarity are sufficient to set it off permanently from other houses of the homestead. It may become first a living lineage when the head of the homestead dies, and in later generations the descendants may form a higher order lineage. These house-derived lineages, however, have one peculiarity at any level of segmentation: as strictly patrilineal groups they lack an apical ancestor, for they trace back to a woman founder, and thus they are genealogically truncated. I suggest that against the tendency for sets of full-brothers in a polygynous family to form separate lineages there is a countervailing tendency to preserve the genealogical integrity of developing patrilineages, and this would require that the distinction between half-brothers of the same father be minimized or ignored. Which of these tendencies prevails in any given society is probably determined mainly by the system of property rights.

In our sample of patrilineal societies, the house principle appears most prominently among the Gusii, and the reason for this seems to be an unusually strict system of bride-price 'bookkeeping'. The bride-price paid in for a girl belongs to her house and should be used in obtaining wives for her full-brothers. The homestead head, however, has a large measure of control during his lifetime over all family property, including incoming bride-price, and he may use a daughter's bride-price to obtain another wife for himself or transfer it to one of her half-brothers. In that case a debt is created between the two houses concerned which is inherited by their descendants, so that there is an economic necessity for a house lineage to retain its unity at least until all debts are satisfied.

The Lobedu have an equally complex system of bride-price bookkeeping, but quite different in character. As was explained in an earlier paragraph, the debt in this case entails not so much the repayment of the bride-price itself but an obligation on the part of a cattle-linked brother or other relative to provide a wife for the son of the woman whose bride-price was taken, with cross-cousin marriage being the normal result. In this system there is no economic need for full-brothers and their descendants to retain lineage unity, and Krige remarks that the Lobedu do not identify a lineage segment by its female foundress, as in the case of the Zulu with whom she has also worked. Gulliver, who is familiar with the well developed house system of the Jie and Turkana, specifically notes that among the Arusha little distinction is made between full-brothers and half-brothers. Thus the extent to which the family patrilineage becomes segmented into house lineages varies from society to society, and the decisive factors determining this process seem to be ecological and economic in character.

The Matrilineal Suku

It would be hard to find an African society which differed from our patrilineal societies in so many of the points we have been considering as the Suku, while belonging to the same

INTRODUCTION

linguistic stock and sharing with them many general cultural traits. Superficially, the Suku seem to contradict many of the generalizations that have been suggested up to this point. But nevertheless, the same generic conceptions and methods of analysis can be applied to them, *mutatis mutandis*, as Kopytoff clearly demonstrates in his paper. Let us consider a few points of contrast.

The first major point of contrast concerns cultivated land, which among the Suku cannot be considered as part of the family estate in the same sense as in the other societies. For the purpose of cultivating manioc, the staple food crop, land is so plentiful that Kopytoff speaks of it as a 'free good'. This unusual circumstance cancels out the system of rights relating to ownership and use of land which in the other societies constitutes one of the major determinants of family and lineage processes; and although the Suku are primarily agriculturalists it puts them in some respects in the category of pastoral or hunting societies as regards land rights. In fact, hunting territories are the only kind of land to which economic rights are claimed, and the unit holding these rights is a matrilineage. Hunting, by its very nature, requires a larger territory than a family group alone could be expected to control; if anyone is to claim exclusive rights to a hunting territory it must be a larger group such as a higher order lineage. Thus the Suku system of land rights, such as they are, conform to local ecological conditions.

Unlike our other societies, the Suku were long accustomed to the use of money—shell money in the old days, later replaced by Congolese francs. With the Suku, money takes the place of livestock as a means of bride-price payment, and this has had the effect of making the bookkeeping for the bride-price exchange system unusually precise. Money (and most other forms of movable property) is regarded as the joint possession of a matrilineage, with the older members exercising effective control over its use and distribution. When a marriage is arranged, the groom's matrilineage pays a money bride-price to the bride's matrilineage; the latter group pays three-fourths of the money to the bride's father and delivers the girl. Any future transactions, such as refunding the girl's bride-price at divorce and collecting a fresh bride-price at her remarriage, are the business mainly of the bride's matrilineage.

The family estate in this system would appear to be non-existent unless we conceive of it on a higher level of abstraction than in the case of our patrilineal societies, for the idea of individual ownership is virtually absent. The basic subsistence resource—land—is plentiful rather than scarce, and therefore we cannot properly speak of ownership or exclusive rights in connection with it. The scarce element is the labour and skills of women necessary for exploiting the land; but to be effectively applied this labour must be channelled through the organization of the family group. The labour of a woman, and her services as sexual partner and wife, can only be obtained through payment of money, into which the scarce goods of the society are transformed for exchange purposes. The ownership of these scarce goods is vested not in the family group or its individual members but in the matrilineage. Bride-price payments, as in the case of the patrilineal societies, represent major occasions of goods exchange. These transactions take the form of ordinary economic exchanges: one group makes a money payment and in return the other group transfers certain rights to one of its women. The family group itself is not directly a party to this transaction, which takes place between the larger matrilineages, but it is the focus and purpose of the transaction. The result is the creation of a family—or the conditions in which a family can develop—having at its command the resources and goods necessary to sustain itself.

For an ordinary Suku homestead is arranged much like a patrilineal homestead. A married man resides there with his wife (or wives) and children, and provides them with the necessities of life. Wives do the cultivating, but there is no need to allocate them land because it is so plentiful. Daughters get married and move to other homesteads, for marriage is virilocal. Sons are expected to live with their father throughout his lifetime, which is somewhat surprising since they can look forward to no inheritance from him. The cohesion of the localized father-and-sons group is partly explained by the organization of hunting activities, and it is also bolstered by certain ritual. This pattern of male residence might lead to strong, localized patrilineages except for several factors which prevent their development and act to preserve the unity of the matrilineages.

INTRODUCTION

Every matrilineage has a 'lineage centre' at which the lineage leader resides and at least a few of the other lineage elders. This provides for every person what Kopytoff calls a 'psychological residence' which is usually different from his actual residence. A son may move to his lineage centre after his father dies, or to another settlement where he has lineage mates. There appears to be no economic incentive for him to stay on at his dead father's residence, though he may do so. The grandsons of the homestead head with whom we started must follow their fathers when they move, and thus the common residence of the local group is broken—the strongest force producing solidarity in the incipient patrilineage.

Patrilineal descent is actually given formal recognition in a series of overlapping, truncated patrilineages known as *kitaata*. At first sight, this might seem to encourage the development of large patrilineages which would compete with matrilineages for the loyalty of individuals, but their actual effect is to prevent this from happening. A *kitaata* is only two generations in depth, and thus grandsons cannot belong to the same *kitaata* as their grandfather; as new generations appear the apical ancestors are continually sheared off, leaving perpetually truncated lineages. The sons are affiliated through their mother with her matrilineage, but as a person the wife-mother is attached to the *kitaata* rather as an outsider; if she should leave after a divorce her sons stay on with their father. The result of this system is to produce a living patrilineage with many of the characteristics of the living lineage normally found in patrilineage societies. Its members, however, are usually affiliated with different matrilineages (unless the family is based on an intralineage marriage), and it is with these groups, lying outside the family, that individuals share common interests in most forms of scarce property. The *kitaata* is united in its ecological dependence on the land cultivated by the family, but it lacks any permanent economic ties to this land, or any durable bonds with the local community where it resides. Thus there is little incentive for it to develop in later generations into a higher order patrilineage, and in any case the genealogical depth limit of two generations makes that impossible.

The resources and goods required to sustain the family are not concentrated, as in the case of the patrilineal societies, in a pre-existing family estate. They are located diffusely in the matrilineages and the countryside. The family estate comes into existence only as the family develops into an organized group capable of exploiting the resources, and as the latent rights of individuals in the property of their matrilineages come into force. When the family and *kitaata* break up the family estate becomes diffuse again.

A 'synchronic' description of the structure of Suku society would have little meaning, for at any one time the actual groupings are highly variable, and each grouping can only be understood by reference to antecedent events, which often go back several generations, and to anticipated events in the future. Thus Kopytoff's analysis of the Suku reveals, even more clearly than the other papers, the family as the nexus of various processes—ecological, economic, and ritual processes, and the processes of human mating, reproduction, and descent.

REFERENCES CITED

BURLING, ROBBINS. 1962. 'Maximization Theories and the Study of Economic Anthropology', *American Anthropologist*, 64:802-21.

DURKHEIM, EMILE. 1947. *The Division of Labor in Society*, Glencoe, Illinois, The Free Press.

EVANS-PRITCHARD, E. E. 1940. *The Nuer*, Oxford, The Clarendon Press.

—— 1951. *Social Anthropology*, London, Cohen and West. (Glencoe, Illinois, The Free Press).

—— 1961. *Anthropology and History*, Manchester University Press.

FORTES, MEYER. 1958. Introduction in *The Developmental Cycle in Domestic Groups*, ed. by Jack Goody, Cambridge University Press.

FORTES, M. and EVANS-PRITCHARD, E. E. (eds.). 1940 *African Political Systems*, London, Oxford University Press.

GOODY, JACK (ed.). 1958. *The Developmental Cycle in Domestic Groups*, Cambridge University Press.

GRAY, ROBERT F. 1953. 'Positional Succession among the Wambugwe', *Africa*, 23:233-43.

—— 1960. 'Sonjo Bride-Price and the Question of African "Wife Purchase",' *American Anthropologist*, 62:34-57.

GULLIVER, P. H. 1955. *The Family Herds: A Study of Two Pastoral Tribes of East Africa, the Jie and Turkana*, London, Routledge and Kegan Paul.

—— 1963. 'The Evolution of Arusha Trade' in *Markets in Africa*, ed. by Paul Bohannan and George Dalton, Evanston, Illinois, Northwestern University Press, pp. 431-56.

INTRODUCTION

LEACH, E. R. 1954. *Political Systems of Highland Burma*, London, G. Bell and Sons.
LEVY, M. J. and FALLERS, L. A. 1959. 'The Family: Some Comparative Considerations', *American Anthropologist*, 61:649–51.
MIDDLETON, JOHN. 1960. *Lugbara Religion: Ritual and Authority among an East African People*, London, Oxford University Press.
MURDOCK, GEORGE PETER. 1949. *Social Structure*, New York, The Macmillan Co.
—— 1959. 'Evolution in Social Organization', in *Evolution and Anthropology: a Centennial Appraisal*, ed. by Betty J. Meggers, Washington, The Anthropological Society of Washington.
NADEL, S. F. 1952. *The Theory of Social Structure*, London, Cohen and West. (Glencoe, Illinois, The Free Press).
RADCLIFFE-BROWN, A. R. 1952. *Structure and Function in Primitive Society*, London, Cohen and West. (Glencoe, Illinois, The Free Press).
TURNER, V. W. 1957. *Schism and Continuity in an African Society: a Study of Ndembu Village Life*, Manchester University Press. (New York, Humanities Press).
VOGT, EVON Z. 1960. 'On the Concepts of Structure and Process in Cultural Anthropology', *American Anthropologist*, 62:18–33.
WINTER, E. H. 1956. *Bwamba: a Structural-Functional Analysis of a Patrilineal Society*, Cambridge, Heffer.

THE SHAMBALA FAMILY

E. V. Winans

I

THE Shambala are a Bantu-speaking people who occupy the Usambara Mountains of North-eastern Tanganyika.[1] The highest peaks in the Usambara Mountains rise to elevations of approximately 7,000 feet, but most of the people live in mountain valleys and small intermountain basins with elevations ranging from 3,000 to 5,500 feet where rain is good and reliable and the climate is cool as compared to the surrounding plains. The economy is based primarily on hoe agriculture, but cattle and small stock are kept in significant numbers and are grazed in unopened bush land, commonage near villages, harvested fields, and on the surrounding plains. The main crops in order of importance are maize, beans, cassava, sweet potatoes, bananas, and sugar cane. In addition to these crops, wattle trees, vegetables, coffee, rice, cotton, and tobacco are grown for the market, and small amounts of other crops are produced. Production for the market is becoming increasingly important and is encouraged by the administration. The mixed economy supports a heavy population which numbered 263,887 in the census of 1957. The greater part of the population is centred in the mountains where densities in excess of 500 persons per square mile are not uncommon, but there are increasing numbers of people residing in the plains at the base of the mountains where rice cultivation and stock herding are the main subsistence activities. However, the plains

[1] A number of variants of the tribal name exist and may be found in the literature. The people call themselves Shambala or Shambara, the British administration called them Sambaa, the German administration called them **Waschambaa**.

are arid lands in part infested by tsetse and mosquito, and in addition large tracts have been alienated to the great sisal estates. Thus the area for expansion out of the mountains is sharply limited.

Under these circumstances of increasing population and limited land suitable for cultivation by the means known to the Shambala, the relation of people to the land is of pressing concern to every man in the country. There is ample evidence to indicate that in earlier times new land in the mountains was available to anyone who wished to clear it of its forest cover. Indeed, there was a continuing influx of people from surrounding tribes who were allowed to take up land on the condition of loyalty to Shambala chiefs and the Shambala state. It appears that a consciousness of land shortage is very new to the Shambala and even now most people are convinced that if only the Government would release land classed as forest reserve, the whole problem would be solved.

Thus it is within a context of rapid population growth and pressure on the land that we must examine the distribution and holding of property by Shambala domestic groups. This is perforce a context of change and of strain between the perception of traditional and desirable patterns of residence and economic activities held by most Shambala and the restraints on these patterns imposed by land shortage, changing political patterns, and the availability of alternative modes of subsistence activity.

The Shambala are highly organized into a state[1] in which a royal patriclan possesses a virtual monopoly of chiefly position and by its dogma of genealogical connection unites all of the people under the rulership of a paramount called the *Simbamwene*. Although the royal clan holds the chiefships as a corporate right of its constituent localized lineages, members of commoner lineages participate heavily in the governmental process because each chief is accompanied by a council of commoners without which he cannot act. Beyond this, there are other bureaucratic positions vital to the functioning of the state which may only be held by commoners. Thus participation in the decision making process and recruitment to bureaucratic

[1] A detailed account of Shambala political organization is given in Winans' 1962.

position strongly affects the behaviour of many Shambala by providing a role structure which is additional to that created by the family. The dynamics of this interplay are of great importance and resemble in many respects the situation described by Fallers for the Soga of Uganda in which there are considerable strains produced within the individual through role conflict and in which role behaviour within one institutional complex tends to contaminate behaviour in other institutions within which the individual is placed.[1] On the other hand, the power of chiefs resides primarily in the regulation of affairs between localized corporate lineages and there is relatively little penetration of chiefly power into the internal affairs of the lineage except by express invitation of the members of the lineage. Thus a good deal of the day-to-day ordering of people's lives and affairs is still a matter of lineage control.

The localized corporate patrilineage (*chengo*, pl. *vyengo*) possesses corporate legal responsibility for the actions of its members and is subject to the control of the chief as a unit. Thus it regulates its own internal affairs carefully and with an eye to maintaining its position *vis-à-vis* the hierarchy of royal chiefs. The corporate lineage is made up of a series of extended families whose heads are united by bonds of patrilineal descent. The heads of the constituent extended families form a sort of informal council which regulates the affairs of the group. This lineage has a regularly recognized head termed the *mgosh wa chengo* (elder of the house) who is the most senior male within the lineage. The *mgosh wa chengo* is *primus inter pares* within the council of his lineage and represents his lineage to the chief. He is also the intermediary between the living and the departed ancestors above the level of a man's own father. Every man has the right and the duty to conduct rituals to his own father but more remote ancestors must be approached through the *mgosh wa chengo*. The lineage as a whole emerges then primarily in political affairs and in religious activities involving distant ancestors. In most day-to-day activities regarding the rearing of children, the allocation and cultivation of land, the handling of stock and other such things, it is the extended families of which the lineage is composed that are operative.

These extended families are usually grouped into a compact

[1] Fallers, 1956.

village settlement and thus village affiliation plays an important part in nearly all kinds of social interaction and has been taken as the basic membership group by the Administration. However, administrative villages do not fully coincide with Shambala conceptions because the Shambala view the village as a social entity based upon kinship affiliation rather than simply as a spatial unit. Therefore administrative villages are frequently composed of several localized lineages grouped under a single Native Authority Headman.

In Shambala terms, the village should be composed of lineage mates all of whom are members of virilocally resident households. Most large villages, and in fact, many smaller ones depart to some degree from this pattern but the immediate verbal response to a question about village composition is that the male residents are all lineage mates. Therefore, we shall examine the ideal conception of land rights, residence and group membership in order to grasp the scheme with which the Shamhala work and then we shall turn to the variations and complications which are found to occur empirically.

The smallest residential group is the nuclear family consisting of father, mother and their children. The ideal familial pattern is the polygynous family. Wives and children are regarded as a man's greatest assets and most men strive to fulfil this ideal pattern. In my own census of three widely separated villages, I found that 38 per cent of all heads of households (thirty-two out of eighty-three) possessed more than one wife. The lowest percentage occurred in a small village with only seventeen household heads of whom four were polygynous. On the other hand, in one village twelve out of twenty heads of households were polygynous. The family is virilocal, residence with the wife's lineage being regarded as very rare, although we shall see later that it is more common than would be expected from attitude responses of Shambala informants. Within this pattern of virilocal residence and polygyny, each nuclear family should have a high degree of autonomy. Each new wife is properly brought to her husband's village and installed in a house of her own. It is the husband's duty to allot his wife enough land of various sorts to enable her to grow a sufficient amount of each type of crop to support herself and her children. This should be done immediately upon marriage and any rearrangement of fields at a later date should be made with her full understanding and consent, for though she has no legal claim which may be sustained in court, her moral right through child bearing to these specific fields is acknowledged and will be supported by her father and brothers. This moral right extends to stock as well, although a man attempts to keep as much of his herd uncommitted as possible so that he can use it for bride payments, ritual, stock client relationships and the like.

The village, then, is composed of a cluster of nuclear families formed through the practice of virilocal residence so that it is the patrilineal relatedness of the men which forms the major tie between them. The position of the women and of the children they bear is established through proper marriage. If a man has failed to perform the recognized marriage ceremonies, the children will belong to the mother's kin. Evidence of legal marriage is the transfer of bride-wealth from a man to the father and other kin of the prospective bride. This action is necessary for the bearing of children but it is not sufficient to establish their legitimacy. It provides access to the woman but rights over her children must be further established by subsequent transferals of wealth attendant upon successful live birth.

The process of familial development begins then with the handing over of bride payments to a woman's father. It proceeds with the construction of a house, the delineation of the wife's fields, and the establishment of lineage membership for the children she bears by the tendering of birth payments. Such birth payments establish not only the control of the father over his children but determine a host of obligations and rights for those children in terms of their membership in the lineage of their father. They are, through these payments, not only defined as the children of some man but also as members of a certain lineage with corporate rights and responsibilities.

During this first phase of family development the children live in their mother's house subject to the close supervision of their mother and the immediate authority of their father. However, when boys reach the age of about ten or eleven it is felt that they should no longer sleep in their mother's house. At this time their father must either erect a small house for them termed the bachelor's house (*nyumba ya bwene*) or he must ake arrangements for them to share such a house already built by one of his lineage mates for his own sons. The bachelor's house will be the sleeping quarters of the boys until they marry eight or more years later. They return home for food which they usually carry away to eat with their peers and they sometimes sleep at home if ill, but they may stay away from their parents for days on end. At the time of movement to the bachelor's house, a boy's relations with his father shift from easy affection to more formal respect, and etiquette forbids joking, bawdy talk, smoking, or eating in a father's presence. The Shambala explain this shift in moral terms, for they regard the discussion of sex between men of adjacent generations as quite outrageous except in the context of the initiation school where it is not the father but some other man of his generation who explains proper sex behaviour to the youths. There is no comparable sequence of events for girls who remain in their mothers' houses until marriage, nor is there a similar taboo upon sex training between mother and daughter.

These more distant relations of authority and respect between father and son which have their inception in the move to the bachelor's house are strongly embodied in the arrangement of the son's first marriage. This first marriage is regarded as the responsibility of the father. It is he who must pay the bride-wealth and it is he who should have the right of decision as to a proper bride. Most older informants claim that infant betrothal was common in an earlier time. Infant betrothal is quite rare at the present and most young men have an important voice in the choice of a wife. Nevertheless, the fathers of the young couple conduct all the bride-wealth negotiations and if these do not prove satisfactory they may forbid the marriage. When marriage arrangements satisfactory to the man's father have been made and after the bride-wealth payments have commenced, the father should allocate a house plot to his son located near the father's own house. He should also aid in the construction of the house, and give the son a portion of his mother's fields and stock, augmented if need be by a part of the father's own unallocated holdings. By the carrying out of these acts on the father's part the son attains the semi-independent status of a married man, but the family still retains a powerful unity under the father who remains the owner of

THE SHAMBALA FAMILY

lands upon which they all live and the possessor of full jural and ritual responsibility for all.

No man should approach his ancestors directly as long as his father is alive, but should always ask his father to carry out the necessary rituals for him on pain of grave supernatural misfortune if he should ignore his father's ritual position, for it is the father's deceased father who is the most active and concerned ancestor. Fields and stock allocated to the son are properly regarded as still under the jurisdiction of the father and may not be disposed of without his permission. Indeed, such allocations by a living father are held to be provisional and are claimed to be open to his revision at any time. As each son matures, the shift in the structure of the family becomes more complex resulting in an extended family where mature, married sons are not regarded as jurally competent in the fullest sense so long as their father may live. Obligations cannot be undertaken by any son without the father's consent, for the father is ultimately responsible for them as head of the corporate extended family, and through him the responsibility extends to the whole of the localized corporate lineage. These relations of authority and responsibility are regarded as remaining the same whether the married sons continue to reside on portions of the father's original holding or move completely or partially off of this original holding by opening new land. This relation is strong even if sons move off of the father's land because most people are reluctant to enter agreements with a man whose father is alive unless the father is present as a witness for fear that the son may be misrepresenting his right to whatever property is involved, and that it may in fact be encumbered with lineage rights which will nullify any agreement the son undertakes.

The relations among members of the extended family shift only with the death of the father. At this time the sons receive their portions of the estate and only then become jurally competent heads of their own nuclear families. The allocation of shares of the estate is accomplished at the formal mourning ceremonies which are attended not only by the sons but by all the male members of the deceased's localized lineage and the deceased's widows. This is the time not only for the final disposition of the estate among the heirs, but also for the final presentation of claims against it by outsiders so that responsibility may be determined and arrangements made for the settlement of legitimate debts. In ideal terms, all the properties of the dead man should have been allocated by him by the time of his death so that the lineage merely affirms the rights of the various heirs to the holdings they already possess. Nevertheless, the localized lineage is held to possess the right of revision in part or in whole of these allocations. Furthermore, in most cases a man will still be in possession of some unallocated holdings at the time of his death which must be divided among his sons. The approved solution is an equal division of such property among all the sons. At these same deliberations, the widows must also be provided for. The Shambala practise the levirate and young widows will be married by the brothers of the deceased. However, the Shambala hold that such marriage is unsatisfactory unless the woman agrees to it, so the widows are present at the deliberations and they are consulted as to their choice of leviratic husband. Elderly women with adult sons are often not married in this way but instead reside with one of their sons.

With the closing of the mourning period, the sons become the fully responsible heads of their own holdings. Each son may now conduct ceremonies to his father with only the limitation that more remote ancestors, and in particular the lineage founder, must be approached through the genealogically most senior man of the local lineage, that is the lineage head. They are, in fact, now competent to perform most of the ritual relevant to a man's own nuclear family. They may enter into agreements on their own cognizance, give and accept bridewealth, and exercise the same powers their father enjoyed before them. However, the earlier unity of the extended family still finds expression in co-operation among the new family heads who clearly form a unit with the potential of segmenting from the localized corporate lineage. Perhaps the strongest such potential lies *within* this former extended family, however, where the tensions over inheritance between half-brothers, the sons of one wife as opposed to the sons of some other wife, may lead to segmentation and the establishment of new settlements.

II

The model of structural states and relations which has been advanced has reality in that informants clearly conceptualize the circumstances within which they live and this conceptualization informs their decisions. However, in the working out of relations among particular individuals various sorts of departures from this model will occur. Indeed, the Shambala are no less aware of such departures than is the field worker and most of these are as regular and as well recognized as is the basic model. In addition to the micro-level of individual personality adjustment, there must also be adjustment to changing political and economic conditions. Thus we must consider several crucial points in the process where alternative patterns may develop. These occur at the establishment of a nuclear family, at the marriage and settlement of the sons it produces, and at the death of the father and the establishment of relations among the now independent sons.

The unitary nature of the nuclear family is a legal fact of primary importance. Yet there are certain factors which may disturb this arrangement. The nuclear family comes into existence through the transfer of bride-wealth from the groom's father to the bride's father. However, bride payments do not have to be complete at the time that the young couple take up residence together. Although bride-wealth is not high in Shambala as compared to many societies, it is often difficult for a Shambala father to accumulate the whole amount at one time and it may be paid in instalments. The young couple may take up residence together when about half of the total amount has been transferred, in which case the groom is obligated to provide services for his father-in-law until the total amount has been paid. These services are usually agricultural labour or aid in house construction, and they are due whenever demanded. Beyond this, payment must be completed immediately upon the pregnancy of the bride or the infant will be considered a member of its mother's lineage. This will also be true if the groom defaults in transfer of the birth payment which is additional to the marriage payment.

If the marriage and birth payments are not met, the bride's father may claim the return of his daughter and her children.

In eighteen such cases for which I could obtain records, this right was affirmed by the court and the woman's father was further allowed to retain whatever portions of the bride-wealth he had already collected. In such circumstances the woman's father then possesses full rights to the bride-wealth of any girls his daughter may have borne during her marriage and full obligation to pay the bride-wealth for her sons. Courts recognize certain residual rights on the part of the defaulting husband, however. If he can raise the total of the debt he owes he may pay it and the father-in-law is obligated to accept. The position of the children as members of their father's descent group is thus re-established even if the wife refuses to return or the husband no longer desires her return.

Even when full and prompt payment of bride-wealth is made, the bride does not become a member of her husband's lineage. She retains strong links with her own lineage which are primarily expressed in terms of her father's continuing ritual responsibilities for her well-being. Her ties to her own lineage are expressed in other ways also. Thus, if she should be found guilty of habitual thievery or of witchcraft the responsibility lies with her father and brothers and not with her husband. By the same token, however, should her husband be guilty of mistreating her outrageously or should he prove to be a witch, her father and brothers may demand her return without refund of bride-price. If there are children, they remain members of the father's lineage as in any divorce where the whole bride-price has been paid.

There are, then, limitations upon a husband's control over his wife which result from her membership in another lineage. This finds expression in the next generation through the recognition of matrilateral ties by a woman's children. The fact that Shambala is a patrilineal society means only that the primary bundle of legal rights and obligations clusters around statuses defined by descent through males. This does not exclude the possibility of recognition of certain rights and obligations as being transmitted through women. The Shambala have a proverb which succinctly expresses their view of this matrilateral link: 'Have you no *mtumba* (mother's brother), then you must fend for yourself.'

Wives return to their father's house for confinement and

parturition and often a man does not see his child until it is two or three weeks old. Usually the mother does not return to her husband's house until the new infant is five or six weeks old and she is able to care for it and her house without endangering her health. When the child is old enough, it is expected to visit the mother's brother and thank him for rituals done at the birth and request that he remember the child in ancestor rituals conducted within the mother's lineage. Small gifts are exchanged and an informal relationship (although *not* a joking relationship) is maintained between mother's brother and sister's children. This matrilateral link reaches its fullest expression when the sister's sons reach marriageable age. At this time they have the right to demand one cow from the mother's brother to aid in fulfilment of the bride-price obligation. They may ask for, and obtain, other kinds of aid from their mother's brother but such other aid is not a demand right and may be refused, although Shambala find it hard to refuse requests of this nature if they are insisted upon. The most important of such requests is for land to augment that allotted by a father. However, this is more suitably discussed later and will be deferred for the present. Although these factors may temper a man's authority, his wives and children are held to remain clearly subordinate to him in terms of property ownership. They live on his land and in his house and derive their subsistence from his crops and stock, yet again there are checks.

As indicated earlier, a man must allot fields and stock to his new wife upon marriage, and in practice such allotments cannot be freely adjusted later on at his pleasure. There are two major factors acting to make men attempt reapportionment, however. The first of these is the traditional one of desire to acquire more wives. If a man wishes to marry another wife and if fortunate enough to have a large holding, he may have sufficient unallocated land to provide for the new bride. However, it is often the case that he will wish to reduce his first wife's holding in order to provide the new wife with a field relatively near his village even if he also offers both women some land elsewhere. Secondly, many men are now attracted to the prospect of cash crops such as coffee, and they often have no land in reserve at all so they must persuade their wives to give up subsistence fields for this purpose. In either case, a wife, by virtue of bearing a man's children, regards herself as trustee of property which her sons stand to inherit at their father's death and she is thus reluctant to see her holding reduced. In point of fact, she has no legal claim which can be sustained in court but her moral position is considered just and the informal sanctions of public opinion may support her if her refusal is reasonable. This is particularly the case if she has borne sons who may expect to inherit her allotted fields. On the other hand, if she is the only wife and has a relatively large holding, or has borne no children she cannot expect support in her opposition to reapportionment.

The management of land which has been apportioned to a woman is largely her responsibility. Her husband will help with the clearing, the heavy hoeing, and the harvesting, but planting, weeding, irrigation and guarding against birds and monkeys is the work of women and children. The wife also decides the proportions of various subsistence crops she will plant and if she realizes some surplus she may sell it and keep the money herself. It is only the money from the sale of recognized cash crops such as coffee, wattle, tobacco and green vegetables grown on unallocated reserve that a man claims. Indeed, men stated in 1957 that they would not allow their wives to independently plant such cash crops and women showed no interest in doing so. They even opposed such planting by their husbands on the grounds that it reduced the land available for subsistence crops. In this respect we encounter another test of the husband's authority over his wife, for husbands often attempt to gain their wives' aid in the cultivation of cash crops. There are no guide-lines within the traditional culture for this sort of activity and wives nearly universally oppose it. Husbands fall back upon their rights to command obedience and in most cases which I observed they were able to get limited labour from their wives with much resentment and complaining but very little open refusal.

Relations between fathers and sons do not really come into focus until such time as the sons have completed their initiation and reached the age of marriage, which is usually in the late teens and early twenties. Marriage of sons produces the greatest possible strain upon the resources of the family, for at this point the father must not only provide the bride-wealth but must also allot land and stock to his son. Many informants stated that marriage negotiations began very early in childhood in former times but today they are usually deferred until the son is old enough to discover his own preferences. Old men decry this practice and I encountered three cases of early betrothal; but the majority of cases which I observed were arranged in consultation between father and son with father retaining the right to veto any proposal of which he disapproved. Most fathers did not regard this as entirely satisfactory and expressed a preference for what they claimed as the traditional order of events in which they would agree upon a marriage between their son and some suitable girl when their offspring were still small children. Thus they could make the bride-wealth payments over a number of years prior to the actual marriage and then would have only to allot land to the son and his new wife at the time of actual consummation of the marriage; but they found the Administration opposed to infant betrothal and their sons reluctant to submit to it under the present acculturative situation.

A man is thus in a difficult position for his sons will be approaching marriage age at just about the time he has consolidated his own economic position. He may have put as much of his land into cash crops as possible, in fact, going into debt to purchase such things as coffee trees. Thus he is reluctant to give up land which now has long-term value. It was perhaps advantageous in an earlier period to give land to one's sons since land had relatively little value aside from the labour put into it to get out each year's subsistence crop. Thus a man could slowly abandon active productive labour to enjoy the status of head of an extended family whose members would support him in his old age. Now this is changed, and he can look towards cash yields from valuable perennial crops which he has planted. Thus he may delay the allocation of fields to his sons and the provision of bride-wealth which reduces his capacity to make capital improvements.

These considerations aside, marriage arrangements appear to be a traditional source of strain between fathers and sons since there is a strong pattern of elopement which forces a father's hand if he has been dilatory in making arrangements. Elopement is generally arranged between the girl and her suitor and follows a set pattern such that the fathers are notified the morning following the elopement and fines in the form of goats are due the girl's father. The girl's father may refuse to allow the marriage and his acceptance of the fines in no way prejudices his refusal. However, this is apparently quite rare, for most fathers are willing to negotiate a regular bride-price and in such circumstances it is advantageous to do so since they may demand the whole payment in a lump rather than in instalments. The man's father cannot refuse to offer bride-price if the girl's father is willing and may be forced to do so by regular legal action if he is reluctant. I have no quantitative measure of the frequency of elopement but judge it to be fairly common since six cases were investigated by me during one three-month period in a single minor chiefdom with a total population of less than 1,500 persons.

The whole elopement pattern is a most interesting case of the jural responsibility of the father. The courts here clearly affirm that responsibility even though it is a wilful act of disobedience on the part of the son which is entered into with calculation and intent. Indeed, although every Shambala emphasizes the full authority of the father over his son, tacit approval is often given to an elopement because the moral responsibility of fathers to arrange their sons' marriages is also recognized.

Elopement is a heavy blow to a father's pride and many sons seek other means of inducing marriage arrangements if these are slow in coming. If the grandfather is still alive, his grandsons can appeal to him for aid. Since theoretically father's holdings still belong to the grandfather, he is in a position to exert pressure to conclude a marriage agreement. This is usually less costly.

In the final analysis, however, none of these patterns of action are total repudiations of the legitimate authority of the father within his nuclear family. Rather they are devices which make use of the responsibility which accompanies that authority so that its arbitrary exercise is channelled.

The marriage of the sons alters the structure, however, making it a more articulated unit with the sons now acting as the heads of their own semi-autonomous nuclear families. In many matters the sons are able to act relatively freely without

THE SHAMBALA FAMILY

their father's consent or intervention. Thus their management of stock which they have been allotted is seldom interfered with. Fathers appear to take the view that mismanagement in this area does not threaten the whole unit nor involve it in permanently disadvantageous commitments since stock undergo natural increase. So stock partnerships and clientships are frequently arranged without the father acting as witness. In similar fashion, marriages subsequent to the first one are the business of the son and his first wife. A father is under no obligation to provide help in collecting the necessary cattle and small stock and does not stand to lose if the son defaults in payment. He is still responsible if elopement fines should be incurred, but I was not able to discover many elopements in second or later marriages. This seems curious at first glance since elopement may not only be a technique for forcing a father to provide bride-wealth, but might also be used to force a marriage after negotiations with a girl's father have broken down. This is very risky, however, since the girl's father has the right to withhold his consent while still collecting the fines and the girl's marriage value is not seriously impaired. Virginity is admired and one goat is added to the bride-price on proof of virginity, but its absence incurs no serious economic penalty nor does it lessen a girl's status. Thus elopement has no great attractiveness to men who are seeking second wives.

Fathers as heads of extended families must be more concerned with matters relating to land, however. The control of land is conceived as the heart of familial authority and transactions in land carried out without a father's knowledge are the most direct kind of denial of his rights. There is very little to be gained by secretly attempting to encumber a field with loans or to sell a field which has been allotted by a father. Few men would enter such a transaction with a son because it would certainly be repudiated by the father and the courts would support this repudiation. Even if a father should fail to repudiate the obligation, there may still be lineage rights in the land because it had been inherited by the father from his father and his brothers could repudiate its total alienation since they have residual rights in it as coheirs. Only land pioneered by a man appears unencumbered by lineage rights and is thus open to alienation without lineage permission. This is a point of bitter contention and it is frequently brought up in court cases, for the jural unity of the extended family may be held to mean that a father acquires rights to any land his sons may pioneer. The chiefs and their councils have been unwilling to support this assertion unequivocably, however, and have instead remonstrated with sons to respect their father's wishes while refusing to nullify transactions over such pioneered land which the sons may have entered.

This has the potentiality of seriously disrupting the solidarity of the extended family for it may mean that a son can move completely off his father's land to land he has pioneered or purchased and thus remove himself from his father's economic control. Such a son has no ritual competence, however, and this is viewed by many men as an extremely grave liability. A case in point involved a man named Hemedi who purchased a tract along a main road and constructed a small retail shop or *duka* where he sold tea, soap, and other cheap items. He was able to do this because he had saved money while serving in the army during World War II. He refused to acknowledge that his father, Mkuna, had any rights in this land and because he was a Christian would not recognize his father as having any ritual rights either. The father was extremely bitter over Hemedi's actions and would not talk about him or allow his name to be mentioned in his presence. Yet he was also regretful and concerned about Hemedi's children who he pointed out as being disrespectful and undisciplined, which in fact was true. Hemedi himself expressed some uneasiness as to his relations with the supernatural but regarded the break as beyond repair. Thus it appears that if a son refuses to acknowledge that his father has rights to land the son has pioneered he in fact alienates himself from his extended family and through this from his lineage. This must have been a nearly untenable position in former times because of the ritual liabilities, but the introduction of Christianity as an alternative dogma makes such a break somewhat easier. Even when breaks of this nature have occurred they may not be beyond repair. I encountered two cases where reconciliations have been achieved by the sons' provision of appropriate sacrifices and demonstrated willingness to submit to their father's authority.

The problem of movement off the father's land at the time

THE SHAMBALA FAMILY

of marriage has several aspects. We have considered only certain of the legal dimensions of the pioneering of new land, and, indeed, the case considered appears likely to have been a symptom of an authority conflict which existed prior to Hemedi's move. That is, his purchase of land might be viewed as symptomatic of his own estrangement with traditional Shambala culture resulting from his experiences as a soldier, his acceptance of Christianity and his acceptance of western values associated with the successful operation of a *duka*. This, in fact, is not a unique case history. There is a good deal of conflict resulting from differential acculturation to western values as presented by the Administration and a rising volume of sales in land and breakdown in the joint holding of property by extended families and localized corporate lineages. Such culture conflict is only reflected in a fraction of people as yet, but it appeared to be on the increase in 1956–7, and could bring about major changes in Shambala social structure in the future.

There are other dimensions, both traditional and modern, to the alterations in family structure occurring at the marriage of sons. Shambala is a state-organized society and there are certain traditional avenues to the recruitment of political positions within it. A royal clan, the *kilindi*, virtually monopolizes chiefly office, but the position of councillor and certain other offices are open only to commoners. Politically ambitious men may achieve these offices by several routes, the most common of which is service to a chief or powerful councillor in a kind of clientship. There is not space here to consider the patterns of political advancement. However, we must consider one part of these. In order to act effectively, the ambitious man must usually reside near his patron. This often means that he must leave his own village to reside in a royal village and requires that he obtain land there for a house site. It is possible under certain circumstances to gain such a house site by grant from a chief who, as the titular head of a localized royal lineage has the right to allot any land held by the lineage which is not in use. Such land theoretically reverts to the royal lineage at the occupant's death. This a chief may be willing to do in return for the service his client provides. Some men thus maintain a house at court where they sometimes stay and another house in their village of origin, but many men attempt to obtain agricultural land from the chief so that they may maintain a wife at court to provide them with amenities and comforts. Such an arrangement has the further advantage of allowing them to reside nearly continuously at court. Men of established wealth and position who are polygynous often have wives in their own village and wives at court and are in a position to act relatively independently of their own extended family and localized lineage. Indeed, they must, for their position depends upon overriding loyalty to their patron. Frequently such men seek marriages with women of the royal lineage as the surest way to acquire land in the vicinity of the chief's village upon which to settle these wives, thus establishing affinal ties with the chief. This is common enough so that one could regard uxorilocal residence as a significant variant on the general pattern of virilocality. In the next generation, the sons may usually expect to inherit land thus held by their fathers in the regular pattern of virilocal residence and patrilineal inheritance, for their mother's brothers find it hard to reclaim this land if their relations with their sister's sons have been good. In fact such men were traditionally a valuable source of political support to a royal lineage and their eviction was a mistake. Such residence and inheritance can give rise to a dependent localized lineage with matrilateral connections to the royal lineage, secondary rights in land, and relatively weak links with the patrilineage from which it has segmented by its founder's move away from his own father's land. In a sample of thirty councillors, over 90 per cent had either affinal ties to, or were sisters' sons of, the royal chief under whom they served. Furthermore, approximately 70 per cent of them resided in the chief's village and had land acquired when they or their fathers married women of the royal lineage.

Many other men who fail to become politically prominent are attracted to the royal villages and marry and acquire land there. It seems clear that there has always been a certain amount of movement away from the father's holdings at marriage with an attendant weakening of control by the father. This movement also has the effect of reducing the land controlled by royal lineages but enhancing their power in the traditional political context. Within the system prior to contact

THE SHAMBALA FAMILY

it was the command over supporters that gave prestige and power to a chief and it was therefore advantageous to allow royal daughters land and thus attract their husbands away from their own villages and in fact out of their fathers' control. This perhaps may be taken to represent a partially unresolved value conflict in Shambala culture in which the solidarity of the extended family and lineage is confronted by the valuation of the state and of participation in its operation with the attendant rewards of prestige and largess from the chief. The conflict could not be fully resolved in favour of the state because of the powerful religious role of ancestor worship and because the lineage retained considerable jural responsibility. It must produce considerable psychic conflict in those individuals who find themselves playing roles in both institutions, but on the other hand, it does provide an avenue for avoidance of too great a demand from either one's father and other lineage members or from the chief.

The pattern of seeking land in a wife's village or with the mother's brothers is not restricted to royal villages, but is quite widespread. Village census material which I collected in 1956–7 revealed three out of twenty-one household heads in one village and one out of eleven in another to be resident in such a manner, while in a royal village eighteen out of fifty-two heads were married in. The moves were not all recent and frequently had taken place two or three generations ago, resulting in substantial secondary lineages which occupied altogether as much as half the land in the vicinity of the village. Such lineages acknowledged the primacy of the lineage which had pioneered the land in that the primary lineage held the headmanship of the village. The position cannot pass to any member of a secondary lineage and its holder is responsible not only for affairs within his own lineage but is also called upon to act in affairs of the secondary lineages on some occasions where conflicts are not easily resolved. In affairs which concern all the members of a village such as the building of paths, roads, fences, or other service for a chief, or in intra-village disputes where all the males in the village convene as a group, members of the primary lineage are accorded precedence in speaking and it is usually their opinions which prevail. These considerations aside, the secondary lineages conduct most of their affairs quite independently and are usually in no danger of losing the land they acquire through female links.

This traditional pattern is made even more complex by the development of a land shortage. The population is growing and has grown in the past both through migration into the mountains and through the high birth-rate, relative lack of malaria, the establishment of the Pax Britannica, and the introduction of western medicine. This is coupled with the facts that much of the land in the Usambara Mountains is steep and subject to rapid erosion while even the more favourably situated lands tend to decline in fertility because of constant cropping without the use of fertilizers, crop rotation, or adequate fallowing. Thus many heads of families find it difficult to obtain food sufficient to their needs from their land holdings. This, of course, tends to force a dispersal of the sons of unfavourably situated fathers. The pattern is a traditional variant on approved residence, but the reason is new. The residential unity of the extended family is increasingly difficult to maintain as sons either attempt to acquire fields from their wives' fathers or their mothers' brothers or both. Some such men are able to return to their own fathers' land as the result of deaths and inheritance, while some do not manage to inherit enough to do so. The result has been a dispersal of lineage holdings so that today most men do not hold sizeable blocks of land but instead work small plots scattered widely which they have acquired by allotment from their father, loan by their father-in-law, loan from blood brothers, purchase, rental, or temporary grant by a chief.

It is no longer possible in most parts of the mountains to pioneer unopened bush. The Administration has made forest reserves out of much of such land in an effort to control erosion, maintain watershed, and protect the commercial potentialities of the stands of cedar and tropical hardwoods which remain. The rest is now regarded as belonging to the chiefs in trust. Nearly all the informants to whom I talked held that chiefs did not have exclusive rights to allocate land in former times, but only controlled that which their ancestors had pioneered. Commoner lineages had equal rights in what they had pioneered and bush was open to anyone. Now, however, such land is scarce and the Government has supported the claims of chiefs, for in western terms rights to command the allegiance of people and rights in land control coincide. The result is that even where unopened land exists it may only be taken up by application to a chief and reverts to the control of the chief upon abandonment by the user or upon his death. Such land cannot be allotted to sons without the approval of the chief and it cannot be inherited by sons. It appears that as time goes by the residential unity of the extended family will become more and more difficult to maintain.

This means that the authority of fathers must also diminish, for as we have seen the dispersal of sons tends to subject these sons to the partial control of others upon whose land they may reside. The image of the extended family as a property holding, mutually responsible, corporate entity is modified, even in the traditional culture, by the centrifugal forces of political activity and the clash of economic interests of fathers and sons. However, it must be pointed out that in those cases where sons move away from their fathers' holdings they tend to establish extended families themselves and thus return to the model. The major effect in these cases is the lessening control over land experienced by their host lineages. This was offset in former times by the enhancement of political power which resulted from increased numbers. Furthermore, regardless of dispersal the heads of families retain important powers which are consistently supported by the courts and by the traditional supernatural beliefs. These include the absolute ritual subordination of sons to living fathers, the right to original allotment of land and stock, rights over the transfer of land and rights over unallocated lands and stock held in reserve.

Only the death of the father brings these jural arrangements to an end and marks the inception of new relations among the sons who survive him. At this time each son becomes the undisputed head of his own nuclear family and the process begins again. But this can only happen if all the sons are married and settled on their own holdings previously allocated by their father, because there must be a final disposition of the property in which all the heirs participate and this can only take place if they are all adults. If this is the case, the localized lineage has simply to affirm their rights to the lands they occupy, make arrangements for the settlement of any debts outstanding at the time of the death of the father, and insure that provision is made for any widows who may survive by either arranging leviratic marriages or approving their residence with one or another of their sons if they are elderly.

Such final settlement is only possible if a man lives to be quite old so that his sons are all married by the time of his death. In my own field-work I only encountered two cases of this sort in which the father was very old and had become almost completely dependent upon his sons who were all mature men with wives and families of their own. It is far more common for men to die while there are still some sons as yet unmarried and living in the bachelors' house. This is particularly the case if a man is polygynous since he often will not have been able to acquire a second or third wife until in his late forties or early fifties and thus may leave young wives with very young children.

The normal expectation under these circumstances is that leviratic marriages with agnates of the deceased will be arranged at the mourning so that the wives and their children will come under the control of other men of the father's generation. In this case the holdings allocated to the wife are transferred to the new husband for his management. If such a wife has some mature sons and some young sons, the older boys who are already married are theoretically no less jurally subordinate to the new husband than are the younger boys who will be allotted land and stock from the remainder as they gain maturity. The stepfather assumes all the jural rights of the deceased father and may rearrange the allocation if he can gain the consent of the wife just as the real father might have done. Furthermore, children may be born of the new union and these are regarded as the sociological issue of the deceased, sharing fully the rights of children born before the death of the first husband. If the new husband is a brother of the dead man he also possesses ritual competency in rituals to their father, but the sons themselves gain the right to perform rituals for their own now deceased father.

This type of inheritance of wives is regarded as a kind of trusteeship even though the new husband does acquire all the rights towards the woman herself which were established by her marriage to the deceased. This is the case because the localized lineage theoretically has the power to revise all the allocations made by a father or a guardian and the final disposition of the properties of the former unitary family will not be made until all the sons are adult.

Since, however, such guardians tend to consolidate the property which accompanies the new wife with the properties they already possess, for reasons of efficiency, the potentiality for later dispute and confusion is great. This is particularly the case since the guardian has full power to use the stock to pay bride-wealth for himself or any of his sons, to collect bride-wealth for the daughters of his dead brother, to encumber the fields with loan debts, and to plant crops like coffee or wattle on any of the fields. The complex rights thus engendered are extremely hard to unravel and the exact nature of the properties passed to the guardian may well be forgotten over the years. If the children of the deceased are quite small, there is not likely to be any serious conflict over property as they mature and marry. However, if the children are older and know the details of their father's holdings they may be suspicious of their guardian and bitterly dispute his management of lands and stock which they feel they should inherit. Beyond this, a leviratic husband finds it very hard to establish any sort of control over the sons who were already married. Thus the younger sons can usually expect no readjustment of holdings when the final disposition of property is made for the estate has undergone a *de facto* bifurcation. In fact the senior sons may attempt to force an equal division of the property which was passed to the guardian while retaining control of whatever they were allotted by their father before his death.

An alternative to guardianship established by leviratic marriage is guardianship by an older brother. If some of the sons of the deceased are married, they may attempt to prevent their father's brothers from gaining control over the holdings of the extended family even if leviratic marriages are arranged. Conflicts of this type are fairly common and are regarded as extremely difficult by the Shambala because the claims of the sons of the deceased as against the brothers of the deceased are based upon the same principle. In either case the unity of siblings within the extended family is at stake. The inheritance of a widow with her family and lands is a strong reaffirmation of the corporate rights of the extended family composed of the dead man and his brothers. This is highly desirable because the jural unity of that generation has been previously weakened by the death of their father. Furthermore, the leviratic marriage of the widow may lead to the bearing of more children to strengthen the local lineage and the widow herself may prefer marriage and integration into an established family. On the other hand, the guardianship of a senior brother over his minor siblings and his father's property is an equally strong affirmation of the unity of the extended family established by the deceased father.

A case in point involved a young man named Juma whose father had died just before my arrival in the Usambara Mountains. At the mourning it was decided that the wife of the dead man should marry his younger brother, Hemedi. She and her brothers agreed to this marriage but Juma, who was in his very early twenties, objected. He pointed out that Hemedi already had five sons of his own and spent much of his time working as a houseboy in Tanga. He went on to say that his two young sisters and one baby brother were already staying in Juma's house and being cared for by Juma's young wife who had no children of her own. He then urged that he be allowed to act as their guardian and use his father's smallholding and stated that he did not object to his mother's marriage but only to Hemedi's control over her children. The father's brothers each spoke against Juma's case, pointing out that he was young and inexperienced, that his mother was agreeable to the marriage, and that Hemedi could raise her children properly. The lineage head (*mgosh wa chengo*) then stated that Hemedi should marry the widow and act as guardian for the property and the children. Juma accepted this decision with some bitterness but said no more.

About two months later, Hemedi appeared at the chief's court and complained that Juma was obstructing this decision and requested that the chief add his voice to that of the lineage and furthermore order Juma to produce his father's two cows and six sheep. He explained that the children had run away to Juma's house three times and that Juma had made no effort to return them but that he, Hemedi, had been forced to go

THE SHAMBALA FAMILY

fetch them. In addition, Juma had concealed his father's stock and would not tell to whom he had sent them. The chief stated that this was properly a lineage matter and he did not wish to intervene; but he did call Juma before the court and there the councillors and the chief added their voices to those of the lineage, and again Juma agreed to abide by the decision of his lineage. As my stay in that particular region of the mountains was nearing its end, the case again came before the chief's court. Hemedi had still been unable to locate all the stock although Juma had produced part of the sheep. Furthermore, the younger children had again run away to Juma's house. On this occasion the chief and his councillors strongly reminded Juma of his duty to respect the elders of his lineage but they ended up by attempting to mediate by suggesting that the children be allowed to stay with Juma, and they suggested that Juma and Hemedi split the stock and the land, with Hemedi to act as trustee over the whole of the property until all the children were grown. Hemedi was bitter about this suggestion but his brothers agreed to it and so Hemedi gave in. In the end, then, neither of the opposing interests was wholly satisfied but a compromise was achieved and the father's agnates were satisfied that Hemedi would be able to insure that Juma did not use the property to his own advantage with no provision for the younger brother, while Juma was likewise satisfied that he would be able to assert his rights to all of his father's property later.

The setting-up of guardianships, polygynous marriage, or the provision of land via a matri-link to a daughter's husband or a sister's son will often prolong the clustering of dependent or semi-dependent men and their families around a senior man. This situation must ultimately end, however, with the final marriage of the youngest man, the death of the *pater*, and the final settlement of inheritance by the members of the localized lineage. The extended family with whatever attached dependents it may have had ceased to exist as a jural entity at this time. Its surviving members are still united by habit and by a positive valuation of co-operation with each other, but there are relatively few residual jural obligations among them by virtue of their earlier unity that are not obligations of the whole localized lineage. The most important of these is the right to be informed of any projected sale of land by one of their numbers whereupon they have the right to offer to buy to prevent the loss of land. This is coupled with the obligation to aid in the payment of any debts incurred by a brother.

More important is their changed status within the localized effective lineage. As long as a father is alive, he represents his sons in lineage affairs. The sons have the right to attend any discussions concerning lineage action but they are expected to defer to the opinions of men of senior generations who are the heads of the constituent extended families which make up the lineage. With the death of their father or the cessation of the guardianship of one of his agnates, they become participants in the fullest sense in this decision-making group. They may speak with full rights concerning the granting of house plot rights, the loaning of cattle, the management of irrigation water, paths, and grazing lands, or the raising of bride-wealth or fines for a lineage member. In a sense they become closely articulated members of a much wider group composed of their father's surviving agnates, and their patrilateral cousins as well as their own brothers.

This localized effective patrilineage is a corporate group of a higher order of articulation than the submerged extended families within it whose heads form the responsible members. Thus we may view the gaining of autonomy of the former members of an extended family as a simultaneous assumption of greater responsibility in the larger lineage. Men are now able to attract cattle clients of their own without involving their father, enter field pledging transactions, lend land to sisters' sons, and otherwise build up external ties and gain prestige. But they also must share responsibility for lineage mates' debts and fines and for the cost of ritual.

There is no space in this essay to consider the developmental process of the effective lineage nor to examine the dynamics of its relations with other lineages. We may only point out that it constantly adjusts relations within its constituent domestic families by its claims on these families' heads, by its appointment of guardians to assume the position of deceased members, and by its power to adjust inheritance. The Shambala express this fully in a proverb which recognizes the tensions inherent within the family but the overriding necessity to adjust these.

'The brothers who beat each other, they are two. The one who stops it is the third.'

REFERENCES

FALLERS, L. A. 1956. *Bantu Bureaucracy*, Cambridge, Heffer.
WINANS, E. V. 1962. *Shambala: The Constitution of a Traditional State*, London, Routledge & Kegan Paul (University of California Press).

THE GUSII FAMILY[1]

Robert A. LeVine

Introduction

THE Gusii are cattle-keeping agriculturalists numbering over 260,000 (estimates of their contemporary population run as high as 287,000) and occupying the south-western tip of the Kenya highlands just east of Lake Victoria. This area consists of long, sloping hills 5,000 to 7,000 feet above sea level with extremely fertile soil and an annual rainfall of more than 70 inches. Although Bantu-speaking, the Gusii are surrounded by formerly hostile people of other linguistic stocks: Kipsigis, Luo, and Masai. They lost some land to the Kipsigis in the nineteenth century, but retained control of an abundant territory when they came under British administration in 1907. The traditional Gusii sociopolitical organization consisted of localized, exogamous, patrilineal clans which were militarily autonomous but loosely integrated with a number of surrounding clans in seven territorially distinct tribes.[2] Class structure, central political authority, and specialized political roles were virtually absent. Each clan was divided and subdivided into segmentary lineages which were, for the most part, highly localized and governed by informal councils of elders. Men of wealth had greater influence in such councils and sometimes achieved an independent judicial status, but only one of the seven Gusii tribes had positions approximating hereditary chieftainship.

[1] The field data reported in this article were collected when the author was a fellow of the Ford Foundation.

[2] For a definition of the tribe as a political unit and a description of the Gusii lineage system, see Mayer (1949).

ROBERT A. LeVINE

The Gusii were exceptional among Kenya Bantu peoples in the importance of cattle in their economic and social life. Agriculture provided their staple cereal diet, but cattle, apart from providing milk and meat, were the primary objects of economic aggrandizement and the most valued units of exchange. The young men lived out in cattle-villages (*ebisaraati*) with the herds, and they conducted raids against the Luo and other Gusii clans. Although sheep and goats had an important place in ritual, cattle were central in the elaborate bride-wealth system, and remain so, despite the incursions of a cash economy. In contemporary Gusiiland, however, cultivable land is a greater focus of economic concern than cattle, because of the cash market for coffee, maize, and other crops and because of the rapidly rising population density (500 to 700 per square mile in many areas) which makes land scarcer and animal husbandry difficult. Many families keep no more cattle than they need for an impending marriage, although wealthy men still invest in sizeable herds of cattle.[1]

In the past, the fertile land of the Gusii was quite abundant, and their system of land tenure was loosely structured. There were no land titles, and land could not be bought and sold, as it was held by patrilineal descent groups whose resident members had permanent use and inheritance rights that were reassumed by the group when a member had no male heirs. Even the idea of renting land is alien to the Gusii; they allow migrants (*abamenyi*, 'dwellers') to live on and use their land rent free if they are not using it, although in this case the privilege may be withdrawn at the will of the permanent user. This free and easy system was based not only on a strong lineage system but on an abundance that allowed descent group members to pioneer new land whenever older settlements began to get crowded. Land was rarely the object of competition between groups and persons. The increased value and scarcity of land has resulted in a great deal of land litigation (in the courts introduced by the British) with arguments based on customary rights in cattle being applied to the inheritance and allocation of land. In 1957, this litigation appeared to be

[1] A detailed description and analysis of the Gusii bride-wealth system can be found in the works of Mayer (1950a, 1951). The traditional economic system and economic change are described by LeVine (1963). See also R. and B. LeVine (1963).

decreasing, since judicial decisions had resulted in setting boundaries between lineage groups which were no longer open to dispute. At the level of family groups, however, rivalries and disputes over land are still extremely frequent.

Gusii houses are scattered across the hillside, in apparently random fashion, with occasional clustering but no discernible pattern of settlement. There is in fact a local group-organization consisting of homesteads (defined and discussed below), neighbourhoods, and local communities. In the past, each clan (or in some areas, sub-clan) was a territorial group with uninhabited bush lying between it and neighbouring, often hostile clans. Within the clan, too, lineage groups tended to be localized and to form the framework of community organization. The pattern of interclan feuding restricted residential mobility and reinforced the tendency of patrilineal descent groups to preserve their residential integrity for, even when they migrated, it was safer to do so as a group rather than individually. In the area studied, Nyaribari tribe, to which all subsequent statements pertain, clans are no longer simple territorial units, primarily because much of what is now Nyaribari, having been left vacant by the Gusii as a buffer strip against the Masai, was not intensively settled until 1930. The migration to the areas of new settlement broke up the territorial unity of clans, so that each clan has a place of original residence plus one or more places several miles away where people of the same clan reside. As this statement implies, the areas were not randomly settled by individual families, but were occupied by pioneers who then offered land to members of their own lineage.

The result of this pattern of settlement (which is also characteristic of many Gusii areas outside of Nyaribari) is that while clans are no longer territorially unified, local communities are homogeneous with respect to clan membership. A local community is a group of families occupying a continuous area with natural boundaries (e.g., rivers, groves, hilltops), and it is the largest *risaga*, i.e. group recognizing the reciprocal obligation to contribute labour on specific family projects in return for beer. Members of the same maximal risaga, numbering several hundred people, also hold initiation ceremonies jointly and refrain from working in the fields for one day of each other's funerals. There is no headman or formal organization in the local community as such, but the homogeneity of membership in an exogamous clan makes it exogamous and acts as a barrier to social contact between adjacent communities of different clans, thus preserving the traditional interclan antagonism at the level of smaller social units.

Each local community is comprised of several neighbourhoods, which are defined not only residentially but also in terms of *risaga riike*, 'small risaga', within which the work-beer relationship is more frequently called into action. In Nyansongo, a Nyaribari community of slightly over 200 persons, there are three neighbourhoods which roughly coincide with three descent group fragments. All male residents of Nyansongo are of one exogamous clan but two of the neighbourhood clusters are of one sub-clan, while the third such group belongs to a different sub-clan. In one neighbourhood the oldest males of the component homesteads trace their ancestry to two wives of a common great-grandfather; in another, the oldest living males are descended from three wives of a common great-great-grandfather. The third and smallest neighbourhood, with the differing sub-clan affiliation, breaks down into two small lineage groups having remote genealogical relationships with each other. All the lineages represented in the three neighbourhoods have many other members living in similar communities elsewhere in Nyaribari. Thus every family resides in close proximity to members of the same lineage, sub-clan, and clan, but not near all of the other members of any of these descent groups.

Outline of the Developmental Cycle

In this section I shall present the ideals and norms which operate in the developmental processes of Gusii domestic groups; the following section concerns the actual structure of such groups as they are found in a contemporary community.

The homestead (*omochie*, pl. *emechie*) is the basic independently functioning domestic unit in Gusii society, with definite economic, judicial, ritual and educational functions attached to it. In the ideal conception, a homestead consists of a homestead head (*omogaaka bw'omochie*, literally the old man or elder of the homestead), his several wives, their uninitiated children, their married sons plus wives and children. Each wife and each

THE GUSII FAMILY

initiated son (married or not) of the homestead head has a separate house with its own yard, although all of the houses are within a fifty-yard radius and often much less.

In the past, the homestead head was formally the absolute ruler of this group and owner of all its property, with sole power to resolve all its internal difficulties including intrafamilial homicide. The internal allocation of livestock and land was entirely in his hands, and he was also the principal performer of sacrifice to the ancestors, although this latter was less important than in many African societies. There were generally accepted customs concerning allocation of property within the domestic group but if the homestead head chose to disregard them, no one within or outside the homestead could challenge his authority and the matter would wait until after his death for the adjudication of other elders.[1] He had the power of putting a curse on his adult sons, which would kill them or drive them mad unless rescinded after a public apology by the son. Everyone in the homestead was obliged to show deference to its head in their everyday behaviour. However, there were also conventional limits on his behaviour within the homestead; e.g., he was prohibited from entering the houses of his adult sons. Fathers still take this prohibition seriously, even when it occasions discomfort.

In the absence of a stable institutionalized authority system at the inter-homestead level, homesteads had a great deal of individual autonomy with respect to their economic and judicial affairs. In fact, homesteads were thought of as potential military units as well, for retaliation was possible in cases of theft and homicide. A homestead head with many adult sons bound in loyalty to him by the father–son relationship had a military advantage in any struggle that might develop; he was better able to protect his herds and pastures and more prepared to retaliate with force against any combatants within or without the community. Although feuding between individual homesteads was rare, people were cognizant of the physical power that a given homestead could muster in an all-out fight. Each homestead head wanted to have the most populous domestic group possible, with numerous sons as a potential fighting force. The homestead was and is also a patrilineage

[1] These customs are discussed in Mayer (1950a: 25–31).

(*egesaku*), and its head can become the founder of a higher-level lineage if his male progeny are numerous enough to form a separate lineage segment. Thus homestead heads, now as in the past, are highly motivated to increase the size of their homesteads by plural marriages and procreation (but not by adoption). They want wives for their reproductive capacity, daughters, because the bride-wealth cattle paid for them enlarges the family herd and can be used to acquire wives for the homestead head and his sons, and sons because they expand the minimal lineage and take care of their parents in old age. This drive for numerical expansion of the homestead is a fundamental tendency in Gusii domestic life.

Three phases of family development are distinguished, with the first an arbitrary starting point in a continuous cycle of events. They are: (1) the nuclear or polygynous family; (2) the extended or compound family; (3) the dissolution of the compound family. A description of these phases follows.

1. *The nuclear or polygynous family.* This phase begins with a relatively young married homestead head whose father is dead and who has no adult children. He may have boundaries with his brothers' homesteads set by mutual agreement or court rulings, or he may have moved away to a new community where a lineage to which he belongs has land.

Polygyny is the explicit ideal of the Gusii and is commonly practised. Traditionally, four wives were considered ideal because the subgroups based on the wives' households (see below) are linked in successive pairs for purposes of bride-wealth loans and inheritance.[1] Thus the first is so linked with the second, third with fourth, etc., and an uneven number of wives is considered a troublesome and incomplete situation. The first four wives have traditional titles: first, 'the ash-sweeper'; second, 'the helper'; third, 'above the cattle pen'; and fourth, 'the gate'. In fact, a young homestead head is not likely to have two or more wives unless he is wealthy or has many sisters and few brothers, but since this is the ideal pattern it will be outlined here.

The man builds a separate house for each wife and allots to her fields to cultivate; she stores the produce in her own granary, using it to feed herself, her husband, and her children. The

[1] See Mayer (1950a: 28).

proceeds from any sales of grain from her fields are usually used to buy clothing and other articles for the wife and her children, although a domineering husband may occasionally appropriate some of this cash. However, the homestead head has his own fields, the unallocated reserve (*emonga*), which he cultivates when he is home during planting season, persuading his wives to weed it if he goes away to take a job later in the year. Aside from grain fields, this unallocated reserve usually includes a coffee garden, the proceeds from which (like his wages from employment) are his alone, although he may use them to provide clothes for his wives and school fees for his children.

In addition to his wives and children, the young homestead head may have his widowed mother living in his homestead in a house of her own and with fields allotted to her from which she produces her own food. When she becomes feeble or blind and is unable to cultivate the fields, her son's wives feed her, although she continues to live in her own house. Her son's children are frequent companions, and the granddaughters often sleep in her house. Another possible homestead resident is an unmarried uterine brother of the head, also living in a separate house of his own.

As his sons approach adolescence, the homestead head builds a small children's house (*esaiga*) for them and he may occasionally sleep in this house himself with his uninitiated sons. Aside from this, however, the homestead head has no house of his own, and he resides alternately with each of his wives if he is a polygynist.[1]

2. *The extended family.* This phase begins when the sons of the homestead head marry and bring their wives to reside in their father's homestead. A foreshadowing of this event occurs when a son is initiated at ten to twelve years of age, at which time a special hut is built for his post-circumcision seclusion. He lives in this small hut, not far from his mother's house, thenceforth and brings his bride there at marriage. Residence at marriage is strictly virilocal, although the bride may spend a good deal of time visiting her parents in the early stages of the

[1] I have omitted description of marriage practices from this account because of limitations of scope and space. Traditional marriage practices are described in Mayer (1950a, 1950b).

union.[1] Initially, the bride shares the hearth of her mother-in-law, but the latter takes pains not to bully or offend her new daughter-in-law. Before she gives birth, her husband builds her a full-size house in the homestead in which they both reside.

The major event of this phase is the gradual hardening of subgroup organization based on the mother–son relationship within the polygynous homestead. A subgroup of this type, consisting of a mother, her married sons, and their dependents, is called *enyomba*, 'house' and is an extension of the mother–child household characteristic of the previous phase. Each 'house' forms a rough spatial unit within the homestead, since married sons live on land allotted to their mother, which is nearer the physical structure in which she resides than it is to that of her co-wives. Furthermore, the house is a unit for the inheritance and transfer of bride-wealth livestock. The sons of a particular woman have residual rights in the bride-wealth brought in by the marriages of their uterine sisters; each son is entitled to obtain at least one wife in this way if there are enough daughters in the mother's house. At the same time, the homestead head is entitled to use the cattle brought in by the marriage of the eldest daughter of each house to acquire a wife for himself. In doing so, he establishes a debt between the house of the new wife and the one from which the cattle were taken; such debts do not expire and repayment may be claimed by the descendants of the creditor house many years later. Even when the homestead head does not want to take a wife for himself, he must formally give his permission for his son to use the bride-wealth of his uterine sister in marriage. He may also transfer cattle from a house with many daughters to one with a preponderance of sons, though a debt is established in such an allocation.[2]

The competition for bride-wealth among adult sons, and the father's actions in allocating the available cattle, tend to solidify the interests of the houses with respect to one another.

[1] In this early period, the marriage may be dissolved and the cattle returned, which frequently happens when brides are not happy with their husbands and offines. Once this period is past, Gusii marriages tend to be stable, both conjugally and jurally, although separations later on in marriage are more frequent than legal divorces.

[2] See Mayer (1950a: 26–29).

THE GUSII FAMILY

The sons of each house, uterine brothers, form a solidary unit acting to protect the property interests of their mother and themselves without directly assailing paternal authority. The homestead head treats each house as a unit; e.g., he may beat one of his wives for the misbehaviour of her adult sons, or allot a poor piece of land to the son of a wife who has displeased him. Inter-house rivalry creates a delicate problem for the patriarch, for obvious favouritism on his part can lead to open conflict between the houses, a consequence he wishes to avoid at all costs. The culturally valued solution to this problem is for the homestead head to maintain an attitude of impartiality, while suppressing any overt conflict by the firm use of his authority to command and punish.

3. *Dissolution of the homestead.* When a homestead head dies, the dissolution of the homestead is expected to follow eventually. No matter what happens, it is unlikely that a widow will move far away or stop cultivating her fields, for she is not welcome as a resident at the homes of her parents and brothers, and she wants to retain the land allotted her by the deceased for her own subsistence and so that her sons may inherit it. Furthermore, the bride-wealth paid for her gives her husband's lineage perpetual rights to her child-bearing powers and custody of her children unless the bride-wealth is returned. Thus she must take a leviratic husband (who may be merely an occasional sexual partner) from among the agnates of the deceased; although the children fathered by him are known as children of the deceased and have the inheritance rights that go with this. It should be noted that the levir must be a real or classificatory brother of the dead husband; adult sons are strictly prohibited from having sexual relations with their father's young widows.

The fate of the homestead after its head dies is dependent on the phase of the developmental cycle it had reached at his death. If he leaves only one young wife with small children, then she may become attached as a leviratic wife to the homestead of his brother or ortho-cousin who lives near by. Under these conditions, the widow may move into a new house at the latter man's homestead and continue to cultivate the adjacent fields which were allotted her by the deceased. She may become socially indistinguishable from his other wives, except that her children look for their inheritance to the property of the man who paid bride-wealth for their mother, not to their stepfather. This is one kind of outcome when the homestead head dies during the first phase. If the deceased leaves two wives and one has a son approaching maturity, a brother of the dead man will act in his place as homestead head until the sons of the wives are married and have agreed to a division of the land into separate homesteads. This guardian is permitted to take only one of the wives in the levirate, with the other finding herself a different appropriate agnate of her husband whose relationship with her will be limited to occasional sexual relations. In such a situation, the original homestead organization persists for a period of years after the death of its head. Although the guardian formally assumes the jural authority of homestead head, his actual activities are ordinarily limited to advising the older wife concerning bride-wealth transactions and court cases, and attempting to settle internal disputes; he does not attempt to rule the wives and children with the iron hand of the deceased.

If, on the other hand, the homestead head dies during the second phase of the developmental process, i.e., when he has married sons residing in the homestead, the outcome is considerably different. Although the dead man's brother takes a protective interest, major decisions for the homestead group are made by the oldest son. Division of the land, at least among the houses, proceeds apace and can result in the formation of separate homesteads within a few years. The wives remain on the land formerly allotted to them by their husband, now the land of their sons, and their leviratic mates may be agnates living at a considerable distance who serve only to father children for them until they reach menopause.

The actual dissolution of a polygynous extended family homestead begins before the death of its head. Although there is an expectation of equal division of property among the sons, with the oldest son of the oldest wife being singled out for a slightly larger share, it is the father's prerogative to decide what each son will inherit before his death and to express himself on this subject before he dies. He may have done so, but the sons will nevertheless assemble the lineage elders and bring land-claims based on the mother's use of certain fields and livestock claims based on inter-house debts. If these cannot be settled by the elders, they are taken to court and decided after a lengthy process of litigation. By and large, this sequence applies primarily to the sons of the several houses as units; intra-house divisions of property are less formal and are treated in the following section. Suffice it to say at this point that, while land fragmentation is increasing, migration of some sons to new lands outside the community after their father's death still serves to retard its pace.

With the division of land among the brothers, each locating his homestead on his share, a full cycle has been completed. In the following section the three phases as presented above will be examined as they occur in a contemporary Gusii community, and irregularities noted.

Families in a Contemporary Gusii Community

What follows is a review of the developmental process outlined above from the viewpoint of their applicability to domestic groups in a single small community, which I call Nyansongo and which consists of eighteen homesteads with a little more than two hundred persons. The three phases previously distinguished are in a sense ideal types, abstractions based primarily on Gusii expectations of 'normal' family organization and process. The question to be taken up at this point is the extent to which these abstractions are congruent with the reality of a particular social microcosm.

1. *The nuclear or polygynous family.* The first question here is whether men do become polygynists before the sons of their first wives marry, i.e., whether the homestead becomes polygynous before it takes on generational complexity. Of the twenty-seven married men in Nyansongo, fifteen are monogamists and twelve polygynists (one has three wives and eleven have two wives each). However, plural wives (or widows) outnumber monogamous wives or widows twenty-four to nineteen.[1] The developmental picture is clarified when one realizes that, despite the roughly equivalent number of polygynous and

---

[1] Two men have plural wives who did not live in Nyansongo during the period of field-work; the men are counted as polygynists but their non-resident wives are not included in the enumeration of women.

monogamous adults, more than two-thirds of the children in Nyansongo have polygynous parents. This is largely because so many of the monogamous men are young husbands whose wives have not yet given birth or have done so only once. Given this situation, it is reasonable to suppose that by the time these young men have many more children they will have taken second wives. Thus it would seem that polygyny usually precedes the marriage of any children.

In fact, however, there are two alternate paths to polygyny for a man who is not blessed with either a cattle-rich father (as few Nyansongo men are) or a superabundance of sisters. One path, found more among men over fifty than among younger men, is to remain monogamous until the first daughter marries at twelve to sixteen years of age, and then use her bride-wealth cattle to procure a second wife. This puts an age differential of at least fifteen years between the two wives and also means that some of the first wife's children will be as old as the second wife. In this situation, the sequence of polygyny first, then the extended family, does not exactly apply, for although the homestead head has the power to delay the marriage of his oldest son by taking the first daughter's bride-wealth for himself, it often happens (since girls marry at a much younger age than boys) that both are able to take wives at about the same time. The homestead becomes polygynous and generationally extended simultaneously. This developmental pattern results from dependence on the daughter's marriages as the sole source of bride-wealth.

The other path to polygyny is taken by young men who do not intend to wait until their daughters marry before taking a second wife. They are usually enterprising individuals, often with a few years of schooling, and they become employed for long periods outside of Gusiiland or become local traders and thus earn enough money to acquire second wives long before the children of their first wives are mature. One Nyansongo man of this kind was a policeman, permanently employed outside the district, one was a trader, and a third worked for the chief. Although this alternative may seem the result of culture contact, it can be seen as corresponding to the cattle raids carried out by men before 1907, whereby they could acquire bride-wealth without waiting for the marriages of their daughters and sisters. Then, as now, this was an alternative for the more enterprising youths, not for everyone. An increasing variation of this path to polygyny is the acquisition of a second wife by elopement, i.e., persuading her to leave her father's homestead and live as a wife without payment of the bride-wealth which legitimizes such unions.[1] The bride-wealth may be paid later on; if it is not, there is little chance that the union will last.

In those cases where a man has acquired a second legitimate wife before the marriage of his first daughter, the structure of seniority and authority between the two houses is less clear than it is where he has used the daughter's bride-wealth for his second marriage. This is because in the first situation the age differential between the wives, and between their older children, is considerably less, and also because the second wife has not come into the homestead with her house owing cattle to the first wife. Since there is no formal ranking of wives in order of seniority, the two wives of similar age are more likely to be competitive and hostile to one another, although there are a few outstanding exceptions in Nyansongo. It should also be noted that the sooner a man takes a second wife, the more likely it is that he will be a polygynist before his father dies. Thus there are in Nyansongo several polygynists who are not homestead heads because they are still members of their fathers' ongoing homesteads.

In the power relationships within the homestead, polygyny makes a great difference. The monogamous male is dependent on his wife for sexual satisfaction, food preparation and other domestic tasks, and a large proportion of the homestead's agricultural activities. When they have a quarrel, she may run back to her parents' homestead for a week, leaving him a bachelor with the responsibilities of a married man. Once he has a second wife, however, he can do without one of his wives more easily, and the wife is hesitant to run away for fear of diminishing her relative standing in the homestead. The rivalry among the co-wives, although potentially dangerous, works to augment the power of the husband whose favour is a scarce commodity desired by both wives. First wives often foresee

[1] Elopement and the sexual and marital patterns of contemporary Gusii are more fully described in LeVine (1959).

this and oppose the second marriages of their husbands; those who are successful in this effort appear to retain a permanent power advantage in the family.

2. *The extended or compound family.* Despite the strictly virilocal pattern of residence in Nyansongo, only six of the eighteen homesteads were complete extended family homesteads in the sense of containing a homestead head and one or more of his married sons. No married men resident in the community had fathers who lived elsewhere, but many of them had deceased fathers. Thus only one-third of the homesteads conformed to the extended family pattern at a particular point in time, which means that many Nyansongo men marry for the first time after their fathers are dead. Some homesteads go directly from the nuclear family phase, with no mature children, to the dissolution phase, with the deceased husband's brother acting as guardian of the family. In others, the extended family phase is a few years or months between the marriage of the oldest son and the death of his father, with the younger sons being married later on.

I have mentioned above that the hardening of subgroup organization within the homestead during this extended phase creates problems of management for the homestead head. Ideally, he succeeds in containing the conflict and maintaining his own authority, but in fact there are homestead heads who are not successful in this regard. Any man who acquires two wives fairly early in life has had a foreshadowing of the problems of this phase, for it is the enmity between co-wives which is extended and intensified in inter-house rivalry during this phase. Although the wives have their allotted fields and the products from them, as well as livestock associated with their respective houses, the husband has control, through his wages and the unallocated reserve of fields and livestock, over the surplus resources of the homestead. His distribution of luxuries such as meat, sugar, tea, and clothing becomes an object of invidious distinction among the wives, and serious inequalities in the distribution lead to bitter hostility among the wives. The bearing and rearing of children is the primary focus of jealousy, for even temporary sterility is regarded by a woman as a serious misfortune, particularly if her co-wife continues to give birth. The number of infant deaths suffered by each of the wives is similarly considered and, when the children grow up, the distribution of school fees among the children of the several houses becomes a problem.

There are several reasons why co-wife jealousy becomes intensified when the sons reach adulthood. One is that the father must pay more attention to his adult sons than to children, and his attention, particularly when it has any economic implications, is seen by the sons and their mothers as signs of advantage or disadvantage in the competition for the homestead property which eventuates in inheritance. The mother is deeply involved in this because she will be dependent on her sons in old age and wants to see them favoured by the homestead head. Another reason is that when the sons are old enough for marriage, the allocation of available cattle for bride-wealth becomes crucial, and debts between the houses take on a new importance. Finally, co-wife jealousy is intensified in this phase because each of the wives has her sons to stand by her and fight her battles within the homestead. Thus a rivalry which was previously an expected squabble among women, which the homestead head might easily handle, develops into a fight between groups of uterine brothers, who are expected to remain unified as members of a common lineage headed by their father.

If the homestead head is diplomatic, impartial, and fortunate, the lines of cleavage within the homestead do not harden to the point of threatening its unity under his leadership. However, I observed cases of homestead heads who had either indulged in favouritism or been lacking in firmness (or both), whose authority was being overtly challenged by their wives and sons. One man outside of Nyansongo, a polygynist with three wives, was faced with a situation in which one wife refused to move her house in compliance with the husband's desire to plan his holding along the lines laid down by the Agricultural Department. She had become convinced by the past actions of her husband that he wanted to give her land to other wives, and her adult sons, though professing loyalty to their father, insisted that her wishes be respected. The father claimed to have been threatened with physical violence by these sons. This example of breakdown of paternal authority can be countered with cases of fathers who remained respected leaders despite inter-house dissension, but it serves to indicate that variations in behaviour of homestead heads during the extended family phase are a source of variations in the degree of homestead conformity to ideals concerning the extended family.

Another type of deviation from the ideal picture of the extended phase is provided by the monogamous extended family. There are some homestead heads in Nyansongo who never became polygynists, although they have adult sons living in their homesteads. One such monogamist, a man in his seventies, had three married sons and one who was arranging a marriage during the period of field study. The oldest son had taken a second wife by elopement and wanted to legitimize the union with the payment of bride-wealth. The family was beset by two major problems: a scarcity of cattle for the four sons to marry with, and a homestead head who was a passive husband and father. The oldest son was angry that the parents had allowed money which he sent home for his second marriage to be used to purchase bride-wealth cattle for a younger son. Later on, when this younger son had become a policeman and was sending money for his parents to hold for him, they allowed yet another son to use the money for his bride-wealth cattle. An adultery suit against the oldest son for cohabitation with his second 'wife' and the homecoming of the policeman son brought fraternal strife to a point where the father could not control it. Their quarrels over bride-wealth resulted in the oldest son attacking his mother with a hoe (for which the chief incarcerated him) and in the erection of a fence between the areas occupied by the first and third sons in the homestead. The fence, erected by the third son, symbolized the disruption of fraternal relations in the extended family. What is most striking about this case is that, though it involves a monogamous homestead lacking subdivision into houses, the rivalry of uterine brothers resembles in many particulars the interaction of houses in polygynous homesteads. The basic principle common to both situations is the competition for scarce resources among members of the same generation in the family, and it takes a strong homestead head to keep this competition within peaceful bounds whether the family is polygynous or monogamous.

3. *Dissolution of the homestead.* The interregnum between the death of a homestead head and the formation of new homesteads out of the previous one is a critical subphase in the developmental process, and it takes a variety of forms. If the several houses have adult sons and there has been a keen competition for bride-wealth and property before the father died, then rapid steps may be taken to divide the homestead jurally and socially. The process of division may nevertheless drag on through years of litigation, and in the meantime one or more of the parties may build a new house as close as possible to a boundary which he wants to establish, in order to lay claim to the land on which the house is built. In such a situation, the proximity of house construction indicates conflict rather than solidarity.

In legal proceedings the oldest son of each house is often the one who claims the land which his mother cultivated and which his father allegedly wanted him to have. His younger uterine brothers, who are often unmarried, live in their bachelor houses on the same piece of land as part of the same homestead. If the share of the original homestead is not large enough for all the brothers, some of them may seek land in the newer areas of settlement where they have close patrilineal kinsmen who are willing to give them land. In Nyansongo, several young men in 1957 moved out to areas near the Masai border which had been occupied by immigrant Kikuyu until their expulsion by the government in 1953; there they established their own homesteads. Under these circumstances, however, at least one son of each house remains behind so as not to lose the claim of that house to its share of the original homestead. Pioneering is not possible for everyone; alternatives available to Nyansongo men include: getting permanent jobs outside the district (leaving a wife behind to cultivate a small portion), using land on the chief's estate (he allows his near-by clansmen to use it rent free); and working as an employee for the chief. These alternatives allow the community to survive in the face of increasing fragmentation of its land.

Some homesteads do not break up into separate and hostile social units after the death of their heads. In Nyansongo there are brothers and half-brothers who have agreed on boundaries among themselves and continue to regard themselves as sharing a homestead although each governs his own family and property separately. Pastures are used by them commonly and their children herd cattle together. An even more striking case in the community is that of its biggest polygynist, who died seventeen years earlier. In 1957, his homestead was still a single social unit. Two of the five widows had died, but the survivors kept their houses near one another and had extremely friendly and co-operative relations. Each had leviratic relations with males near or far and had continued to give birth, but none had been incorporated into a different homestead. Their sons and some of the sons of the dead wives had houses there as part of one big homestead, but a few had pioneered new land in the area mentioned above. One would be tempted to think of this arrangement as a co-wife matriarchy, in that the senior generation is represented solely by women, but the widows do not rule the homestead; it is governed in fact by their older sons who regard themselves as the owners of the land and have managed to agree about the allocation of land within their father's homestead. There has been no need so far to make a formal division of the land, and so the 'interregnum period' has lasted for almost two decades. This homestead was recognized as unusual in Nyansongo, and the widows attributed its persistence to the fact that their husband had fostered harmony and co-operation among his wives to an unconventional degree. Although a deviant case, this family indicates that homesteads do not always dissolve quickly upon the death of their founders.

Conclusions: Paternal Authority in the Homestead

The Gusii homestead is organized around a founder who is its head while he is alive. The above discussion suggests that, while the fission of homesteads is an inevitable part of lineage segmentation at the level of the polygynous extended family, there is much that the homestead head can do to accelerate or retard this process. His policies concerning his co-wives in the first phase and their houses in the extended family phase can aggravate or alleviate grievances over bride-wealth and land which may affect the rapidity and extent of homestead division after his death. In many cases, scarcity of family resources creates fraternal competition so intense that only respect for

THE GUSII FAMILY

paternal authority, skilfully used by the homestead head, can contain the conflict while he is alive, and nothing can contain it thereafter.

Social change in Gusiiland is presenting a number of challenges to paternal authority which may affect domestic group structure in the future. One challenge is that of the son who has been employed outside the district, earning money independently of the family economy, and coming into contact with authority figures more powerful than his father. Though many of them contribute a substantial proportion of their earnings to the family in the form of school fees for their brothers and gifts to their parents, such sons are less likely to conform to traditional standards of filial piety. Open defiance of paternal authority develops when the son decides to appropriate for his own use some of the cattle from the bride-wealth brought in by his uterine sister. Knowing that he is customarily entitled to these cattle, he neglects to ask his father's permission for them. Most frequently, the father, furious at this threat to his control of homestead resources, reports his son to the police as a thief, and the son is imprisoned briefly (while the cattle are returned) reprimanded by the chief, and released. In some cases, fathers have burned down the houses of their sons within the same homestead for taking cattle. With support from outside authorities, then, fathers are currently winning this fight with their sons, but the conflict is likely to continue.

Another serious challenge to the authority of the homestead is the elopement of daughters. With bride-wealth rates high, young men are frequently resorting to persuading young girls to run away with them without payment of bride-wealth. In some cases the chief's police are brought in and they manage to recapture the girl and have the youth prosecuted in the African tribunal courts for the 'customary law' offence of removing a girl without the consent of her parents. Many elopements are successful, however, and this means that the girl's father is dependent on the goodwill of her lover for payment of bride-wealth. If the bride-wealth is not forthcoming, the father of the girl may resort to a number of actions which will not be detailed here. The basic point is that, the fewer bride-wealth marriages take place, the less the homestead head has an important resource under his control which will command the respect and obedience of his sons. If the daughters do not bring in bride-wealth cattle and the sons do not need such cattle for conjugal unions, an important paternal power has been lost, especially in light of the fact that fathers have the traditional right to deny bride-wealth to misbehaving sons. At present the bride-wealth system is far from collapsing, but the trend towards elopement is clearly evident.

A final challenge to paternal authority is land fragmentation. The less land the father has to allot and to leave his sons at his death, the less will they be dependent on him. When the land shortage becomes serious, a son will have a choice of pioneering new land if he can find it (thus breaking the pattern of residence at the father's homestead) or obtaining permanent employment. Both alternatives, in so far as they are actually available, free the son of paternal control. In the meantime, before the alternative of permanent employment becomes a highly developed pattern, fathers will have to contend with increasing fraternal conflict over the decreasing amount of available land, and this also poses a threat to their authority. The decay of paternal authority in the extended family seems likely to produce a somewhat different developmental process in Gusii domestic groups than the one described in this article.

REFERENCES

LeVine, Robert A. 1959. 'Gusii Sex Offences: A Study in Social Control', *American Anthropologist*, 61.
—— 1963. 'Wealth and Power in Gusiiland', in *Markets in Africa*, ed. Paul Bohannan and George Dalton, Northwestern University Press.
LeVine, Robert, A. and Barbara. 1963. 'Nyansongo: A Gusii Community in Kenya', in *Six Cultures: Studies of Child Rearing*, ed. B. B. Whiting, New York, John Wiley.
Mayer, Philip. 1949. *The Lineage Principle in Gusii Society*, London, International African Institute (Memorandum No. 24).
—— 1950a. *Gusii Bridewealth Law and Custom* (Rhodes-Livingstone Paper No. 18), London, Oxford University Press.
—— 1950b. 'Privileged Obstruction of Marriage Rites among the Gusii', *Africa*, 20.
—— 1951. 'Bridewealth Limitation among the Gusii', in *Two Studies in Applied Anthropology in Kenya* (Colonial Research Studies No. 3), London, H.M.S.O.

FAMILY AND LINEAGE AMONG THE SUKU OF THE CONGO

Igor Kopytoff

THE Suku are a Bantu-speaking people living in a region of rolling savanna in South-western Congo (formerly the Belgian Congo) between the upper stretches of the Bakali and Kwenge rivers.[1] Their territory measures roughly fifty by one hundred miles, with a population of about eighty thousand. Population density is, thus, relatively low—some fourteen or fifteen persons per square mile. Suku subsistence is derived primarily from the cultivation of manioc and from hunting and fishing.

The ancestors of the Suku, like those of many neighbouring groups, appear to have occupied this area some one hundred and fifty or two hundred years ago in an eastward migration which originated in the Kwango river valley and which is related to the imposition of Lunda hegemony over the region. According to tradition, the Suku paramount chief, known as the MeniKongo, led his subjects into the largely empty lands in the east. The population that remained in the Kwango valley under Lunda control are at present known as the Yaka. Many of the Suku and Yaka lineages belong to the same clans and some maintain occasional contacts. Culturally and linguistically, the two groups are closely akin to each other.

[1] This paper deals with the main body of the Suku group, most of whom live in Feshi territory of the Kwango district of the Province of Leopoldville. The data presented do not necessarily apply to some thirty thousand Suku who form an isolated enclave straddling the Congo-Angola border to the south and whom I did not visit. The field-work was done during 1958 and the first half of 1959. It was supported by a Ford Foundation fellowship grant and was conducted under the auspices of the Program of African Studies, Northwestern University.

Similarly, the eastern Suku resemble the Sonde, their neighbours to the east, who, like the Yaka, are ruled by chiefs of Lunda origin. The Suku have successfully resisted Lunda encroachment and have their own independent paramount chief.

We are thus dealing with a group which is not a discrete cultural unit but rather a political one, for all Suku recognize the authority of the MeniKongo. The formal political system is based on the delegation of power by the paramount chief to regional chiefs and sub-chiefs. One of the principal expressions of this power is the periodic collection of tribute in each region and its flow, at least ideally, upwards to the MeniKongo through the successive links in the chains of delegated authority. While this structure served, in pre-colonial times, to maintain relative order and peace and fulfilled some judicial functions, the sparseness of settlement and the limited means of communication permitted the operation of other political patterns independent of the formal organization. This complementary political system regulated relations between lineages as quasi-autonomous units; it included resort to armed strife, self-help, capture of hostages, enslavement of strangers, and mediation of disputes by non-chiefly tribunals.[1]

According to the earliest available administrative records, dating back to the middle 1920's, Suku villages normally varied in size between fifteen and seventy-five inhabitants; only the villages of important chiefs were larger. Since then, the Belgian administration has grouped villages into bigger clusters within which, however, subdivisions corresponding in structure and size to the old villages persist.

Spatially, villages are relatively stable; some have not changed their general location for thirty years and when changes occur (for example, during epidemics or after the death of an important chief) the village moves within a radius which is seldom more than a mile. Shifting agriculture, it may be noted, does not make it necessary to displace villages. The soil, once planted, must lie fallow for fifteen or twenty years;

---

[1] The operations of this 'informal' political organization are described in a previous article, 'Extension of Conflict as a Method of Conflict Resolution among the Suku of the Congo', *Journal of Conflict Resolution*, Vol. 5, No. 1, March 1961, pp. 61–69.

FAMILY AND LINEAGE AMONG THE SUKU

but land is plentiful, manioc yields are sufficient to support a family of four or five on little over an acre a year, and fields are at any rate planted at some distance from the village to prevent depredations by domestic animals. There is always enough cultivable land within what is regarded as a convenient distance of about a mile.

In this paper, dealing with the family cycle, certain broad facts of Suku social organization are best mentioned at the outset, to be dealt with later in greater detail. Suku descent is matrilineal. The fundamental social units are corporate autonomous matrilineages which are further grouped into clans. Residence at marriage is virilocal and the male children of a man reside with him, patrilocally, at least until his death and often thereafter with his brothers or other older members of their father's matrilineage. Consequently, the membership of a matrilineage is always dispersed among several villages and the constituent lineages of a clan are scattered throughout the Suku area. In any one village, the adult male population does not all belong to the same lineage. At the same time, every lineage possesses its own territorial centre—the village originally founded by it. The persistence of this centre depends upon the continued residence in it of a certain number of lineage members, particularly the older ones. It is clear that one of the important factors affecting the cycle of residence of the nuclear family is the necessity of reconciling its patrilineally-biased residence rules with the need of maintaining the lineage centre.

An observer wishing to classify the specific types of residence found among the Suku quickly discovers great variation with no dominant statistical trends. He also finds, however, that the variation is not fortuitous and that each type is the product of a specific series of events and of residential shifts each of which exhibits discernible regularities, even though there is an accidental aspect to their arrangement in a particular series. To explain why a particular person lives where he does it is often necessary to examine the shifts in residence by other persons over two and even three generations back. This essay is concerned with presenting a model which accounts for all the variations in structure and residence found among Suku nuclear and extended families. To achieve this, the following features of Suku culture must be described in some detail:

(1) the overall lineage organization, (2) the functions of the corporate matrilineage, (3) the system of property control, and (4) the nature of Suku marriage and the structure of legal rights that it establishes in the nuclear and extended family.

Lineage Organization

By the rule of matrilineal descent, every Suku belongs to a series of kinship groups of different magnitude. All these groups are called by the same term *kikanda* (pl. *bikanda*). Another less frequently used term is *mvumu* (pl. and s.). Although usually used synonymously, the latter tends to be restricted to groups of lower magnitude. Analytically, the following matrilineal units may be distinguished: the presumptive clan, the operative clan, the major lineage, and the autonomous lineage.

The presumptive clan is one in which the relationship is uncertain but given lip-service with the appropriate etiquette. In important economic and political matters, however, it is disputed unless established by firm evidence not the least of which is repeated divination. The operative clan, on the other hand, groups several lineages whose common descent is unquestioned even though the exact genealogical connections may have been forgotten.

Generically, of course, it is not the separate lineages that 'constitute' a clan but rather it is a single lineage, back in time, which has become a clan because it has segmented into several units. The present structure of lineages must be viewed in this light and for this the process of lineage segmentation must be examined. To understand this process one must take into account the fact of territorial dispersion and the practical necessity for an isolated kin-group to have a relative degree of autonomy both in its internal organization and *vis-à-vis* its neighbours, given that the relations with them are culturally defined as being among corporate groups. Historically, many lineages appear to have subdivided at the time of the eastward migration, some segments remaining under the Lunda conquerors and thus becoming Yaka while others moved into new territory and became Suku. Segmentation also seems to have occurred when the present Suku territory was being occupied;

traditions constantly refer to the separation from the bulk of a lineage of several adult members, usually siblings, as they set out in search of empty lands. In these conditions, the practical autonomy of a segment in economic matters and marriage arrangements would eventually be confirmed by the formalization of their ritual autonomy through the division of the lineage 'medicines'. A similar process of segmentation may be started when a woman marries a man from a distant area and through her descendants, residing patrilocally, establishes an enclave of the lineage there—an enclave which, if it persists and grows, eventually develops into an autonomous lineage. As long as the relationship between such segments is remembered and recognized, they constitute what we have called an operative clan. In time, however, the clanship tie may become merely presumptive and finally disappear altogether.

Although some territorial dispersion of the lineage is inevitable, given the rules of residence and descent, whether a particular lineage segments or not depends on the extent of the dispersion. A lineage can function effectively as a corporate group as long as contact and periodic consultations among its members can be maintained without great difficulty over the distance separating them. At the present time, this distance seems to be some twenty or twenty-five miles; in pre-colonial times, when travel was not always safe, it was probably less.[1] Consequently, as long as a lineage is not scattered over too wide an area, it need not segment, although it may sometimes do so as a result of internal quarrels. It is therefore impossible to speak of the normative or even 'normal' genealogical depth of an autonomous corporate lineage. Some have remained unsegmented for five or six generations (that is, for about the maximum period of trustworthy reconstruction), while others in the same time have given rise to several new lineages. The question of genealogical depth is further complicated by another feature of Suku lineage structure, namely that autonomous lineages of an operative clan, and even sections of them, may re-merge back into a single lineage. Such

---

[1] There is some indication that with the increase in safety of travel and the consequent expansion of communications re-mergers of previously autonomous lineage segments have become more frequent and segmentation resulting from distance less prevalent.

remergers are not tied to the previous order of segmentation nor do they affect the autonomy of the remaining lineages of the clan (some of which, in fact, may be more closely related to either of the merging lineages). If a lineage finds itself without any mature adults to succeed to its headship, an elder from a related lineage is called in to assume the position and he usually brings with him several real or classificatory brothers and sororal nephews. Similarly, a member of one lineage, by setting up permanent residence very near a related lineage, becomes incorporated into it as full-fledged member.

This structure reflects a central point in the Suku conception of the blood unity inherent in common matrilineal descent, a conception emphasized by the lack of different terms to separate the various analytical levels of kinship grouping. Segmentation and lineage autonomy are seen mainly as concessions to practical necessity (be it territorial separation or a quarrel with the almost inevitable concomitant development of accusations of witchcraft and the felt need for protection against it); but segmentation is not viewed as a desirable or even normal condition in itself. Thus, ideally, the entire operative clan is a single corporate group which, because of circumstances, is subdivided into units somewhat analogous to the 'local chapters' of a fraternal organization in the west. Every autonomous lineage is, as shall be seen, a corporate group but it is that primarily in its relations with neighbouring unrelated lineages rather than with the other lineages of the same operative clan. Within the clan, its autonomy is expressed in that it has a separate head and separate 'medicines' and in that it acts as an independent agency in everyday economic matters and in contracting marriages. But if the lineage owns hunting territories or holds a political chieftaincy from the king, it controls such rights in trust for the entire operative clan. As a matter of necessity and convenience, the active exercise of these rights remains within the lineage. But that the latent ties are there is shown by the re-mergers described above, by the full sharing of hunting or political tribute with members of other lineages who happen to be present, and by the sending of at least symbolic portions of such additions of wealth to distant related lineages.

What we have called the major lineage is a kinship grouping

which stands midway between the autonomous lineage and the operative clan. Fundamentally, it is a corporate lineage which has not completed its segmentation and, in fact, may never do so. While its two constituent segments act as autonomous groups in certain respects, they retain their corporate unity in others. Thus, if the lineage controls a chieftaincy, succession to it devolves upon the oldest male in the entire major lineage; similarly, ownership of hunting lands is actively maintained by the whole group. Yet, in such matters as marriage and control and inheritance of movable property, the two segments act as separate units. This situation usually arises when the original lineage has been rent by dissension or when a new lineage offshoot has arisen at some distance but is not large enough to establish its formal autonomy by dividing the lineage 'medicines'. In either case, the process of segmentation may be completed or reversed, as quarrels are patched up or as the minor offshoot fails to grow and eventually moves back to the parent village.

The Autonomous Corporate Lineage

In this paper, it is the minimal autonomous lineage which is most relevant to the discussion of marriage and the family structure. Ordinarily, this group consists of three matrilineally related generations. The oldest may contain two or three elders of each sex; the middle generation may comprise a half-score middle-aged and younger adults; the roster is completed with some ten to fifteen children and adolescents borne by the females of the previous generation. The total number of members typically fluctuates between twenty-five and thirty. As an estimate of the size of the Suku operative clan, this writer can state that he has not seen any that contain more than five such lineages.

A corporate lineage has a name which may be that of the person who, in retrospect, has been its founder, or that of a 'medicine' associated with its headship. Its formally designated head is always the oldest member, barring mental incompetence or extreme physical disability. Discounting a few exceptional cases, the head always resides at the lineage centre. Here are also found several other lineage members as well as residents belonging to other lineages but living here in patrilocal residence. The rest of the lineage is scattered among several other villages in the vicinity.

The unity of the lineage, expressed in the concept of *menga mamosi* ('one blood'), is directly reflected in the supernatural system. Every corporate lineage has a *musiku*, a special pot of 'medicines', which is ritually indispensable for the marriages of its women with members of other lineages; in addition, the *musiku* gives supernatural force to the power of elders and ancestors. Every lineage also possesses a certain number of 'sacred medicines' (*mikisi*) which affect it as a unit; any violation of ritual taboos connected with these 'medicines' are believed to result in sickness or death in the lineage as a whole and not only, or even necessarily, for the violator himself. Similarly, the dissatisfaction of elders and ancestors affect the fortunes of the entire lineage. Finally, witchcraft operates only within the boundaries of the lineage.[1]

Politically, the lineage is an entirely autonomous unit as far as its internal affairs are concerned. Political chiefs and the king may intervene only in inter-lineage quarrels, with the sole exception of matters affecting the operation of the formal political system, in whose stability the king has an interest. Within the lineage, authority is vested in the group of elders who represent its oldest living generation. It is they who make the important decisions affecting the lineage as a whole, though not without consulting the more mature men of the generation under them. The lineage head has no special authority in this regard, his position being that of a spokesman for the lineage.

The intricate system of sanctions supporting the authority of the elders may be briefly summarized by the concept of 'protection', in its widest sense, which one enjoys as a lineage member and which may be withdrawn by the elders. The

[1] This does not mean that a witch cannot attack a person who is not a member of the same lineage. The ideological structure of witchcraft allows for this but at the same time it is believed that the witches of the victim's lineage would prevent such attacks as an infringement upon their rights, in the same way that any lineage member opposes a theft of lineage property. A stranger witch is permitted to 'eat' members of another lineage only as a means of repayment of a flesh-debt previously contracted by witches of that lineage, and it is the latter therefore who are blamed.

withdrawal may be silent, even unconscious, or it may take the form of an open curse; in either case, it results in misfortune, disease, or death for a younger member. Elders are also often held to be witches and this further supports their power. The importance of these supernatural sanctions, with which we can deal here only in passing, cannot be overemphasized.

The Suku often compare the relationship with one's lineage elders to that between an animal and its owner. This metaphor is used to explain not only the corporate right of the lineage, as represented by its elders, to the labour and wealth of its younger members but even the *sub rosa* right of elder witches to 'eat' their juniors (this, however, must be done moderately since a succession of deaths, as during epidemics, may be countered by a poison trial). In pre-colonial times, the elders had the right to sell junior members as punishment for repeated and costly breaches of conduct or simply because of financial need.

The corporate unity of the lineage appears clearly in its relations with other lineages. Here, reciprocity is stringently maintained by both sides. Obligations contracted by any member bind the lineage as a whole; individual transgressions become the responsibility of all the members; self-help may be resorted to indiscriminately against any one of them by a wronged lineage. Debts between them never lapse; even a borrowed basket of peanuts is remembered for two or three generations and sooner or later reclaimed. Homicide, be it accidental or not, must be compensated with the payment of two persons or by a reciprocal murder; a theft is cancelled only by the return of an equivalent object, plus a fine, or by a counter-theft.

Property and Wealth

Suku subsistence is heavily dependent upon the cultivation of manioc which represents by far the most important item in the diet; other crops include peanuts, sweet potatoes, pumpkins, beans, and peas. Cultivation is the exclusive responsibility of the women, who select sites in the bush and work them individually. Since fields are made in the open grassland (exceptions to this are negligible), men do not participate in their preparation by clearing trees. Land is extremely plentiful and, as far as cultivation is concerned, it may be classified as a 'free good', with no system of tenure attached to it. The men's contribution to subsistence comes primarily from hunting, which is pursued with an enthusiasm surpassing by far its objective economic importance now that game has become increasingly scarce.

Suku land tenure hinges on hunting rights rather than agriculture. The bush is divided into areas, usually bounded by streams, which are owned by specific lineages. 'Ownership', in this context, means free hunting by members of the lineage, its exclusive right to burn the bush at the time of the communal hunts in the dry season, and its right to collect a portion of the meat from any game caught in it by a hunter of another lineage. In short, ownership confers the right to collect hunting tribute but it is not a hunting monopoly. The owner-lineage gives a hunter luck by granting him formal permission to hunt, but such permission is not always sought and need not be. Under no circumstances is control of hunting land necessary to subsistence, and many lineages own no hunting lands at all. Initially, hunting rights were acquired through prior occupation of empty lands at the time of the first migration. Since then, many of them have been transferred *in toto* to other lineages through sales, as gifts, or as compensatory payment in legal cases. The Suku see no mystical unbreakable bond between hunting land and the lineage that owns it or its ancestors.

The other types of immobile lineage property are fishing sites and trees. Fishing is free to all in the larger rivers where, in any case, the yield is poor; the more productive small muddy streams and swampy grounds, on the other hand, are controlled by specific lineages in the same way that hunting lands are. Palm trees and bamboo groves supply the Suku with 'wine', highly prized for itself and important in a variety of social and ritual contexts. These, and kola trees as well, are owned by the lineages that have first found them, planted them, or bought them from others.

The types of property considered so far—hunting lands, fishing sites, and trees—are controlled directly by the lineage as a corporate body; they are exploited by any and all of its members. There is, however, property that is directly controlled by individuals although the ultimate rights in it are still held by the lineage. This consists of domestic animals (dogs, goats, pigs, and chickens); houses, household goods, and tools (all made by men, with the exception of pottery); and money.

Money was an integral part of the Suku economy long before the colonial period. Although much of the trade was carried on through barter, which was characterized by several closed circuits of exchange, the value of any item could be expressed in terms of small shell-money called *nzimbu*. No object that could be bartered could not also be sold; and some things, such as wine, domestic animals, most of the tools and utensils, and slaves were normally acquired with money. The importance of money as wealth is seen in that it could be saved for future use, loaned out at interest, serve as payment for services (for example, to diviners and judges), and be used as legal tender in marriage transfers and in giving tribute to chiefs. At present, shell-money has been entirely displaced by Congolese francs. Also, new important sources of revenue have appeared, such as employment with the administration and migrant labour.

The use of all property is controlled by the conception that, whatever a person acquires, he does so not simply as a lineage member but rather, given the supernatural sanctions of lineage unity, 'because' he is a lineage member. Thus, the lineage as a group is always seen as possessing the ultimate claim over the entire property of all its members. In the case of immobile property, collective ownership is expressed in the rules regarding the revenue from it. The hunting tribute is subdivided between all the adult members who are present and a certain amount is also sent to those who live in the vicinity. When a person taps trees for wine, the major portion of the produce is shared with those members of the lineage who are there to make good their claim; if the wine is sold, the revenue must again be shared.

Most of the domestic property, necessary in everyday living, remains under individual control. This includes nets, calabashes, hoes, knives, baskets, bows and arrows, clothing, pots, and drums; and, at present, such things as dishes, lamps, bicycles, gramophones, and sewing-machines. But a certain portion of such property does continuously circulate within the lineage. A Suku cannot for long refuse the request by another member of his lineage for any object unless he can show that he cannot do without it; even such valuable articles as bicycles and sewing-machines, unless actively used, tend to make the round of lineage members who believe they need them at various times. When a migrant worker returns from town or plantation with money and goods, these are shared out within a few days, voluntarily and in satisfying the insistent demands by lineage relatives.

Legal fines and compensations; bride-wealth, collected or disbursed; tribute and, more recently, taxes—all these impinge on the lineage as a unit, every member contributing as much as he can convince others that he can afford, collecting as much as he can demonstrate he needs. When a person dies, the inheritance reverts to the lineage as a whole (it is thus not genealogically 'matrilineal'), but individual need is an important factor in the redistribution. If the dead has left several goats, the person without any will insist upon a greater share than someone who already has several animals himself.

The principle of sharing, deriving from the conception of lineage unity, operates in conjunction with another, that of seniority, upon which the hierarchical organization of the lineage rests. Authority as well as responsibility lies with the elders, and their insistence upon greater control of lineage wealth carries more weight than that by younger members. It is they who are expected to provide for taxes, supply much of the bride-wealth, pay the fines in tribunals, and have ready cash in various contingencies. It is they also who, by reminding others of these obligations, are in the best position to accumulate wealth. This, combined with a longer time spent in trading, breeding domestic animals, or engaging in crafts, gives the total wealth of the lineage several 'centres of gravity' which are its elders. There is no formal 'common purse' in the lineage; in this respect, the position of the formal head does not differ from that of other elders.

The rules of sharing, it must be emphasized, are not enforced with an accountant's fervour. Not every piece of meat need be subdivided, nor must every calabash of wine be counted. What is required is that the principle itself be honoured; in practice, this means that demands and compliance must be 'reasonable',

FAMILY AND LINEAGE AMONG THE SUKU

and this term, for all its vagueness, must suffice. What is not tolerated is outright refusal to fulfil what are considered 'natural' obligations. This would mean renouncing one's lineage membership and its protection in both the supernatural and the material sense. In the old days, given the fact that the lineage was juridically autonomous in its internal affairs, the recalcitrant would simply be killed. In the colonial period, coercion would come from the administratively instituted 'customary tribunals', with their conservative orientation. Supernatural sanctions, in the form of a curse by lineage elders, are no less potent, bringing with them misfortunes, accidents, death, and exposure to witchcraft. These mechanisms are not, however, one-sided. Reasonableness in demands is required of elders as well as their juniors. The former are controlled in their turn by fear of being accused of witchcraft and killed by ordinary poison given under the guise of a witch-poison trial. Finally, the role of formal sanctions must not be overstressed. They preserve lineage unity when it is threatened but it is not on them that this unity rests. The lineage is welded together by face-to-face interaction, by the general acceptance of cultural premises, and by the everyday working of the society in which these premises are not questioned. The concepts of 'common blood', of economic unity, of the role of elders and ancestors—all these are clearly perceived psychological factors in Suku behaviour and not mere 'rationalizations' and 'symbols' of abstract structural principles—unless, that is, the position is taken that culture is recreated every generation in some mystic urge to 'reflect' a society's structural arrangements.

As in other matters, the economic relations between lineages and between members of different lineages are dominated by the rule of reciprocity. Jealous precautions are taken to insure that no wealth belonging to individual members should pass into the hands of others. For example, sons are rigorously excluded from sharing in anything of value in their father's inheritance (the only exception being the bow). In recent times, with more visible wealth available, this watchfulness has become all the stronger.

IGOR KOPYTOFF

The Legal Aspects of Marriage

The corporate organization of the lineage has been emphasized as strongly as it was because marriage, involving in most cases different lineages, gives rise to a new co-operative unit whose structure must reconcile the divergent loyalties of its members which the lineages concerned continue to demand. It is not surprising, then, that the contractual side of Suku marriage is clearly defined and sets strict limits within which individual predilections are allowed to express themselves.

Although lineage exogamy is not a cultural requirement, most Suku marriages do occur between members of different lineages.[1] To understand the structure of the family, it is best to begin with the examination of the kinds of transfers that take place in inter-lineage marriages. The modifications found in other kinds of marriages will be seen to be the logical outcome of this basic model.

Marriage involves an arrangement among three lineages: those of the groom, of the bride's father, and of the bride herself. The rights connected with a woman, which are subject to transfer, are the following: those to her domestic labour and to part of her labour outside the purely domestic sphere; sexual rights; paternal rights to her children, always excluding their filiation. These transfers are made in several consecutive steps.

[1] Within the lineage, sexual relations between persons of the same generation (classified as 'siblings') are incestuous and marriage is prohibited; the same applies to classificatory siblings who are not members of the lineage, that is, patrilateral parallel cousins. Inter-generational marriage within the lineage is, however allowed; between such close relatives as a man and his sister's daughter, marriage is frowned upon, yet it does occur, and with a classificatory sister's daughter it is not uncommon. As for statistics, out of a random selection of fifty-seven marriages, intra-lineage marriages account for roughly 30 per cent, marriages between lineages of the same clan for 12 per cent, and inter-lineage marriages for 58 per cent. Such data, however, must be accepted with great care. We have not analysed our data fully, but we know that the figures must be broken into several categories. Lineages show different degrees of preference for one type of marriage over another. Thus, in one lineage, over half the marriages are within it, while in another the figure is less than a fifth. Generational differences are also important. Older men, in marriages subsequent to their first, show a tendency to marry within the lineage women who are themselves often divorcées from a first inter-lineage marriage. At present, younger people tend to marry more consistently outside of the lineage, partly under the influence of missionaries who, from reading anthropology, feel that the 'traditional African' pattern is for lineages to be exogamous.

FAMILY AND LINEAGE AMONG THE SUKU

In the old days, bride-wealth consisted of about 10,000 shells (approximately the price of three goats); at present, it is equivalent, in Congolese francs, to between thirty and forty dollars. Payment is made after the bride's father and mother and her lineage have agreed to the marriage. At the time of payment, all the three lineages concerned are represented by at least one elder; in addition, the groom's father may be present, although formally he is not involved in any way in the transactions. The groom hands the money to the representative of the bride's lineage and he in turn gives some two-thirds of it to the bride's father. This portion is viewed as having been paid to the father by his daughter's lineage (and not by the groom) for having begotten her and reared her safely. In case of a future dissolution of the marriage, the groom and his lineage claim the entire sum back from the bride's lineage alone.

With the payment of bride-wealth, the father tentatively surrenders his paternal rights over his daughter to her own lineage; tentatively because, should the marriage proceedings be stopped before the next step is taken, he must return his portion of the bride-wealth. To the groom, the father transfers the right of sexual exclusion, that is, the claim to legal fines from the girl's future lovers for every act of sexual intercourse. It is at this time also that the groom may begin to profit from the woman's domestic labour; the bride usually moves to his village and begins planting the fields and cooking for him, but not living with him.

The sexual rights of possession are acquired by the groom in the next step. He presents to the head of her lineage a goat which the latter, at a time he considers propitious, will sacrifice to the *musiku* of his lineage. This pot of 'medicines', held by every autonomous lineage, symbolizes its blood unity; the sacrifice to it is regarded as a precautionary blood payment to the dead of the lineage, in the absence of which inter-lineage sexual intercourse—a mixing of alien 'bloods'—results in the sickness or death of some member of the woman's lineage. A similar sacrifice, it may be noted, is performed in the case of any illicit sexual relations. After this rite, the marriage partners may finally begin living fully as man and wife. The rite also marks the permanent surrender by the father of all legal rights and responsibilities to his daughter. In case of divorce, it is her lineage that must reimburse the entire bride-wealth and it cannot claim back his portion from the father; at the same time, it will also collect entirely any new bride-wealth payments upon her subsequent remarriage.

To summarize, the arrangements among the three lineages involved are the following: the groom's lineage pays the bride-wealth; that of the bride's father receives two-thirds of it and that of the bride a third; if the marriage breaks up, the bride's lineage returns all the bride-wealth to the groom's lineage. On the ritual side, marriage necessitates the sacrifice of a goat without which inter-lineage sexual relations would endanger the members of the bride's lineage. These transfers become modified whenever one lineage occupies the structural position of two or even all three of the parties concerned. To illustrate, three examples may be mentioned:

1. Marriage of a woman whose father and mother belong to the same lineage. Here, both the paternal and lineage rights are vested in the woman's own lineage. Hence, the sacrificial goat and the entire bride-wealth are received by that one lineage.

2. Intra-lineage marriage. No goat is given or sacrifice since no mixture of 'alien bloods' takes place. But the bride-wealth must still be paid to the lineage of the bride's father by the lineage which is both the groom's and the bride's; the bride-wealth is however reduced by the third which the bride's lineage would normally retain. In case of divorce, no return of bride-wealth is possible, the bride's lineage being also that of the husband.

3. Intra-lineage marriage of a woman who is herself the daughter of such a marriage. Here, all three parties involved are telescoped into the same lineage. Both bride-wealth and sacrifice become meaningless and neither takes place.

The rules governing the reimbursement of bride-wealth are an integral part of the conceptual structure described, with its emphasis on balanced exchanges, and they also reveal the conception of paternal rights. Marriages may be dissolved by divorce, the initiative lying with either partner, or by death. If no children have been born, the totality of the bride-wealth and all the incidental gifts given at the time of betrothal must be returned. If there are children, the amount returned is reduced by half for each daughter and by a quarter for each son. However, the husband's lineage may demand a return of all the bride-wealth, thereby renouncing its paternal rights over the children, and these rights are then transferred to the children's own lineage; the children's legal position from then on is like that of children born to an intra-lineage marriage (that is, both paternal and maternal rights are vested in the same lineage); the father, however, still retains a claim to a small portion of his daughter's future bride-wealth (about a quarter) in his capacity of her genitor and to an additional sum which varies with the number of years he has cared for her. In the same way, a foster-father, such as the mother's second husband, claims a portion of his foster-daughter's bride-wealth for bringing up his wife's children.

Some 20 per cent of married Suku men have more than one wife, but about three-quarters of these have no more than two. Thus, large polygynous families are characteristic of some 5 per cent of married men. A second wife is seldom acquired until middle age; consequently, among the older men the incidence of polygyny is higher than the percentage indicated for married men as a group.[1]

Every subsequent marriage by a man is a new discrete legal arrangement duplicating his first. New relationships are established with additional lineages without affecting those of the previous marriages. Sororal polygyny is extremely rare; while there are no moral objections to it, it is rejected as unstable, since a quarrel with one wife would, the Suku claim, lead to another with her sister and the same would also apply to divorce. True sororate is also seldom found. The reasons are related to the rules of bride-wealth reimbursement; this being the responsibility of the wife's lineage and not her

[1] Since until now Christianization has primarily affected men who are no older than in their middle forties, an age group which was generally monogamous even in the old days, these statistics are probably valid on the whole for the pre-colonial situation, that is until the middle 1920s, which mark the beginning of effective administrative control and of missionary activities. Where changes have occurred is in the diminution in the number of wives among the men with more than two; men with four or five wives are more rare now than they used to be. This decrease of wives in the upper age group corresponds with their increase for the group of younger men taken together since these now marry at a younger age than they did before.

father's, a true sister will not serve as a substitute for the bride-wealth unless the father is once again compensated in the usual manner. Ordinarily, the dead woman's lineage will provide a woman over whom it has both paternal and maternal rights—that is, a daughter of an intra-lineage marriage, a divorcée, or a widow who, to be sure, is often the dead woman's classificatory sister by virtue of lineage affiliation.

The pattern of bride-wealth payment and reimbursement similarly precludes the 'mother's brother's daughter' form of marriage (while patrilateral cross-cousin marriage is a favoured though statistically minor form). Since a man and his mother's brother are of the same lineage, the payment of bride-wealth by the former is considered meaningless because most of it goes to the 'same purse', that is to his lineage elder in his capacity of bride's father. Should divorce take place, however, the bride's lineage must reimburse the money to the groom's (and father's) lineage which did not, in fact, pay it in the real sense.

From the above, one point emerges which is crucial to the understanding of the structure of the Suku family. It is that the ties between the spouses and between the father and his children depend on clearly-defined contractual arrangements between strongly corporate groups—the lineage of the father and that of the mother and her children. Since the affiliation of each family member to his or her lineage implies very strong economic, social, and supernatural interests outside of the family group, the functions left to the family are correspondingly restricted. It is not surprising that, as shall be presently seen, the relations among family members are rather precisely delimited and this in largely contractual terms. It must be emphasized that, within this structure, individual feelings and differences in personality play their part fully, as they do in any contractual relations in any culture. But they do so *within* the limits imposed. Going beyond these limits would impinge on the accepted rights not only of individual members of the family but of their lineages as well, and every lineage, with the full force of legal sanctions at its disposal, immediately intervenes to redress the reciprocal balance when it is violated.

FAMILY AND LINEAGE AMONG THE SUKU

The Nuclear Family: Relations between the Spouses

By the time the ceremonial sacrifice of the goat makes possible the cohabitation of husband and wife, some of the material base for the new family has already been laid. The wife has planted a field so that its own food supply is assured. The larger part of the household paraphernalia, such as baskets and pots, necessary to her work, has been brought in by her; another part, and more particularly the hoe, is supplied by the husband. The house has been built in advance by the husband. Though in the same village, it is set at some distance from his father's compound. This is to avoid the 'shame' of being too readily observed by his parents in the intimacies of day-to-day married life and to make it more easy for the wife to practise in-law avoidance.

The Suku rules governing the division of labour between the sexes are on the whole rigid. There are few activities which both men and women may pursue; the principal ones are fishing and collecting. But even these tasks are usually done separately. As far as the main activities during the day are concerned, husband and wife live in two separate spheres. The wife must cultivate her fields, feed her husband, and keep house. The husband must provide her with meat, cloth, hoes, and some of the household utensils. He must also repair the house and, when necessary, build a new one.

The continued obligations of their separate lineage memberships define, in turn, the economic relations between the spouses. The property of each is held separate. A husband has no legal right to his wife's livestock nor can he use her stored food without permission. If the wife is a potter, or if the husband is a basketmaker or blacksmith or carver, the money each accumulates from these trades is not shared. If the wife sells agricultural produce, half the proceeds belong to the husband; this is explained as the result of 'partnership' between her labour and the hoe he has supplied. But once the division is made, each person's share is entirely his or her own.

In a harmonious family, these rules of separate ownership may be relatively relaxed. For example, a husband may kill his wife's fowl in her absence to feed visiting friends, but he must still eventually replace what he has taken, for the fact of separate ownership remains. In a family in which strains are evident, the same action will generate a quarrel. In case of divorce, these rules are given full expression and each partner retains all the property that he or she formally controlled.

Both partners tend to channel to their respective lineages whatever wealth they have stored up. This is particularly true of the wife. Residing alone among strangers, she makes periodic transfers of money or animals to her mother's brothers or her own adult brothers for fear that her property should fall into the hands of another lineage in case of her divorce or death. With the man, such fears need not be as strong; he lives with his own brothers, whose lineage interests are like his, and he has direct kinship ties in the village through his father. While young, a man does channel some of his accumulated wealth to his lineage in response to the demands by his elders. With time, as he approaches being an elder himself and as his responsibilities and authority rise, the process is reversed and wealth begins to gravitate towards him.

The wife's continued membership and interest in her own lineage is not only economic. She often visits her maternal relatives. If seriously ill, she prefers to be taken care of by them rather than by her husband's relatives. Moreover, the interest of the wife's lineage in her well-being may actively interfere in family life. When a husband commits adultery or breaks a ritual taboo, his continued sexual relations with his wife may affect not only her health but that of other members of her lineage. Hence, her lineage imposes, in such an event, a blanket prohibition of sexual relations until the husband ritually repairs such transgressions and pays the appropriate fines. In short, the wife's lineage is always in the background of family life, jealously guarding its interests and economic prerogatives. The wife herself neither gives nor is expected to give her undivided loyalty to her husband. Her continuing ties to her lineage are regarded as entirely normal and, though living with her husband, her 'psychological residence' lies to an important degree elsewhere.

FAMILY AND LINEAGE AMONG THE SUKU

The Nuclear Family: The Position of Children

A child is from the beginning a full member of his mother's lineage. Legally, the latter is entirely responsible for its acts and it, not the father, must furnish compensation and fines if the child commits a crime. In minor breaches, it is true, the father usually takes this responsibility upon himself, but he always informs the elders of the child's lineage when he has done so. In matters of importance, such as sickness or a serious misdemeanour, he must call them in at once. It is significant that while the payment of minor fines is regarded as a good father's duty for which he would not normally be reimbursed, should there be a divorce in which the father demands full return of the bride-wealth (and hence renounces his paternal rights), such expenses will be taken into account in the final settlement.

The birth of a child does tend to fortify the tie between the parents; it certainly does so in the negative sense that a wife's barrenness would loosen it. By the same token, the lineages of the spouses establish a potentially more lasting relationship. But another consequence is the increased interference by the mother's lineage in the life of the family. The effects of the father's misbehaviour in sexual and ritual matters are now widened to include the children. A child's sickness may be taken as an indication of such breaches of conduct and the threat of further prohibitions of sexual relations between the parents is increased. A child's death immediately results in such a taboo and in conflict. Responsibility is in the end determined by a diviner who often blames not the father but the child's own lineage elders for some ritual transgression or for witchcraft. In such cases, the father may only receive a symbolic gift signifying a promise not to 'kill' his children in future. But if the father is found guilty, the child's lineage may demand the compensation customary in homicide (two children as slaves), though ordinary it will be satisfied with less if it wishes to preserve the marriage. This inequality in the relationship with reference to the child, and the potential conflicts it generates, emphasize once again the disjunctive effects on the family structure of the near-monopoly by the matrilineage of the important social functions.

In effect, the father's legal role with respect to his children is that of a trustee for their lineage. With a daughter, this trusteeship lasts until her marriage, when the father collects the major portion of the bride-wealth and she is thereupon legally 'reclaimed' by her lineage. The paternal rights over a daughter essentially consist in this claim to her bride-wealth. With a son, trusteeship gives way to a more lasting legal relationship. The father has a claim to a portion of all the game that the son kills and to periodic gifts. This claim continues throughout the son's life; after the father's death, it is transferred to the father's lineage as a whole, more specifically to its current elders.

Another obligation on the part of the son is to remain living with his father until the latter dies. However, in contrast to the obligatory hunting tribute and occasional gifts, this duty is binding only in the case of a 'good' father—a rather flexible category characterized by kindness, provision of adequate food and clothing, avoidance of too many illicit sexual entanglements which are believed to threaten the children's lives, and willingness to go beyond purely legal responsibilities. A father is not obliged to pay his son's fines, but a 'good' father does help at least with the minor ones. While legally a father does not have to contribute to his son's bride-wealth (which is credited entirely to the son's lineage), a 'good' father gives a share. It must be stressed that the Suku do not view the son's continued residence with the father as a reciprocity for such favours. For the father, it is more a matter of adequately fulfilling his expected role; for the son, it is more a matter of obligation. Nevertheless, when a man fails to be a 'good' father in almost every respect, the son's obligation is not seen as binding, and he may leave his father upon maturity.

As a rule, the father–son relationship is notably harmonious and warm. A man tends to trust his sons far more than his sororal nephews who often chafe under the authority of their lineage elders. For example, a sick man decidedly prefers to be cared for by his sons, who have nothing to gain materially from his death, than by his sister's sons who may be impatient to move up the ladder of authority and take control of lineage property. Though individual variation naturally exists, the cultural stereotyping of the relationship between lineage elders and juniors is that of considerable covert hostility, in clear contrast to the father–son relationship which, unencumbered by a pervasive authoritarianism, allows a freer play for purely personal attachment.

While fulfilling his obligations to his father, the son must also play his role as member of his own lineage. As he approaches maturity, he begins to visit periodically his maternal uncles. He increasingly participates in the discussion of lineage affairs; he learns its traditions, the history of its relations with other lineages, and any past events which have given rise to current conflicts and disputes. If his lineage is vested with political authority, he helps to maintain it by doing various errands and by helping it to implement its judicial responsibilities. His economic interests become more and more bound to his lineage membership. He exploits the palm and bamboo groves, sells the wine he has tapped, and shares the proceeds with the elders. After a hunt, he sends them portions of the game; if his lineage controls hunting lands, he also demands a share of the hunting tribute that it collects. He may receive a goat or a pig with which he starts a series of partnerships, sales, and purchases, thus building up his resources. When he is ready for marriage, he importunes his elders to assemble the necessary bride-wealth. Thus, as in the case of his mother, some of his most important economic and social interests lie outside of his family and his place of residence. In this, however, he is not alone for he constitutes with his mother and brothers an enclave of his lineage whose interests are undivided.

In a polygynous situation, there are several such enclaves and the polygynous family is, structurally, a constellation of mother–children groups around a common husband–father. There are no direct ties of economic interest among these groups. Each occupies a separate house in the same compound. Each wife cultivates her fields independently and cooks separately from the others, and the husband is expected to spend, in turns, an equal amount of time with each. Harmony among co-wives is desirable and common, although not regarded as indispensable. In fact, it may be suggested that it is precisely this functional independence of each mother–children sub-group which makes for the relative harmony that exists. Competition to advance their own children's interests at the expense of the children of co-wives is meaningless when the joint family is not the group in which economic and social advantages can be sought. The autonomy of each wife in the domestic sphere precludes many situations in which quarrels would tend to arise. Even more than in the father–son relationship, the absence of formal rights and obligations among co-wives leaves more room for purely personal likes and dislikes in a situation in which there is relatively little to quarrel about. Hence, a harmony which, it is true, is quite often based on a fundamental indifference.

The Truncated Patrilineage and the Residential Group

We have until now emphasized the essentially disjunctive aspects of Suku family structure by stressing the juxtaposition within it of the varying claims of different lineages. The family has emerged as consisting of two sub-units—the father as opposed to the mother and her children—whose dominant economic and social affiliations lie outside of the family unit. This sub-division, rooted in matriliny, is however cross-cut by another one which is patrilineal and which, leaving the mother aside, relates the children not only to the father but also to a wider group of patrilineal relatives. This is the *kitaata kya mukongu* relationship (lit. 'fathership of the *mukongu*), which is different from the other type of paternal relationship, that with the father's matrilineage, whose main features we have already discussed. Although *kitaata* is sometimes used to denote the latter as well, in this paper the term will be used exclusively in its patrilineal meaning without continually modifying it by the phrase 'of the *mukongu*'.

Mukongu is the tree stump planted in front of a man's house, on which his sons deposit the game they bring from the hunt before it is subdivided among the hunter's relatives. A *mukongu* is believed to insure the hunting luck of the members of the family; and just as dissatisfaction by lineage elders brings misfortune through the force of the lineage *musiku* pot, so a father's supernatural power over his children, affecting a daughter's fertility and a son's hunting luck, is expressed through the force of the *mukongu*. A married man usually has a *mukongu* planted in his own compound when his male children are approaching adolescence and begin to do some hunting; formally, however, the right to a *mukongu* begins upon a man's marriage. The ritual of the planting is usually performed by a man's father but it may also be done by any member of the man's *kitaata*. Other functions of the *kitaata* are also ritual or supernatural. They include participation in the 'coming out' ceremony of a newborn and in funerals, and the power of an older *kitaata* relative to 'curse' a younger person, thus affecting, as with the father himself, a woman's childbearing and a man's hunting.

The *kitaata* excludes the father's father but includes his patrilineal descendants down to Ego's own generation. Thus, it embraces the following persons: Ego's father and the latter's siblings by the same father (and regardless of mother); and all the children of males of the previous group. Ego's father's brother is a senior member of this group but he is also a junior member of an older *kitaata* from which Ego is excluded. Analytically, these relationships give rise to a group based on the members of the lower generation and including persons of the generation above; the upper generation of this group is, in turn, the base of another such two-generational group. This organization is summarized in Diagram I (page 108).

We have here a proliferating series of two-generational, interlocking patrilineal groups, B being one of at least two possible *kitaata* groups springing from A, and B in turn giving rise to C and D. Each group, by definition, excludes its common progenitor in the generation above it although it is from him that its patrilineal unity is derived; for this reason, we have referred to the *kitaata* group as a truncated patrilineage. The entire structure is not a lineage of a larger order for it is given no cultural recognition; the patrilineal relationship does not extend beyond the boundaries of a person's *kitaata*. Thus, the relationship between Ego and his grandfather is a joking one (as it is with any true or classificatory grandparent), but in this case it is entirely devoid of any economic, legal, or ritual functions, this grandfather being a member neither of Ego's matrilineage nor of his *kitaata*. Similarly, a person in the *kitaata* group C, although classified terminologically as Ego's 'father' or 'sibling', does not have with Ego a relationship involving any of the legal elements that are present when one is dealing

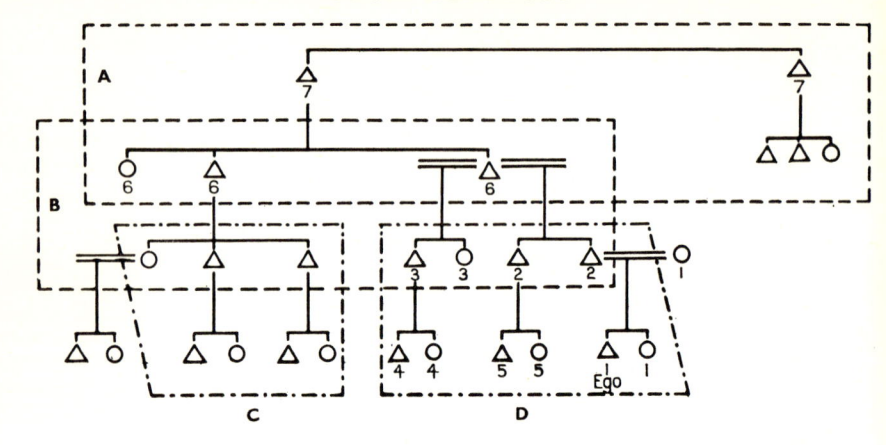

DIAGRAM I.

A, B, C and D represent truncated *kitaata* patrilineages. A polygynous marriage has been introduced to emphasize the strictly patrilineal nature of the *kitaata* relationship. Thus, Ego's *kitaata* D includes his father's half-siblings whose matrilineage is different from that of Ego's father. Numbers are used to indicate common membership in a matrilineage; for example, Ego, his sister, and their mother are all marked 1.

with similar relatives who belong to the same matrilineage or the same *kitaata* group.

At its inception, the *kitaata* patrilineage (its women usually excluded) coincides with the residential unit of several brothers, with their families, who live in the same village beside their common father. It is also possible, at times, for several interlocking *kitaata* groups to form one residential unit (for example, B, C and D in the diagram). The concept of the *kitaata* thus corresponds to the facts of patrilocal residence but, as shall be presently seen, of patrilocal residence in its specific Suku variant. The patrilocal continuity among these groups is transient and is eventually broken in a way that makes logical the institutional refusal to carry the recognition of patrilineality for more than two generations at a time. As a result, the emergence of what may have been a double-descent system is inhibited in its classic form. This limitation of the patrilineal-patrilocal continuity is related to the residential cycle of the nuclear family which will now be considered.

FAMILY AND LINEAGE AMONG THE SUKU

The Residential Cycle

What we may call the 'phenotypical' aspects of Suku residence show considerable complexity, particularly if one tries to describe the 'normal' residential unit in relation to the overall social structure at any given point in time. On the other hand, a diachronic model of individual residence is relatively simple and may be described in a few words.

A woman, until she marries, lives with her father; a married woman lives with her husband and changes in her residence are dependent on changes in his. A divorcée resides with one of her mother's brothers, real or classificatory, who himself may or may not be living at the lineage centre. A widow, unless she remarries, settles with one of her mother's brothers or with one of her own mature brothers, with an increasing tendency, as she gets older, to settle at the lineage centre.

A child lives with the mother until adolescence, wherever she happens to be; thus, a son or a daughter follows a divorced mother to her new place of residence. After adolescence, if they had been living elsewhere, sons always (and daughters usually) join their father.

A son resides at whatever village his father lives in, and, except in cases of serious conflict, he does so at least until his father's death. Should the father move to another village, the son follows him, taking with him his wife and his own sons. When the father dies, the son has several choices before him. The approved pattern is to remain with his father's brothers by the same mother, whose cycle of residence has been like that of the father himself. Not uncommonly, however, and especially if the son's personal ties with these father's brothers are not very strong, he may at this point join one of his lineage elders, usually a mother's brother, and preferably but not necessarily one who lives at the lineage centre; in this move, the son's own family follows him and it may by then include married sons and their children. If the son continues to live with his dead father's brothers, he must again make a decision when they die. Ordinarily, he will at this point move to his lineage centre. This is especially true if his father's brothers had not been living at their own lineage centre. If they had, by then, moved there, he may continue to live at his father's lineage centre with his other classificatory 'fathers' of that lineage, and may die there. In general, however, the majority of lineage members are found, in their old age, at their own lineage centre.

The above picture represents not so much an 'ideal' sequence as a complete and uninterrupted one, presupposing considerable longevity on the part of males. In reality, this sequence is rarely carried through every step. In the specific case of a family, whose residence depends on that of the father, the sequence may be relatively short, consisting of few residential shifts, or long; the father's own decisions are based on a variety of factors, including his personal relations with his father, with the latter's brothers, and finally with the father's lineage as a whole, and he may make the final decision to move to his own lineage centre at several possible points in his life-cycle. As to the 'typical' residential group that these rules of residence bring about, the situation is complicated by the fact that while the son's residence is unambiguously dependent upon his father's during the latter's lifetime, the simplicity of this connection is deceptive. Just as the son has several choices of residence when his father dies, so does of course his father upon his own father's death. Thus, the specific form of residence that a man and his family adopt (and this, in turn, influences his later decisions) is linked to a series of previous decisions by other persons in a chain of at least three patrilineally-related nuclear families—his own, his father's, and his father's father's.

The possible variations in residential groups that may emerge can be examined with reference to Diagram II (page 111).

Two brothers, 1 and 2, members of the same matrilineage, reside together with their married sons (3, 4, 5; and 6, 7); the latter, in turn, have their sons, some already married, and unmarried daughters living with them. The first and second generations in the diagram form one *kitaata* patrilineage; overlapping with it are two other patrilineages, one composed of the three brothers (3, 4, 5) with their children, and the other of two brothers (6, 7) and their children.

The group shown here represents a patrilineally-based residential group at its greatest point of expansion. It is clear that what holds it together is the common residence of 1 and 2. Its members are affiliated to several different matrilineages,

FAMILY AND LINEAGE AMONG THE SUKU

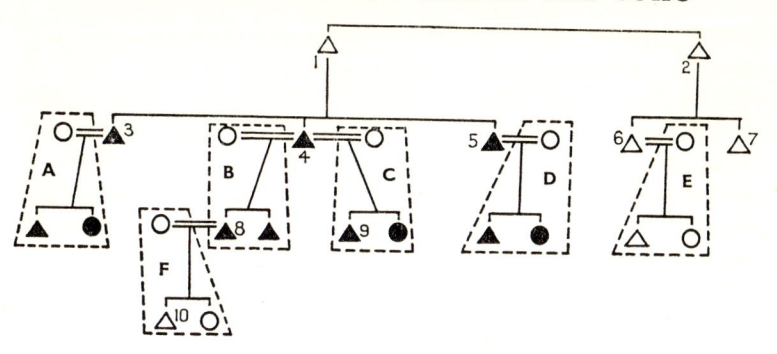

DIAGRAM II.

Letters (A, B ... F) represent enclaves of common matrilineal affiliation inside a large patrilocal residential group. Numbers indicate persons discussed in the text. Dark symbols show members of one *kitaata* patrilineage.

and in these terms represent several sub-units (A, B, C, D, E, F are those marked on the diagram) whose preponderant economic and social interests lie outside of this residential group. Where this group lives depends on the previous decisions and life-histories of the brothers 1 and 2; it may be found at their lineage centre or at their father's lineage centre—these being the most probable places since 1 and 2 are at this point beyond their middle-age.

Should 1 die, his sons normally will continue to live with his brother, thus preserving the residential unity of their *kitaata*. But this need not be the case if their relations with their father's brother are strained and they decide to move away and join one of their lineage elders. The older *kitaata* will thus split, giving rise to two separate residential groups which are the two *kitaata* groups of the lower generation (3, 4, 5, with their children; and 6 and 7 with theirs). It is in this sense that the *kitaata* patrilineage largely coincides with the patrilocal residential group, staying together for most of its duration and shifting its residence as a block. The kind of residential change shown here also illustrates the essential 'fit' between the truncated patrilineage and Suku rules of residence.

It may be noted that the sons in the younger *kitaata* group (for example, 8 and 9) have only the obligation to live with their father. They have no legal ties and no obligations to their father's father (1) nor to his matrilineage. If 4 were the only son of 1 and died before 1, his sons 8 and 9 would have no direct ties to the village where 1 lives. They can remain living there, it is true, but only as *batungi* (lit. 'builders', that is, strangers in the village). Ordinarily, they would join their own lineage elders elsewhere; if they move to their own lineage centre, their cycle of residence is thereby foreshortened, for its final step of bringing them to their lineage centre would then take place in their middle age or even earlier instead of in old age.

It should be noted that what holds the brothers 3, 4, and 5 together (and, consequently, the families they head) is not only their common father but also their common membership in the same matrilineage. This latter fact also separates them from 6 and 7 of the same *kitaata* group. Towards the end of their residential cycles, these two groups of brothers will go their separate ways, pulled apart by their different matrilineal ties. A similar process will, of course, take place in the following generation. In the case of the children of 4, that is 8 and 9, polygyny introduces an additional disjunctive element into the *kitaata* group. Though sons of the same father, 8 and 9 belong to different matrilineages and their places of residence at the end of their lives will not be the same. This indicates that the residential unity of the *kitaata* patrilineage usually ends before the persons forming the base of the group die and that the consistent unit of common residence is not the *kitaata* itself but its matrilineal subdivisions.

The above examples also illustrate the 'chain-reaction' effect of a residential move by a person of the upper generation. A shift in residence by 3, 4, and 5 (itself related to previous decisions by their father) has automatic repercussions for the two generations under them. Thus, while the rules followed by a person are rather simple, to explain the particular residence of a specific person at any one time often requires going up three generations to isolate the various decisions made in the chain and the events behind these decisions, such as the time at which persons died and the conflicts in which they were involved.

With all the inter-related changes of residence and the resulting varieties of residential groups, what matters in the

FAMILY AND LINEAGE AMONG THE SUKU

Suku cultural context is that a certain number of middle-aged men and most of the old men are, in a sense, 'fed' back to the lineage centre, thus assuring its maintenance and continuity. The cycle of residence results in a kind of delayed avunculocality, though by no means in every case. Furthermore, it must be remembered that avunculocal residence *per se*, given the territorial dispersion of every lineage, does not solve the problem of maintaining the lineage centre. When men move from their father's village to join one of their real or classificatory mother's brothers, they as often enlarge subsidiary lineage enclaves as they do the lineage centre itself. Unless these subsidiary enclaves are far away and grow into autonomous lineage segments, they eventually disappear as the mother's brothers move to the lineage centre (for example, upon their father's death) and take with them their attached sister's sons. Consequently, the process of 'feeding' lineage members to the centre may take place by way of subsidiary in-gathering points.

The variations in the residential cycle that we have described were related to specific events, such as divorces, deaths, and private decisions, which are important variables in the model but impinge upon the family structure from outside. There are, however, still other types of cycles which are inherent in the structure of the family itself.

In a family founded upon an intra-lineage marriage there is no contradiction for a son between living with his father's lineage and with his own. The father, to be sure, may initially be a resident in his own father's village. But once he moves to his lineage centre, the residential cycle of his sons comes to an end, since they too become residents of their own lineage centre.

Another way in which the cycle is shortened is through the marriage of a man with a woman from his father's lineage (one variant of this pattern is the approved 'father's sister's daughter' marriage). Such a marriage reinforces the ties between a man and his father's lineage, which is also that of his wife and children, and when a man lives in his father's lineage centre he is likely, in such a case, to remain there after his father's death, while his sons are thus able to live simultaneously in patrilocal residence and at their own lineage centre. If their father dies without having shifted his residence, the sons simply continue living at their lineage centre for the rest of their lives.

It is evident from the above that the residence of the nuclear family as a group is dependent on that of the father and that the latter's residence is determined by such a large number of variables and their fortuitous clustering in any one case at any one time that a one-word description (such as 'patrilocal' or 'avunculocal') cannot serve as a basis on which to project or predict Suku social morphology. One cannot speak of a 'typical' larger residential group, uniting several nuclear families, since this may vary from a three-generational patrilocal extended family to an isolated nuclear family living as 'builders' in a village with which it has no formal ties left. The only valid description of 'residential patterns' becomes an individual diachronic model with multiple variables whose number and possible combinations may produce a large variety of specific residential groups.

Conclusion

Outside of the scarcely enlightening statement that the family consists of two parents and their children, there is little that can be said about the Suku family *qua* family without introducing a number of qualifications at every turn. The family is not a unit with certain constant residential or structural characteristics but rather a constellation of discrete relationships, each subject to many variables producing quite distinct family structures. A family based on an inter-lineage marriage, in which relationships show a high degree of social and economic autonomy, is quite different from one springing from a marriage within the lineage, where the highest degree of integration exists because of factors which have little to do with the concept of the family *per se*. Furthermore, within each of these two types, additional important variations are possible. All such variations can be related to the specifics of each situation in a precise manner.

The most useful model for understanding these variations is the one in which a marriage is seen as being contracted between different lineages. Here, the divergent loyalties of family members appear most clearly, the sub-units based on common lineage membership are most distinct, and the lack of continuity in the patrilineal–patrilocal organization as it gives way to the matrilineal principle becomes most evident. Each family member's preponderant and generalized obligations are to his or her corporate lineage, while the obligations to other members of the family are delimited and clearly defined on an essentially contractual and usually revocable basis. The economic unity of the family, such as it is, consists only in sharing the daily necessities of food and shelter. Those rights to property which are definite enough to be called ownership rights are vested not in the family but in the lineages to which individual members of the family belong.

The fact that most of the basic rights and obligations in Suku society tie an individual to his lineage rather than his family is probably responsible for the instability of the family. Suku divorces are frequent; a rough estimate is that some 50 per cent of middle-aged women have been divorced once. The economic and social autonomy of the wife correlates in this case with her behavioural and psychological independence which makes divorce a relatively easy matter. Our data, parenthetically, do not show that bride-wealth has any empirically demonstrable 'stabilizing' function. The high frequency of divorces contributes further to the complexity of the network of bilateral relationships that has been described, for the breaking of one tie has no necessary repercussions for others. For example, a divorce between parents does not affect by definition the father–children relationship. Also, the residence of the children may be variously affected, depending on whether each particular child is or is not adolescent. Such not infrequent complications make the large patrilocal residential unit far from being the norm.

The essential structure of Suku society, as viewed by the Suku themselves, is as it was described at the beginning of this paper: a series of territorially overlapping lineage groups, each with a central village and several subsidiary transient points at which elders, who are not at the lineage centre, reside and constitute additional points of reference for the still more widely scattered younger membership. Within this framework, there is a continuous process of both dispersal and in-gathering of members. Occasionally, the centrifugal forces of marriage residence fling out a group of members sufficiently far away for it to become a segment which may grow into a new autonomous corporate lineage. Marriages and the families in all their structural variations are regulated by principles which accommodate them to this on-going process that maintains the fundamental matrilineal features of the social organization.

PROPERTY AND THE CYCLE OF DOMESTIC GROUPS IN TAITA

Alfred and Grace Harris

IN this essay[1] we shall examine the development of domestic groups among the Taita of Kenya, from the foreshadowing of a new household when a young man takes a bride to his parental homestead, through the setting up of a 'satellite' household which later becomes independent of control by seniors, and on through other stages to decline and extinction.

The developmental process is, predictably, represented by a number of 'types' of domestic group, differing in size and composition. The commonest type is the domestic unit composed of a man, his wife, and their unmarried children. Less predictably, perhaps, the numerical predominance of households composed of a single nuclear family is apparently not attributable to conditions of change or culture contact. Such households, while recurring regularly in the course of the developmental cycle, bear only a superficial resemblance to the small and highly autonomous nuclear family units of Europe and North America.

The rights and obligations of household members over property, labour, and produce make manifest significant features of the developmental cycle and differentiating characteristics of Taita households at various stages of development. It is in terms of these rights and obligations that we shall discuss

[1] This paper is based on field research carried out between July 1950 and August 1952 and financed by the Colonial Social Science Research Council, to whom we wish to express our indebtedness.

households at each stage, and this forms the major part of the paper.

Taita households are not isolated, however, and in an introductory section we sketch the wider economic, jural, and political orders with which domestic group structure is articulated. A short concluding section summarizes some of the principles emerging from consideration of domestic group development, briefly examining their connections with the wider social order and suggesting points of interest for comparative work.

I

Crossing the dry bush plain of southern Kenya, the Taita Hills are sighted about a hundred miles north-west of Mombasa. The main massif of Dabida, together with near-by Sagala, and Kasigau (some thirty miles to the south) were inhabited by about 53,000 Taita in 1948.[1] Calling themselves Wadawide[2] the people speak a Bantu language and follow a way of life resembling that of the Kamba and Kikuyu. There are also cultural and historical affinities with the Coastal Bantu of Kenya (especially Wagiriama) and Tanganyika; and with the Pare and Shambala peoples of northern Tanganyika.

The hills rise from the encircling plain to over 7,000 feet, and everywhere the two contrast. Virtually all of the cultivable uplands are utilized, but in most places on the plains only a narrow band around the base of the hills can be cultivated. The alienation of plains land and draining of swamps have reduced the amount of arable land in this part of Taita. The main limitation, however, is technical. Taita cultivators, using bush knife, digging-stick, and hoe, today find it impossible to expand their area of cultivation greatly.

Within their lands, the Taita—and primarily Taita women—try to grow enough grain, roots, and legumes to meet daily needs. Men and boys tend the small herds of cattle and small stock, nowadays adding to this traditional male occupation the growing of cash crops such as vegetables, coffee, and chillies. Differences of altitude, soil, and moisture conditions

[1] Derived from East African Statistical Department, 1950.
[2] W or w represents a voiced bilabial fricative.

within the hills make different areas more suitable for various subsistence crops, for pasturage, or for cash crops of one kind or another. Yet Taita cultivators, especially those whose domestic groups are in the middle stages of development, try to grow a sufficiency of foodstuffs in as great a variety as possible. Householders also work to gain as much as possible of the livestock which constitutes the most important form of wealth (*mali*). Men and women, therefore, require access to both garden land and pasture; and if they can acquire and utilize land suitable for one or more of the cash crops, so much the better. But this quest for household self-sufficiency is itself structured by membership in and relations between the residential units larger than the household.

There are two main forms of settlement: dispersed and aggregated. Most of the population lives in dispersed hamlets and villages comprising one to twenty homesteads. The remainder occupy aggregated villages, a few of which include hundreds of homesteads.

Dispersed settlement tends to be associated with land-use arrangements under which residents depend for the most part on upland gardens. A male householder usually holds a number of plots scattered about within a radius of half a mile of his village. Ideally, some should be moist valley-bottom land, some irrigated hillside, and some dry hillside, so that both female cultivators and male growers of cash crops (if any) have land suitable for the variety of crops desired. In such areas also a householder often has access to plots at a much lower altitude, on the plains border, or even on the plains, where supplementary foodstuffs can be grown. Livestock kept at the homestead is herded on hillsides away from the cultivations or on fallow plots, while other animals may be kept at herding stations.

In contrast, the aggregated villages are mainly located in higher-altitude areas of craggy, dry ridges. Their residents depend heavily on plains border fields supplemented by upland plots, few of which can be irrigated. Their land tends to be poorer and less varied. But good or adequate pasturage is more plentiful than in areas of dispersed settlement, and it is possible to have some relatively large upland herds in addition to livestock kept out on the plains.

Despite the variation in physical aspect and pattern of land-use, all settlements in Taita are socially similar. Not only the small villages, but groups of neighbouring villages in the areas of dispersed settlement are predominantly inhabited by men who are patrikinsmen, living with their wives and children. Similarly, each section of a large village is dominated by the homesteads of men agnatically related. A few aggregated villages are said to be inhabited wholly by agnates.

The complexities of composition and internal arrangement are very much alike too. Men *and women* who reside near one another may be close or remote agnates, agnatically remote but matrilaterally or affinally close, or even agnatically-matrilaterally-affinally linked. This is so because, Taita patrilineages being non-exogamous, the male agnates who form the core of the wider local unit can take wives from among their agnatic kinswomen. Everywhere, also, these localized patrilineages[1] are linked in a regular fashion to form 'neighbourhoods'. The villages of one patrilineage often include some members of a neighbouring patrilineage.

The group of agnates whose males claim the right to occupy a particular territory is usually seven to nine generations deep, counting living generations and the dead, up to the named male founder. This is the *kichuku kibaha* or large lineage.[2] Its unity is focused ritually on a central shrine assemblage and an ancestral skull repository.

In areas of dispersed settlement, each large lineage has from one to three square miles of upland where its male members have the right to build their homesteads and have gardens. The area of plains used for supplementary gardens and pasturage is usually more extensive. Aside from unfenced pastures and wooded areas, only tracts of especially poor land remain not subject to individual rights other than temporary use-rights. That is, most of the garden plots are individually held by men of the lineage, and the ownership rights held by a man at his

[1] Obviously, in the absence of complete endogamy, all members of a patrilineage, male and female, cannot be members of a single local unit. However, the term 'localized patrilineage' is by now sanctioned by usage and is appropriate here in any case because of the high degree of actual intra-lineage marriage and the consequent retention of female members within the same local unit.

[2] Such a group may acknowledge ultimate ties with others elsewhere, but the nature of these links need not concern us here.

death must pass to a male or males of the lineage, preferably his legal sons. Livestock and other movables normally pass in the same way. Thus, although males of a large lineage do not exercise 'communal' rights over land other than pasture and woods, they form a territorial unit which is also a property-transmitting group.

We have said above that lineages are not exogamous. More precisely, there are two rules: (1) Marriage is forbidden between persons who share a common great-grandparent; and (2) it is forbidden between two persons whose sibling groups are already linked by one marriage.[1] These rules are important for the internal organization of large lineages.

The first means that men who share a common grandfather cannot become affines by giving the sister of one as wife to the other. Men who share the same father's father's father can exchange women for bride-wealth, provided they observe the second rule, though even a marriage within this degree requires a special ritual performance of 'killing kinship'. This ritual has no effect on *group* relations. It simply changes the *degree* of relationship between two parties. Beyond this degree, marriage within the patrilineage is untrammelled, always allowing for the rule concerning sibling pairs. Thus a sub-lineage of four generations' depth is the widest segment in which the marriage rules restrict the superimposition of affinal ties on agnatic ones. A three-generation segment is the only one for which such complexities are impossible.

Three- and four-generation segments are important in other ways, as well. Men whose fathers were brothers or half-brothers—who, therefore, have a common agnatic grandfather—are members of one *ifwa* or inheritance group (*ifwa* means 'burial rites'). Because of the way in which the actual distribution of inherited land and livestock proceeds, it usually happens that the final disposition of the remnants of an estate is not made until the generation of a man's grandsons.

Further, if the survivor of a sibling group dies without legal (male) issue, his heirs are his brothers' sons—members of one *ifwa*. Should the survivor of an *ifwa* group die without an heir, an heir or heirs will be chosen from among the sons of the

---

[1] That is, two brothers may not marry two sisters, nor may a man marry his sister's husband's sister. Sororal polygyny is, of course, forbidden.

deceased's fellow *ifwa* members. These men make up the fourth generation of the segment known to Taita as *kichuku kitini*, the small lineage.

It is seldom necessary to go beyond the range of small lineage relationships to find an heir for land or livestock. Therefore it is unnecessary for property purposes to agree on the precise genealogical links between more remote agnates, save under most unusual circumstances. Neither do the marriage rules require such agreement. Observation confirms that in fact the small lineage is for most Taita the limit of precise genealogical knowledge (or agreement). It is also the limit of strongly enjoined mutual aid, within which bringing suit for repayment of a 'gift' (thus turning it into a debt) is considered in dubious taste.

The use of socio-mythological techniques to structure segmentary relationships at higher levels of lineage organization need not concern us here. What is important is that, for most practical purposes, Taita descent groups are composed, as it were, of numerous little boxes—the small lineages—within a large container. Members of the different small lineages are potential but unlikely heirs of one another; they share an interest in the territorial integrity of the wider group and in its ritual affairs, and they can be linked to one another by affinal (and matrilateral) ties.

Many of them are in fact so linked. Intra-lineage marriages amount in some cases to as much as 30 per cent of all the marriages entered into by males of the lineage. Many of these involve the closest permitted degree of relationship, and it is rare to find two sibling groups in that range without the single allowable marriage connecting them. The nature of the remaining marriage ties brings us inevitably to the involvement of large lineages in local units of another order.

Each large lineage in Taita is linked to one or more others whose territories adjoin its own, to form what we call a neighbourhood. Besides marrying within their own descent group, men of a large lineage are found to choose wives predominantly from the other lineage or lineages making up the neighbourhood. Indeed, it is this concentration of marriage ties which Taita stress in defining the nature of a neighbourhood. Speaking of the constituent lineages they say that they 'have come to understand one another'; that they have 'become like one

TAITA DOMESTIC GROUPS

lineage' through intermarriage; or even that they are ultimately related agnatically since they do marry so much among themselves!

Taita say that the boundaries of each lineage's territories are known. But in practice, the homesteads and gardens of neighbour lineages inter-penetrate to some degree and each one's area displays small enclaves of the others' holdings. This is made possible in large part because land rights can be acquired not only by inheritance, but by loan, pawn, and even purchase. In fact, a large number of land transactions are effected among men of a neighbourhood. Not only is that the case, but residence within a neighbourhood is normally the prerequisite to acquisition or mobilization of land rights. Neighbourhoods are, in effect, land-use units.

Across the alignments of descent, kinship, and neighbourhood cuts the age-status system. So long as a man's father lives he is in some measure subject to his control. He has not come into his inheritance of land and livestock. Further, he is forbidden to try too strenuously to develop holdings which rival or surpass those of the father. Lacking independence and wealth, he cannot acquire private shrines and ritual knowledge.

Once a man is independent—has attained his jural majority—he can proceed to engage in livestock transactions within *and beyond* the confines of his neighbourhood, in an effort to gain riches. The prestige of age, independence, and wealth can be translated into ritual prerogatives through the acquisition of 'medicines', shrines, and sacred lore. The acquisition of partners in enterprise and of debtor-followers enable a man to exercise influence.

Ageing, independent, rich and influential men of ritual attainments are the *wagosi* (sing. *mugosi*) or elders. They constitute the *ad hoc* councils which make decisions of lineage and neighbourhood importance, and they hear and decide disputes among their junior kinsmen and co-residents. Their involvement in decision making marks them as political persons, and the effective scope of their decisions serves also to define the neighbourhood as a political entity.

Taita neighbourhoods, highly autonomous in so many spheres, were never held together by a centralized political organization. Rich elders engage in livestock and other enterprises across neighbourhood boundaries, make 'foreign' marriages providing them with extra-neighbourhood affinal ties, and enter blood-pacts. Observance of the latter by kinsmen of the pact partners is supernaturally sanctioned, with the result that pacts between individuals become the medium for wider political integration.

This outline of economic, kinship, local group and political relations outside the domestic group is more than general background for the main discussion. We shall be treating the development of domestic groups, as has been said, in terms of the rights and obligations respecting property, labour and produce. Resources and supplies come into the domestic group from various sources and, going out of it, reach various destinations. A male household head progresses through the age-status system, and his efforts to move upward and to widen his range of action affect the disposition of household resources. External pressures affect the domestic group, its developmental changes mobilizing the rights and obligations of its personnel as members of descent and local groups and participants in the status hierarchy. General structural principles are manifested in it.

II

Before proceeding to discuss the development of domestic groups it is well to define the nature of the units we shall be talking about. By domestic group—or household—we mean the persons occupying one or more buildings making up a homestead[1] under the direction of an adult member, sharing in the exploitation of land and livestock controlled by that head and, directly or indirectly,[2] contributing to and sharing a common food supply.

[1] Old-style Taita dwellings are usually round, built of mud and wattle, with some internal divisions and thatched inelegantly. Rectangular houses are increasingly popular, a few of them built of stone; corrugated sheeting often replaces thatch on these. Variant forms serve as kitchens, byres or extra sleeping space. A beaten earth area surrounds the buildings, and this may be bordered by a fence, hedge, or other border-marking device. But one homestead in a village may be separated from others by only a small open space. Taita make an important distinction between the household and the village.

[2] Every co-wife in a household headed by a polygynous male has her own storage shelf for food from her own gardens. But co-operation in feeding the husband and sharing in the 'insurance' crops grown by him suffice to justify our speaking of them as having a common food supply.

TAITA DOMESTIC GROUPS

In one representative lineage area, our census data furnish complete information on 68 out of a total of 82 lineage households, with a population in these 68 of 362 (including men temporarily at work outside the area). In size these households ranged from one to twelve members, with an average of 5·3. If we exclude the six households of polygynists, the average is 4·9. As to composition, 48 (77 per cent) consisted of a man, his wife or wives, and their unmarried children, and of these only four had one or more additional residents. Six households, 9 per cent of the total, include a married son and his wife, with or without small children. Widows and widowers accounted for all single-member households.

For present purposes, the important fact is that so many households consist of a man, his wife or wives, and unmarried children. Given the low rate of polygynous marriages in Taita (approximately one in seven), this means in fact that most of these consist of a nuclear family or the remains of one depleted by deaths and the marriages of offspring. A small number are 'extended family' households, some with three generations. It should be noted, however, that such extended family households include only *one* married son, a fact which suggests that each such arrangement is transitory, assuming that every son has an equal right (or duty) to bring his wife to his parental homestead. This is indeed the case. Since no other complex forms of household arise with any regularity (ignoring for the present complications arising out of leviratic unions) we are left with the characterization noted at the beginning of the essay.

Since households made up of nuclear families predominate in Taita, this may add point to what is in any case a legitimate question: Why do we choose to speak of households or domestic groups rather than families? We do so, first of all, to facilitate comparison between societies in which members of a nuclear family do in fact make up the usual form of the domestic group and those in which the case is otherwise, and to distinguish stages of development at which the nuclear family is *not* coterminous with household. To talk, in comparative work, of 'different forms of the family', when reference is to the differing degrees to which membership in a nuclear family corresponds to membership in a residential unit, only compounds the confusion.

For analytic purposes, also, it is desirable to differentiate between the family as a set of relationships, on the one hand, and residential arrangements on the other. That is, the family as a system of relationships may persist over time although the persons occupying roles in the system may be dispersed through a number of domestic groups. Furthermore, domestic groups may be linked to one another by means of familial relationships, while within a single domestic unit complexities arise from the familial ties which members have with persons outside the group.[1]

The Newly Married Pair

In an overwhelming majority of cases, the bride is taken to live at the homestead of the husband's parents. Thus a newly-married pair begin their life together as members of the man's parental household; their marriage marks a stage in the further development of that household and it foreshadows the establishment of a new domestic group.

Co-residence does not mean jural completion of the union. When non-elders marry, it is normal for bride-wealth payments[2] to be extended over many years. However, certain major payments (or even the promise of them) signify intention to complete the payments and give the man rights to sexual and domestic services as well as claims to offspring.

Property relations affect the fortunes of the nascent household. First of all, there are the claims of the young husband to having bride-wealth payments made on his behalf. One of these is the strong moral claim on his mother's brother for assistance to the extent of one bull. If this is forthcoming the matter ends there—no repayment is due and no complexities arise. No repayment is due, either, to the man's father, who should take responsibility for at least the major payments for

[1] In this paper we touch upon, but because of space limitations cannot discuss fully, several issues of current interest in social anthropology. Our starting points were Fortes 1949 and 1958. The continuing discussion between Fortes and Leach is especially important, the most recent paper being Leach's essay 'Rethinking anthropology' (Leach, 1960). That volume refers to papers by both discussants of which Fortes, 1959, is especially important. On bilaterality, see Murdock, 1960; and on residence, Barnes, 1960.

[2] Bride-wealth payments consist of cattle, small stock, money, cooked and uncooked foods, purchased goods and labour.

his son's first wife. But if, in order to make these payments, the father has had to use beasts on which others have claims (such as a cow given for the groom's half-sister, to which beast the girl's own full brother has first claim) this makes the young husband liable for ultimate repayment.[1] If any other senior agnate offers to contribute to a youth's bride-wealth the same is true—ultimate repayment is expected to the donor or his heirs.

Relations with the wife's father, brothers, and mother's brother[2] will be an important concern for years to come. Continuing his indebtedness benefits them as well as him, but periodically they will dun him for further instalments and eventually payment must be made.[1]

The major bride-wealth payment is a heifer calf born to a cow taken, while pregnant, to the bride's father's enclosure. If the resources of the groom's father permit, the cow is left with the father-in-law, establishing a relationship of stock-guardianship; and its offspring will furnish the nucleus of the groom's own herd. Often this is not possible, however, and commonly the fiscal arrangements entailed in marriage result in encumbering the resources of the nascent household with debts rather than supplementing them.

Marriage mobilizes the respective claims of husband and wife respecting land which will provide them and their children with food. As his father's heir a married man has the right to establish claims to portions of the land owned by his father. A woman, whose duty it is to grow subsistence crops with which to feed husband and children, has the right to use land under her husband's control. The two claims are met at the same time when, a few months after co-residence is established, the husband's mother begins to transfer to his wife the use of portions of the fields owned by the husband's father but cultivated by her.

The ultimate right to dispose of this land still belongs to the husband's father, though to take it back without compensation

---

[1] This is one of the instances in which it is bad taste to take an agnate to court and demand repayment as if for an ordinary debt; but it is legally possible.

[2] The bride's mother's brother receives a special beast of his own, not merely a portion of what is given to the bride's father, to whom all other livestock payments are due.

[3] For details, see Harris, 1962.

with other land would be morally wrong. His rights are appropriately called *ownership rights*, while the newly married son may be said to have acquired *overseer* rights. The young wife has obtained *use rights* from her mother-in-law, but legal responsibility (e.g., for lending a portion of this land to someone else) belongs to the husband, who must account for it to his father.

The land so apportioned ought to be in the form of segments of a number of fields formerly cultivated by the husband's mother in order that the young wife may cultivate a variety of crops on appropriate land. In amount, however, it is not expected to meet all the needs of the future. Rather, it may suffice for the early years of marriage and will form the nucleus of the land holdings which the husband will claim by right of inheritance.

Labour obligations go with membership in a domestic group. Each member of the new couple is expected to contribute labour under the direction of the senior member of the same sex, with the fulfilment of labour obligations being related to a share of the produce of all.

At the beginning, the young wife is but one more member of the female work-team headed by her mother-in-law and composed otherwise of the unmarried daughters living at home. (These women and girls till the fields in which the mother-in-law has use rights, do household chores, and engage in small-scale marketing of (and shopping for) foodstuffs.) After having fields allotted to her she continues to help in the mother-in-law's fields, receiving help in turn from other members of the female work-team. The young man continues membership in the male team under his father's direction, doing heavy clearing and other masculine agricultural tasks, caring for livestock, and doing errands. The word 'team' is perhaps misleading here, for all females or all males do not always work together on any single task; 'pool' is perhaps the better term.

Extra-household familial ties of the individual residents make additional helpers available from time to time and also take household members to the aid of members of other households. In particular, both members of the young married pair owe help to the wife's parents. For the wife this is part of a series of reciprocal rights and obligations: she returns to her natal homestead to give birth to her first child, she will always be received and cared for there in time of illness, and members of the household frequently come to help her and give her gifts of food. In return she is expected to contribute domestic and garden work periodically, and to visit the sick. For the husband, occasional work for the parents-in-law is part of his continued indebtedness to them.

Produce is also controlled by the senior residents. The mother-in-law has a storage shelf in her house, a separate store-room, or both. There goes all the produce of the fields, to be shared out for cooking, gift, or sale under her supervision. Milk from the livestock is similarly gathered and distributed under the father's direction. Control by the seniors, however, goes with responsibility to give out appropriate shares to those who have contributed their labour. Failure to receive a just portion of food or milk justifies a household member in withdrawing his or her labour in protest, a protest which will receive external support should the senior make a public complaint. In the case of the young married man, his position as an heir of his father also gives him a voice in the disposition of the resources from which the supplies come, for his father ought to consult him before disposing of land or livestock, lest impoverishment result.

These days, the money earned by a son whose wife is resident in his parental homestead but who is himself out at work, tends to be treated as a substitute for his traditional contribution of labour. Parents therefore consider that the son ought to send his money home to them. But parents-in-law also plague him for gifts and small amounts of cash, while his wife presses him to buy things for her or to save for the future. Therefore at this stage the competition among various persons to enjoy the profits of the young people's productive capacities is intensified where money is concerned.

Satellite Households

Permission to provide his wife with the house of her own to which every married woman is entitled is secured from the husband's father. The approach of a younger brother's marriage and, especially, the birth of children to the resident young couple are the most likely occasions. The result is not a fully independent household, but a 'satellite' of the parental household.

Youngest and only sons find it difficult or impossible to obtain more than a separate house immediately adjacent to the parental one, for they are expected to be the mainstay of the parents' old age. Eldest sons, ideally, go to the site of the paternal grandfather's house, and in practice are usually to be found on an adjacent knoll or at a little distance along the ridge occupied by the parents, whether or not the site was previously lived on by the grandfather. Middle sons often go farther away to build, within lineage territory but frequently nearer to some other agnate than to the father.

The nature of the terrain, the scattered land holdings, and the practice of moving once or twice after the establishment of a separate homestead all contribute to a situation in which neither a man and all of his sons, nor a group of brothers, need live close to one another in a single village or hamlet. Such arrangements are to be found, but it occasions no surprise when a son builds at some distance from his father's homestead. The residential separation of fathers and sons and brothers from one another is evident in both types of settlement.

Responsibility for launching a new homestead belongs to both sets of parents. They take turns supplying materials, labour, supervision and refreshments for the workers, who include kinsmen of all kinds and unrelated neighbours. The culmination of their efforts comes with the setting up of a new hearth by the two mothers, who kindle its first fire and initiate its use by the young woman.

With respect to livestock rights and resources no major changes follow upon establishment of one's own homestead. All animals, including those the young married man has special claims to, should still be kept in the enclosure belonging to his father and herded jointly. The young householder may, it is true, try to acquire some livestock of his own other than the cow and calves which may be under guardianship for him by his father-in-law. With his father's permission he may use such animals in transactions profitable to him. There are, however, both practical and jural limitations to be noted.

Livestock transactions include stock guardianship (*wuturi*), which gives a guardian the right to use milk from female animals in his keeping, but which entails responsibility for the beasts. Guardianship may involve long-term loans, mutual-aid partnerships whereby each partner takes turns supplying the other with animals as they are needed (as for sacrifices), and contracts for calves or 'grand-calves' of pregnant animals. In all these transactions, recompense to the transferrer or transferrers (more than two individuals may be involved) is received over a long period. Final settlement is often deferred until the generation of the parties' sons.

It should be noted that Wataita speak, respecting any good, as though the transferrer (even in a sale) always confers a benefit upon the purchaser; they do not operate in terms of sellers who must seek buyers. In the sphere of livestock transactions this idiom is used to establish and maintain long-term relationships of superiority-subordination or, as with mutual-aid partners, equivalence.

Added to this is the advantage to a transferrer, in transactions extending over time, of having a reserve in the form of debts owed, a bank account of sorts which may be drawn upon in time of need or which may eventually constitute part of his estate's assets, to be inherited (and collected) by his heirs.

The two aspects are interwoven in the efforts of men both to increase the size of their herds through skilful trading and to use livestock to extend the range of their relationships. Both aims preclude the desirability, in Taita terms, of outright sale for cash. Although small stock can be purchased for 'cash in hand' (*pesa mkononyi*), cattle are rarely sold except on the instalment plan.

A young man whose father is still alive can enter into the resulting network of transactions to only a limited extent. Those wishing to engage in transactions will normally prefer to deal with his father, who still has jural authority over him and who can withhold permission. A father continues to be the *de jure* principal in such transactions. Further, a young man will find it most difficult to arrange transactions in which he would be creditor rather than debtor, since prospective debtors prefer to link themselves to an already established, older man who is an independent agent. Finally, to rival one's father is an impertinence to all seniors.

A very minor item in the livestock resources of a young couple may be a goat or two or even a cow, 'given' to the wife by her father as a gesture of affection. She has no jural claim whatever to such animals, and they can easily be reclaimed by her brothers at the death of her father.

Movement out of the man's parental household usually does entail important changes where land resources are concerned. More fields may be allotted to the wife from her mother-in-law's portions. Even these are unlikely to suffice, whether or not the husband has brothers who also have rights to a share of the land.[1] Not only insufficiency, but inconvenience of location or type may require the husband to seek additional land. He must therefore enter the system of land transfers whereby land in Taita is redistributed from older to younger men by means other than (although in addition to) inheritance.

In rare instances, land can be given freely, as in the case of an immigrant who has cut his ties with his old community and who intends to settle down in the new one. More often, a plot is pawned when its owner urgently requires some item of livestock or goods, but does not wish to relinquish his rights in the land permanently. Use-rights then pass to the person who agrees to take the land in pawn, but this person acquires no right to transfer the field to anyone else. The return of a pawned field is secured upon repayment by the original owner[2] or his heirs, to the third generation. Thereafter unredeemed land is considered to belong to the heirs of the man who originally took it in pawn.

Nearly everywhere in the hills, most kinds of land are subject to outright sale as well. Those tracts of very poor land which can be cultivated profitably for only one or two seasons, after a very long period of fallowing, are subject to use-rights only. The rights are held by whatever members of the local community choose to clear plots. All the better types of land can be sold, although there may be restrictions on freedom to sell (see page 123), and the sale of land seems to be neither recent nor the result of contact with Europeans.

[1] Discussion of other factors involved in the distribution of land to sons is deferred until later.

[2] That is, the man who pawned it rightfully, for we are ignoring any previous owners from whom the plot may have passed by inheritance or sale.

Land is also loaned for periods ranging from a single season to many years. As with all other transactions, loans must be ratified by a beer drink at which the parties are joined by witnesses who beat the bounds with them. For loans this beer, supplied by the borrower, formerly sufficed. Nowadays, especially when the borrowed land is to be used for cash crops, a rental in money, goods or livestock is often demanded. Not surprisingly, the rental and other difficulties give rise to frequent disagreements as to whether a particular transaction was a loan or a sale.

Entering into the network of land transactions, the head of a satellite household has certain possibilities and limitations set on his search for land. The needs of his household for food, and his own desire to undertake cash crop production or to grow supplementary subsistence crops by himself dictate the amount and kinds of land sought—in part. His wife's desires are important, too.

A wife has the duty to supply her household with food, but she may distribute her crops, arrange her work schedule, and exchange agricultural aid with other women as she sees fit. Part of this freedom is the right to a voice in deciding what additional fields shall be acquired. Therefore, although the husband effects the transfers himself, her needs and preferences as a cultivator are vital.

The most important limitation on land acquisition has already been mentioned: a householder must seek land within his own neighbourhood. Those kith and kin who transfer land to him are normally older men who might, if they chose, distribute more land to their wives and sons, but who lend or sell it instead. The recipient thereby becomes indebted to a number of seniors within his community.

The very common loan of a field or more to a householder by his wife's father is of particular interest. As must always be the case, the arrangement is effected by the men concerned. But this kind of loan is spoken of as a loan to the daughter herself. Often it is said to be undertaken voluntarily by the woman's father (and with her brothers' agreement) in order to mitigate the hardships which a married daughter must be undergoing as wife to a man of meagre resources. Or its convenient location may be stressed. Whatever other reasons are offered, such a loan is, in addition, spoken of as being 'for the sake of the grandchildren'. In jural terms, overseer rights pass to the householder, while use-rights pass to his wife. She cannot pass these on to anyone, including her children. Ownership rights are retained by her father, and pass to his male heirs. Indeed, this follows the pattern of all other land loans save where use-rights also pass to the man, as when he wishes to cultivate cash crops.

It is significant that this customary and morally sanctioned transaction follows the line of a particular familial tie uniting a female member of the household to those in her parental unit. Although the loan cannot be demanded as a legal right, young householders can usually count on it to expand their resources. It is only feasible, of course, when a man has taken his wife from within the neighbourhood. It adds yet another element to relationships with a household to which his wife and he are already closely bound.

Work in their own homestead and fields now claims more and more of the couple's time, but they must still give labour to the husband's parental household. Otherwise, those with whom each spouse exchanges occasional help are now to a larger extent of his or her own choosing, the choices being less dominated by the relationships primarily important to members of the husband's parental household. As the couple's own children grow, they align themselves with their parents to form male and female labour pools on which the household comes to depend primarily.

A crucial event for the satellite household soon after its inception is the building of a storage shelf in the new house. Permission to have a separate shelf is granted by the husband's mother, and she supervises its construction. The young wife now may oversee her own food supply, contributing to others and receiving contributions along the lines of her own kinship ties. Milk is still controlled by the husband's father as supervisor of the entire joint herd, but the young man's labour still gives him a claim to share in the produce. Gifts of food ought to go to the man's parents and, in fact, in times of great emergency (as when a severe drought occurs), the husband's mother regains the right to direct the food supply for her own and the satellite households.

Members of the viri-parental household frequently complain that the young wife allocates too much of her labour and gives too much food to her mothers and sisters, and too little to her husband's people. They also complain that her kinswomen spend too much time at her homestead and try to interfere in domestic affairs which more properly come under the supervision of the husband's own parents. Similarly, the husband's increasing devotion of time, energy and resources (including money) to his own wife and children brings complaints of hard-heartedness from his parents. Wataita sometimes speak of this state of affairs as 'warfare' between a man's wife and his parents. Their doing so is a sign of the real increase in independence of the younger couple, combined with retention, by the wife, of rights in and duties towards her natal household.

Independent Households of Non-Elders

A satellite household becomes an independent one after the head's father dies. Its 'independence' does not mean isolation, of course, and internal changes must still be seen against the background of altered relations with members of other households.

The death of his father eventually brings a man to the status of independent property owner, as heir or coheir to the father's livestock and land. The formal rules of livestock inheritance are simple enough. If, as is usually the case, the deceased had but one wife, all sons by her share according to birth order, with the eldest receiving the largest portion. When the heirs comprise two or more sets of half-brothers with different mothers, division is according to birth order irrespective of matri-segment in some parts of the hills, while in others it is by matri-segment first and then by birth order within it. In either case, animals kept at homesteads are treated as 'house property'. A widow, for example, has the right to the use of one milch cow, the beast to be taken eventually by her youngest son. Men claim the bride-wealth of their own full-sisters, each man having a special claim over that brought in by his paired sister (*i.e.*, the one closest in birth order or age).

While the widow's use-right is usually respected whenever

possible, the particular claims over bride-wealth are often overridden, at least temporarily. Complications may have been introduced during the father's lifetime by his own transactions, but we will deal here only with *post mortem* arrangements. It is each man's right, as heir to his *pater*, to have at least major bride-wealth payments made on his behalf. Therefore when a livestock estate is very small, adjustment is made by means of an agreement to treat female animals as joint holdings, with brothers taking the offspring by turns. Other transfers between full- and half-brothers can also be made. Most Taita speak of such transactions as 'gifts' and hold that the transferrer ought not to reclaim repayment. However, it is expected that adjustment will eventually be made by the parties' heirs.[1]

Further practical complications often arise from herding arrangements or from the transactions of the deceased father. While a very poor man may keep all of his few beasts at his homestead, others normally divide their holdings into a homestead lot including one or a few available milch cows, and an 'outside' lot, kept grazing at a high upland or plains herding station. Although at least one son, chosen by his father for his responsible character, is supposed to know about these 'outside' animals, as is the widow, it is sometimes difficult to sort them out from those belonging to herding partners. Then too, there are the beasts being kept as *wuturi* by other men and those over which the deceased was guardian on others' behalf. Finally, there are certain to be debts encumbering the estate, as well as claims to be pressed by the heirs. Debts and claims must therefore be divided along with the beasts in hand, with larger shares of both debts and claims going to senior coheirs.

These complications delay settlement of an estate and even though a man becomes independent of his father it may be some time before his household feels the effects fully. If there are younger brothers as yet unmarried, settlement will be further delayed on that account. The herd can be drawn upon when necessary, but only after consultation with the widow or

[1] For instance, in the generation of sons' sons of the original owner, the son of A sues the son of B—A and B were brothers—saying that A allowed B a portion of the bride-wealth obtained for A's linked sister in order that B might marry without delay. If no direct or indirect restitution was ever made by B, then B's son is reckoned debtor to A's son and must repay, even though A's son is thought boorish to have made the affair public.

widows, the senior agnate who as co-trustee helps to supervise the estate,[1] and the senior heir. Their wishes must be respected and their knowledge of the estate relied upon.

Even after all coheirs are married and all beasts, debts and claims are apportioned, the actual dispersal of the herd may not take place for some time. It is considered desirable for coheirs to continue to manage their animals jointly and, depending on the number of men involved and their relations with one another, they may maintain one or a small number of joint herds. Sooner or later, however, their individual interests lead them to division.

As to land, the household has, as a satellite of the husband's parental unit, already been enjoying the use of fields owned by the husband's father and formerly cultivated by his mother. The husband's married brothers will also have acquired some land in this way. Land which had been retained by the father for his own use is divided into shares in such a manner as to insure equitable distribution of plots of the various types. In most parts of the hills, the amount of this land received by a man is proportional to his seniority, irrespective of matri-segment. But the differences are of very minor practical importance.

Paralleling the livestock arrangements, there are use-rights of women which must be respected. They are both more numerous and more important practically. First, a man and his co-heirs do not have the right to deprive their mother or any other widow of their father of land actually being cultivated by her. This land (which includes fallow) is hers to use so long as she may live. Second, men ought not to reclaim land being cultivated by their sisters, i.e., portions lent to their brothers-in-law by their father. A sister should not be ousted

[1] If possible, a brother of the deceased man is chosen to watch over the survivors, and to share supervision of the estate with the widow(s) and senior heir. Failing a brother, someone is chosen from among the next closest agnates in the deceased's generation. The man chosen should ideally also act as 'begetter' (*mvi*), raising children to the dead man. However, practice diverges from this alleged ideal even to the extent that the widow may select a lover who is not an agnate of the dead husband and who has no say in the estate. Widows' establishments vary considerably according to age, children's age, identity of co-trustee and begetter; but when the widow is a young woman with small children the result, for practical purposes, is that they form an especially well-endowed matri-segment in a polygynous household whose head has access to but incomplete control of their endowment. In such cases the dead man's name may drop out of common use, though discussion reveals him as the 'real' father of the widow's children.

as cultivator provided her continued use of the land does not impose a real hardship on the heir or heirs. Ultimately, the remnant of land cultivated by the mother belongs to her youngest son. If land cultivated by a sister was originally a portion of her own mother's cultivations, it must revert to her own full-brothers. But if it came from the father's unassigned land pool, all heirs have equal claim unless some special reason (such as a former unavoidable inequity) entitles one son to preferential treatment.

Again, there may be complications resulting from the deceased's transactions. Payments may still be due for land sold, and there may be pawned land to reclaim or return. Of greatest moment is land lent by the father to men other than his sons-in-law. On all lands putatively a part of the estate, ownership claims are decided on the same principles as with the father's unassigned land, and then it may be left to each heir to decide whether to oust the cultivator or cultivators or to renew the arrangements. Alternatively, the brothers may press the estate's claim jointly against one or more borrowers and then, having regained the land, proceed to parcel it out among themselves. If arrangements are renewed, reclaiming may be left to the next generation.

The heirs we are considering must, of course, be concerned to settle transactions left over by their own father and his brothers from the settlement of the (heirs') grandfather's estate. Claims may be put forward for the return of livestock 'gifts' made in the last generation. The father's sisters were very likely cultivating land which, if it was not reclaimed from the sons of these women following the latters' deaths, should now be recovered. But a man's sisters frequently survive him, so that usually not all such land can be reclaimed at this point. There may also be parcels of land lent by the paternal grandfather, whose sons chose to leave them in the hands of the original borrowers. It is important that these plots be reclaimed, for were their loan to be extended yet another generation reclaiming them would be difficult.[1] These final dispositions of

---

[1] This is so both because of the difficulty of producing reliable testimony concerning the original transaction, and because sentiment would favour the notion that the transfer must have been intended as an outright gift based on special friendship, or else reclamation would have been made before.

the grandfather's estate, then, add to the many complications arising from settlement of the father's portion, and involve other members of the *ifwa* or inheritance group.

Eventually, then, a householder whose father has died acquires title to livestock and to land. Beasts and fields, his portion of the estate, are the focus of interest, as property and resources, for members of his now independent household. Particular complications, involving claims on and by kin and neighbours, link them and him to members of other households for years to come.

Not only property relations are important. Though the founding spouses of an independent household are wholly free of any direct control over their labour and produce, they have important duties. If the head's mother survives as a widow, he and his wife ought both to help with the work of her homestead, particularly if she continues to live alone. They ought also to give her gifts of food and welcome her to meals at their place.

Death of the father also causes responsibility for relations with his daughters' affines to devolve upon our householder and his coheirs. The head of an independent household becomes especially closely involved with the husband of his linked sister, and more particularly so after that man himself becomes head of an independent household. The sister's husband owes help and deference, and he probably owes some bride-wealth also. But the pattern is for him to be sought after also as friend, confidant, and helper on ritual occasions. Gifts of foodstuffs and the exchange of garden labour also follow these and other links through women, adding to and calling upon the household's resources.

Relationships within the independent household are intricate. The birth of more children and the survival of some adds to the numbers, of course, and their arrival at adolescence adds to the male and female labour pools. Marriage of daughters depletes the female labour pool. The entry of son's wives does not in the long run make up for this depletion, since there is only one such daughter-in-law resident at a time, other sons and their wives moving one by one from the parental homestead into homesteads of their own. There may be, then, many years during which an independent household has a resident son and daughter-in-law, with an infant or two, as members.

But the resident young couple changes every few years, so that the household retains the same kind and degree of complexity.

As owner of his own herd, the independent householder can now duplicate the arrangements of his own father. Animals may be divided between homestead and 'outside' herds, with yet others in the keeping of other men. His is the ultimate control over them as well as land inherited and otherwise acquired by him. Wives and sons have rights respecting use of resources and enjoyment of produce, rights which correspond to their duties to labour and contribute the fruits of their work.

The wife (or each wife in a polygynous household) has the right to the use of one milch cow so that she and her children, as well as the husband, can have milk, curds and butter. When sons have married, they should continue to receive milk from the father's herd as a return for the labour contributed to its care. Should a wife refuse to cook or a son to herd (or to contribute cash to pay a herd-boy), milk can be refused. If the household head is stingy, his wife and sons have no recourse but to withdraw their labour.

Portions of the land inherited or otherwise acquired by the head are assigned by him to his wife or wives for cultivation by them. Other portions he retains for his own use, to grow 'men's' crops, as insurance against crop failure or shortages, or for cash crops. He may retain some land as fallow also, and is likely to hold back some portions in anticipation of later marriages and for use in transactions.

A wife must supply food for her children and her husband from what she grows on the fields assigned her. As we have mentioned, she has virtually complete control over food-production, over the harvested food and its daily apportionment, and over any surpluses there may be. Surplus foodstuffs may be sold in the local markets, and money so earned is hers although Taita say she 'ought' to give some cash or gifts to her husband.

A husband's crops—on which his wife is likely to have expended some labour at critical times—are his, but his first responsibility is to supplement his wife's produce should it not suffice. Moreover, a man's obligations to his wife and children are numerous, and he is usually under pressure to spend the proceeds of sales on their behalf. His dependents must be clothed, other necessities must be supplied, and payment made for fines, and medical and divinatory expenses. Just recompense for a wife's domestic and garden work should also include an occasional goat, slaughtered for a feast. The household head cannot avoid expending livestock; his dependents cannot long evade their duties—this is the way in which Taita themselves speak of such affairs.

Apart from rights to produce in return for labour, sons and wives have rights as heirs and mothers of heirs. The independent household head is responsible for the major bride-wealth payments for each of his sons, having no right to marry polygynously himself unless his sons' marriages are provided for. If possible, he ought also to leave each cow bearing the bride-wealth heifer under the guardianship of his sons' fathers-in-law, to form the core of the sons' portions.

To review: sons gain the core of their land inheritance as parcels are turned over to their wives for cultivation shortly after marriage, from the portions of land assigned to their mothers. Sons acquire overseer rights in these fields, and possession of them helps make effective their right to enjoy the produce of their own wives' labour. While a father retains ultimate control, back of each son's overseer rights is the expectation that his rights as heir will be exercised over these particular parcels. His father cannot in justice claim their return—although there are unjust fathers in Taita who do so. Over time, a substantial proportion of a father's land is divided among his future heirs, since every son has the same right to have land assigned to his first wife for cultivation.

Women endeavour to protect the right of their sons and heirs. As the mother of heirs, a wife expects her sons to receive care and help from the husband and father, an instance being shares of milk from the herd, a matter over which there is frequent wrangling. Her interests in land are more direct, for she is concerned to have enough for current needs, with an ample margin for her daughters-in-law so that after all her sons have married she will still retain some fields for herself.

Equally important, potential heirs and their mothers have a voice in the disposition of property. A man is guided by his wife's needs and preferences in the acquisition of additional fields for her use, as we have mentioned. She must also be considered when fields or livestock are to be disposed of, as must prospective heirs, lest the transactions lead to their impoverishment. The protection of wives and heirs is secured in part by requiring them to witness transactions, since this necessitates their knowledge and consent.

In practice, an independent householder usually has little difficulty doing as he pleases with livestock. It is simply expected that he will employ his 'capital' so as to realize the greatest profit, ultimately to the benefit of his wife or wives and heirs. Matters are not so straightforward where land is concerned. A household head may prefer to lend or sell land to acquire debtors, expecting his heirs to seek additional land elsewhere if they are short. If the land to be disposed of is an especially choice plot, his wife and sons may resist.[1] Just as with the head's stinginess with produce, or money, wives and sons have recourse to passive resistance. They can refuse to serve as witnesses, a warning to prospective buyers of possible future disputes. Their other course is withdrawal of labour or other co-operation. Should the husband and father complain about such actions publicly, they have the right to explain the reasons for their behaviour. In effect, he is forced to change his ways, tolerate the withdrawal of services, or risk public censure.

As the years pass, a household head's participation in the networks of transactions usually increases, and is of continuing concern to all household members. Not only bad fortune, but bad management too, may now impoverish them and result in a multiplication of debts which heirs will some day have to face. Good fortune and successful management enables the head to expand his activities' range. He may now find men wishing to contract for his calves, willing to enter mutual-aid partnerships with him, and asking for long-term loans. Some of these livestock transactions, in which he can now be the creditor or at least one of two equal parties, will involve him with men beyond the boundaries of his neighbourhood. Within the local community, he may be of sufficient note to rise in the ritual order. In land transactions he is also more likely to enter as creditor than as debtor. Further changes affecting the house-

[1] The limitations placed on disposition of land by sons and wives are in addition to the rights of members of the small lineage to first refusal when land is for sale. Their right is morally strong but jurally weak.

hold as a unit (and its individual members also) depend in part on the continued success—or failure—of the head.

The Waning of Non-Elders' Households

In later years, the course of development also displays general patterns. Again, there are changes related to events in other households with which familial ties exist, while other changes proceed internally. In this section we will deal with the latter first.

These years inevitably bring diminution in the household's size. Children surviving to adulthood have been married, preferably in order of age. If there were several sons, there has been a succession of resident daughters-in-law and small grandchildren. Though all the children have at last married the youngest son and his wife should be living close at hand. In the original homestead, only the ageing couple remain. Others are often about the homestead as visitors and helpers, and a grandchild or two may visit for prolonged periods. Among the latter, daughters' children are especially welcome.

Let us deal here with men who, where resources are concerned, are not rich in livestock. In Taita terms they have not been able to become elders. The marriages of daughters have brought animals in through bride-wealth payments, of course, and some may still be outstanding. But there has also been a flow of animals out. Bride-wealth has been given on behalf of sons' marriages, while responsibility for sacrifices and fines may have proved very costly.

Taken as a whole, the livestock estate is likely to include a few animals kept at the homestead plus claims on others, minus outstanding debts. Any elderly man is certain to be involved in a network of transactions. For the less fortunate this is largely a matter of bride-wealth debts and claims on the one hand, and, on the other, of a series of loans resulting from periodic need to sacrifice. Sacrificial needs always involve a man in loans from and to other herds, since men dislike killing animals from their own herds even when they can afford to do so. For a poor man, debts outweigh claims established in this manner. The complication of a poor man's affairs is merely an aspect of progress through the life cycle: in later years, a man is head of a household at a late stage of development, but is not necessarily a 'grand financier'. Quite commonly an estate is minimal; the case of the man who, at his death, left no stock on hand and was owing only two beasts is extreme, but not unique.

The land resources have been reduced also, as fields have been turned over to sons for their wives to cultivate. Loans to sons-in-law and others will also have made inroads. However, land needs are not so pressing now, for an elderly couple needs only small patches on which to grow food and some sugar-cane fields to supply the wherewithal for beer. The household does not now have available enough labour to maintain more than a minimum under cultivation. Cash crops cannot be grown on an especially large scale, either. So also with produce: needs are not so great, but fulfilment of them, using only household labour, may often be difficult. Loss of health and vigour can mean reduced or straitened circumstances.

Members of a waning household seek to supplement their resources, usually successfully. This is the stage at which the head and his wife, as founders of a parental household, depend on reaping the benefits of seniority, of which the subordination and indebtedness of others are aspects. First in importance are the married children and their spouses.

As we have seen, a married son with a homestead of his own is simply head of a satellite household. A father retains ultimate control over the land and livestock whose products his sons enjoy. For a poor man with few animals left, labour which his married sons might contribute to care of the herd is not a pressing matter in later years. Their cash earnings, however, are vital. Indeed, if the household head has himself been employed in wage-labour it is now appropriate for him to retire. By virtue of his control over his sons' labour capacities, he may expect cash contributions from them to replace his own earnings. Sons' wives, having received use-rights in land, are expected to contribute labour and produce to the elder couple.

We remarked earlier that married sons' engrossment in the affairs of their own households and the calls their own family members make upon daughters-in-law can result in friction. Refusal of sons and their wives to fulfil their duties in more than a minimal fashion sometimes works hardships on an elderly couple. But the indebtedness of sons as their father's heirs, and the moral weight of parental claims, ordinarily make such claims effective.

The ties maintained by a married daughter with her parental household give her claims to certain kinds of care and attention, as was noted above, and these extend to her children. The old people press her to visit, expecting her to help with agricultural and household tasks, and to bring them gifts of food whenever possible. From sons-in-law, too, the ageing couple can expect various services and gifts, since they are considered to remain indebted. If the old man has lent them land the degree of their indebtedness is increased, and they may be counted on for more deference and help.

Maintenance of close ties with married daughters and their husbands makes it possible for an older couple to supplement the claims on the filial dutifulness of sons with claims on sons-in-law. The usefulness of an attentive son-in-law is epitomized in the pride with which an old man remarked on an army greatcoat given by a son-in-law as a minor part of bride-wealth.

Junior agnates as well as sisters' sons and other persons outside the lineage can be called on actually to pay debts incurred in previous years. More generally, and especially if they have received land or livestock from the elderly household head, they are important because they owe him deference. When he requests gifts or the performance of some tasks, they should comply with his wishes if at all possible.

Elderly men can, then, call upon a variety of junior kinsmen and neighbours when they need labour for a work-party. And should some special task need to be done, or some item particularly required, they have a number of young people, male and female, to call upon.

Ties with the households headed by contemporaries are also important. In later years the creditor-debtor relationship between brothers-in-law tends to be overridden in everyday affairs by generational solidarity. A man therefore engages in various kinds of mutual aid, economic and ritual, with his sisters' husbands and wife's brothers. Familial ties of the wife are also important: sisters, mother's sisters' daughters, and other consanguineous kin, together with brothers' wives and husband's sisters, can be called on (as they call on her) for small gifts of food and help in garden and homestead.

In sum, just as, when their household was a satellite of the husband's parental one, a couple did not look only to his father for resources, so in the waning of their domestic unit an elderly couple look not only to their own offspring but to a variety of juniors and contemporaries. They hope to enjoy, when they need them most, the fruits of independent householdership: a host of persons who owe help and deference.

Elders' Households

For men who have achieved the wealth, influence, and ritual positions of elderhood, their households have important potentialities for developments made possible by the prosperity of their heads.

In Taita terms, an elder owns large herds, and is not embarrassed by the expenses entailed in household headship. His household can enjoy more meat, for he can afford to slaughter small stock for occasional feasts. His numerous ritual activities, particularly, requiring the sacrifice of stock or their slaughter for divination, add to the household larder. Although substantial portions of animals slaughtered by the head are given to others, portions also come in as shares in the animals sacrificed by other elders.

Greater livestock resources do not justify their wanton expenditure or use for display. They may not even mean that the household head meets his responsibilities gladly or does more than the minimum required of him on behalf of his heirs and dependents. Even an elder may press his sons to help with their own bride-wealth payments, especially if they are working for wages. And he will certainly not encourage his sons to acquire additional wives. Being responsible only for their first marriages, he prefers to use his livestock to acquire additional wives for himself.

Most important as a differentiating feature of an elder's household is the head's full-scale involvement in the network of livestock transactions both within and outside of his own neighbourhood. These include not only bride-wealth debts and claims and arrangements made to meet ritual needs (see above,

p. 143), but far-flung stock-guardianship partnerships, long-term loans to poorer men, and mutual-aid partnerships. They culminate in 'foreign' marriages and the formation of blood-pacts, both of which have implications for the internal relations of his domestic group and for its relations with other households.

Most plural marriages and most of the marriages to women outside the neighbourhood are elders' marriages. For non-elders, the advantages all lie with marriage to a local woman, the connection between ties through women and the search for additional land being especially significant.[1] An elder, having married locally early in his life, can seek a marriage with a woman from a distant neighbourhood for the sake of political and economic advantages. Correspondingly, his suit finds favour by virtue of the advantages which his wealth and local influence offer his 'foreign' affines. Blood-pacts with other elders outside the neighbourhood also provide political benefits to the partners and can lead to further economic relations. Foreign marriages and blood-pacts often follow, one from the other.

A 'foreign' marriage brings to the man's household (without an initial period of residence in the parental unit) an 'alien' wife who is likely to lack local kinship ties. To Taita, who speak habitually in terms of local marriages, such a union poses special problems: The wife from a distant neighbourhood may suffer loneliness, for she cannot reach her mother and other kinswomen easily, as is normally the case; also, she 'does not know the ways' of her husband's locality and so may cause friction. On the other hand, the special nature of the marriage gives her some prestige. Occasional visits to and from her kinsfolk are matters of importance, and cause more stir than the ordinary comings and goings of kin-cum-neighbours.

Blood-pacts also bring special visitors to the homestead, visitors whose presence is remarked by the neighbours, and who require special hospitality which they reciprocate on other occasions. Part of this hospitality is the provision of sexual services by the wife for the husband's pact-partner, especially should the household head himself be away from home. Wife-sharing of this kind would be a heinous sin between two brothers, resulting in the death of one of the three parties;

[1] This is treated at length in Harris, 1962.

but it is heartily approved for pact-partners. One of the consequences is that some of the young children in an elder's household may have been begotten by their legal father's pact-partner. This in itself is of less importance to Taita than the fact that wives and children alike can look to the head's pact-partners for help and hospitality in the future should they need it. Thus, whatever other political, economic, and prestige purposes blood-pacts may serve, for individuals and for communities, the man engaging in them is also in effect purchasing a kind of last-ditch insurance for his household dependents should local kin and neighbours some day fail them.

The land situation of an elder's household is very like that of non-elders. However, greater prosperity is likely to have made it possible for the elder to have retained more purchased land. He therefore has larger resources to use in transactions through which to establish special ties beneficial to himself and his dependents.

Of course, if the elder is a polygynist, he must use some of the land held back from earlier assignments to supply his later wife or wives with land to cultivate. These women, then, do not receive use-rights from the mother-in-law, but acquire rights after the manner of women whose husbands have borrowed or purchased land for them to use. Sons of an elder may eventually fare better than other men's heirs, inheriting more substantial portions of land. But the household head often deliberately follows a policy of lending, pawning, and selling land to other junior kinsmen and neighbours. Realization of claims so established is likely to benefit heirs later on, once they inherit the estate. In the meantime, they serve to attach other juniors to the head and supply his household with extra sources of food, gifts, and labour.

A special aspect of the position of an elder regarding land is his ability by virtue of influence in the community to use extra land resources to settle an immigrant or a small group of immigrants from another neighbourhood, under his protection. Like others, a powerful elder observes neighbourhood boundaries with respect to ordinary land transactions. Unlike others, he may succeed in introducing a 'foreigner' (or, rarely, an uxorilocal son-in-law) whose presence is an asset to his household.

TAITA DOMESTIC GROUPS

Within a polygynous household more female labour is available than elsewhere, but this is not so important in an agricultural system in which women are highly independent cultivators aiming at the fulfilment of subsistence needs and seldom much beyond them. The husband cannot direct their activities, and he must recognize the right of each wife to dispose of her produce as she sees fit, provided she furnishes food for the children and himself. Wives should help with the weeding and harvest work in any fields planted by their husband, but this is rarely onerous work in the case of elders' small plots. Hence the arrangements of wives do not overlap greatly, while the husband benefits from each woman's farming, cooking, and brewing.

However young his later wife or wives may be, an elder is likely to have grown sons by his first wife who are heads of satellite households. An elder's larger herd means more work for his sons, but also more milk for them to share. Further, as heirs to a considerable estate their interest is maintained. Sons-in-law may hope for further loans of land, and they may depend on their elder father-in-law to allow delay of bridewealth payments, on which he does not depend in order to meet debts. Junior agnates, sisters' sons, and others also hope for favours. An elder's household benefits rather more than most from the labour and gifts of many juniors, given out of deference and the promise of some benefit, and not only as the result of demands. One or two young men paying a visit, perhaps with a pot of beer, can often be found in the homestead, a visible sign of its head's influence.

Structurally, an elder's household combines features of a non-elder's diminished household and an independent household at the height of its development. The elder's first wife, if she survives, is likely to be elderly, all her children married and removed. A younger wife may have some unmarried children still at home, while a very young wife who has barely begun her child-bearing life may have offspring who are contemporaries of the other wives' grandchildren. Sooner or later, however, the process of final diminution begins, with death and its consequences.

III

It is clear that the 'typical' nuclear family in Taita is not the same in structure and jural features as the highly autonomous nuclear family found in some segments of western industrial society. Many of the most important differences are related to the manner in which domestic groups are articulated with a wider social order, that itself has differentiating characteristics. These characteristics set Taita apart also from many other superficially similar African systems. Property ownership and political rights are held by males and transmitted patrilineally. But the word 'patrilineal' cannot sum up the Taita social system. Examination of the cycle of domestic groups in relation to property calls attention to the principles of the wider system, while revealing their working in everyday life.

In Taita there are highly exclusive local units—the neighbourhoods—within which most marriages take place and in them almost everyone is likely to be related to everyone else in some way. Yet the membership of such a local unit does not constitute simply a bilateral kin group, since land ownership and residence rights are transmitted patrilineally within two or three large lineages. Focusing on this latter aspect, one might see the situation as one in which a small number of descent groups stand to one another in a (putatively) permanent or long-term relationship, exchanging spouses. But since there is no rule of exogamy as such, affinity is not a matter only of relations between groups. Neither is it merely the total of particular in-law bonds set within the limits of some universal tendency to marry close at hand. Incest prohibitions prevent the concentration of affinal bonds among *both* close patrikin and matrikin, and the additional marriage prohibitions prevent duplicating ties among close affines. These prohibitions at least create, for individuals, 'pockets' of close agnates, matrikin and affines who are differentiated from one another. The preference for marriage within the neighbourhood brings us around again to the appearance of bilaterality. The importance of women's rights contributes to this appearance.

In terms of categories of persons, the following is the case: *Close* kinship (and close agnation) is incompatible with affinity;

non-close kinship (and agnation) is compatible with affinity but not equivalent to it. Thus the Taita system is not like more common African ones in which agnation and affinity are mutually exclusive (so that when marriage is desired within a hitherto exogamous agnatic group the latter must be split); but neither is it like systems in which affinity implies bilateral kinship, as in prescriptively endogamous groups (where a refusal to continue marrying implies severance of kinship). In Taita, non-close affines are likely to be kinsmen of other sorts also—perhaps agnates. Matrikin are likely to be affines and may also be agnates. Agnates may be matrikin and perhaps also affines. But these are possibilities and probabilities, and not necessities.

The working of the entire system depends, in considerable part, on the essentially political rule making the exercise of property rights contingent on residence within the neighbourhood. It is also of critical importance that both men and women have property rights, *but that these are different in kind* and not only degree. It is the *conjunction*, through local marriage, of male rights of ownership and overseership with female use-rights in land within a single community which turns a mere vicinage into a neighbourhood. Men's daughters cannot transmit ownership rights in land, but they gain use-rights somewhere within their parents' own local group; they transmit to their sons claims to particular portions of their husbands' land while transmitting use-rights to younger women (daughters-in-law) of their own or neighbouring lineages. Men's rights in livestock used for bride-wealth are also part of the 'understanding' of neighbours, through the exchange of livestock for rights over women; paying bride-wealth for marriage to a local girl gives a man access to overseer rights in a bit of her father's land.

Following the developmental cycle of domestic groups, we have seen how, at each stage, the rights of women are important: rights acquired *qua uxor*, *qua filia* and *qua mater*. In the first category are the use-rights which a woman acquires, upon marriage, to a portion of her husband's mother's fields, and also use-rights in other parcels of land turned over to her by her husband, however he may have acquired his rights of owner or overseer. Secondly, there is the contingent right to use a portion of land owned by the woman's father. This is bound up with a married woman's continuing ties with her parental family. It allows a woman's children to benefit from the land of their mother's patrikin through the exercise of their mother's labour on it. As a mother, a woman has the right to transmit her use-rights to the wives of her own sons, and she also holds trustee rights in the estate should she outlive her husband.

It seems to us that the constellation of women's rights are a major factor in restricting the growth, in size and complexity, of Taita domestic groups. A domestic group grows when a son marries and brings home his bride, but diminishes again when the new couple set up house alone. With a number of sons, there is a series of additions and diminutions: the egress of married sons and their wives is inevitable for all save the youngest. We suggest that the fact that each daughter-in-law has identical use-rights *qua uxor* acts to expedite the differentiation of sons' households. That is, the vesting of use-rights in a series of daughters-in-law defines the domestic separation of their husbands from each other and from the parents.

The practical consequences of women's rights are many: the claim of a woman as wife cuts into the supply of land used by her mother-in-law; a wife's claims restrict the freedom with which her husband can treat his holdings; a daughter's claims lessen the supply available to her parents and brothers; a woman's claim as mother affects the portions received by the sons of her co-wives. The existence of women's rights of use and trusteeship channels the flow of property from male to male all along the way: father to son via the latter's mother; father-in-law to son-in-law via the former's daughter; final distribution of paternal grandfather's estate via this man's daughter, on whose death it reverts to the heirs, and so on.

In considering the domestic cycle in relation to property rights, we have had to consider the intersection, at each stage, of men's and women's property rights as the needs of a household change, claims and duties alter, resources expand or contract. The cycle may be seen also as passage from the initial stage in which men's political interests are minimal and women's use-rights in land are most important in beginning the movement towards independence, to the late stages in which men's ownership rights in land and livestock connect domestic arrangements directly to the political field.

The 'business' of the domestic group as an institution in the Malinowskian sense is performed within the framework of generalized legal and political principles. The Taita social system embodies a rather unusual combination of principles, and this is manifested in the development and property relations of domestic groups.

REFERENCES

BARNES, J. A. 1960. 'Marriage and Residential Continuity', *American Anthropologist*, 62, pp. 850–66.

EAST AFRICAN STATISTICAL DEPT. 1962. *African Population of Kenya Colony and Protectorate: Geographical and Tribal Studies*, Nairobi.

FORTES, M. 1949. Time and Social Structure: An Ashanti Case Study; in *Social Structure: Essays Presented to A. R. Radcliffe-Brown*, ed. M. Fortes, Oxford University Press.

—— 1958. Introduction, in *The Developmental Cycle in Domestic Groups*, ed. J. Goody, Cambridge University Press.

—— 1959. 'Descent, Filiation and Affinity', *Man*, 59.

HARRIS, GRACE. 1962. 'Taita Bridewealth and Affinal Relations', in *Marriage in Tribal Societies*, ed. M. Fortes, Cambridge University Press.

LEACH, E. R. 1960. 'Rethinking Anthropology', in *Rethinking Anthropology*, London.

MURDOCK, G. P. 1960. *Social Structure in Southeast Asia*, Viking Fund Publications in Anthropology, No. 29, New York.

PROPERTY, CROSS-COUSIN MARRIAGE, AND THE FAMILY CYCLE AMONG THE LOBEDU[1]

Eileen Jensen Krige

THE Lobedu are a South Bantu people characterized by the institution of 'divine kingship'. They live in a mountainous area of the North-eastern Transvaal lowveld. Originally from *Bokhalaga* (S. Rhodesia), they migrated south when the empire of Monomotapa broke up and established themselves as rulers over the sparse Sotho population they found in occupation. The rain-making powers of their queen, enhanced by the mystery and secrecy of her ritual seclusion, attracted many accretions from diverse tribal groups from surrounding areas who sought security and peace particularly during the period of unrest following the wars of Shaka, the Zulu, and the raids of Matabele and Swazi. For enemies feared to attack the Lobedu queen lest they be visited by drought and locusts. The descendants of the Lobedu proper therefore form only a small portion of the total population which, however, except for relatively recent Tsonga immigrants from Portuguese East Africa, is remarkably homogeneous in culture. The Lobedu had no military traditions and built up their kingdom by peaceful means.

The form of government is that of a central authority with the queen as the head of state and spatially defined political

---

[1] The field-work on which this essay is based was carried out jointly with my husband, the late J. D. Krige, under the auspices of the International African Institute in 1936–8, and was supplemented and brought up to date by short field trips in 1961 and 1962.

units which, each under a headman, enjoy a considerable degree of autonomy.[1] A large proportion of these districts into which the country is divided are ruled by the descendants of original sections of the nuclear group; a few have been allocated to alien groups under their own headmen while some are held by royal women, *batanoni* or 'wives' of the queen. Many districts now held by commoners originated from *batanoni* but since women do not succeed one another as heads of districts these have been inherited by their sons of husbands given to them by the queen. Royal wives (*batanoni*) are of various kinds. Some are of royal blood, daughters of close relatives of the queen to whom they have been given as a token of homage (*ho loba*). Only these are set up by the queen as rulers over districts. (Women may also rule areas in their own right where there is no male heir, as we shall see). Other royal wives are the daughters of district heads, while a number are daughters of foreign chiefs who come, sometimes with cattle, sometimes with money or a daughter to *loba* the queen for rain. Once a woman from within the tribe has been accepted by the queen as a royal wife, the tie is renewed from generation to generation on the pattern of cross-cousin marriage. Men may offer a daughter to the queen also in return for, or in the expectation of, economic help or political favour (though these are not always accepted) and there is a tendency today for districts to be subdivided into smaller and smaller units to satisfy the political aspirations of ambitious subjects. Royal wives bind to the queen not only her closest relatives but most of the important people in the tribe. Some wives are given away in marriage to her councillors, relatives and district headmen. Some remain with her and have allocated lovers. Children of these latter call the queen 'father' and she is responsible for helping them to marry.

The Lobedu proper appear originally to have regarded themselves as an aristocracy but today it is only the royal lineage (*ba Mohale*) and a number of important Lobedu district heads that are looked up to. Many non-Lobedu lineages have, by virtue of marriage links through royal wives, a higher status and are more closely related to the queen than sections of

[1] For a general account of the Lobedu, see Krige, E. J. 1941, Krige, E. J. and J. D., 1945 and 1950, and Krige, J. D., 1939.

Lobedu themselves. The society is remarkably egalitarian and there is no concentration of wealth in the hands of the ruling group. Nor would this be easy in a tribe in which the limited resources in property (in cattle) are used primarily for, and are constantly being converted into, marriage alliances.

Other distinctive features of the Lobedu are their marked agricultural bias; a fertility cult with sacred drums; masked dancing; ritual arrangements in ancestor worship (in the form of impersonation of the spirits, the predominance of beer offerings and the *phasa* rite of spurting water out of the mouth as an accompaniment to prayer) which link them more closely to the tribes to the north than to their southern Nguni and Sotho neighbours where the blood sacrifice and cattle cult are more clearly marked.

Agnatic Groupings

Despite the fact that they are ruled by a queen and that women can and do hold important political and religious positions the Lobedu are a patrilineal people in the sense that a man belongs to his father's lineage, property is inherited in the male line and marriage is patrilocal. The tribe is made up of a large number of different totemic groups, Lion, Elephant, Crocodile, Wild Pig, none of which, not even the royal Lobedu totem, is confined to the Lobedu tribe. All these totems are found in neighbouring tribes and many also in other parts of the Transvaal and elsewhere. A few groups have no totem (*motupo*) but designate themselves by their place of origin, e.g., *Mokhalaga*. Groups which have the same totem do not consider themselves related if they come from different places of origin. Elephant of Khalaga are thus unrelated to Elephant of Tsubye or Elephant of Thobolo. People sometimes swear by (*ana*) their totem and are supposed to but do not always abstain from eating it. The totemic name is useful only as a distinguishing mark; e.g., in divination the bones may indicate a person of the Elephant or Lion totem as responsible for illness or theft. Beyond this the *motupo* has little meaning and today many of the young people do not even use the term. The totemic group is not exogamous.

The lineage has no distinguishing name, the term *moloko* or *leloko* which is in common use referring to the group of agnates as well as to the relatives on the mother's side of the family. The lineage segment of four to five generations tracing its descent from a common male ancestor (grandfather of the adult males) shares a common major shrine and occasionally meets at the harvest thanksgiving or when a *mokhobo* (a gathering of the descendants of a particular common ancestor) is indicated by the diviner as the wish of a troublesome spirit. Such a group of agnates of four to five generations in depth tends to be concentrated in the same locality and in many cases may be found in the same homestead (*motse*). As neighbours and relatives they share in many common activities such as helping in each other's work-parties, taking part in girls' puberty ceremonies, consulting each other in the marriage of their sons and daughters. Only in the minimal lineage of father and sons are there jural ties. The lineage is not a land-owning unit, has no political functions, is not exogamous, marriage within the lineage being common especially in the Lobedu royal group.

An interesting feature of the Lobedu lineage is the important part played by its women who continue even after marriage to be active in lineage affairs as leaders in religious ritual and as guardians over their brothers' households. The merging of the ancestors on the father's and mother's side of the family which results from preferential marriage with the mother's uterine brother's daughter and the inclusion in ancestor worship of relatives on both sides, which will be described later, also affect the character of the lineage. A religious gathering (*mokhobo*) of the descendants of Sekhobo which I attended showed the lineage segment of five generations in operation and illustrated some of these points. Descendants through both sons and daughters in the line of Sekhobo's chief wife took part in the ceremony and, in addition to calling upon the deceased father and other male ascendants of the head of the lineage, the officiator mentioned by name also the deceased father's uterine sisters and the father's mother. The inclusion of the father's mother was all the more remarkable because this was a gathering of the descendants of Sekhobo and it had been the specific complaint of the troubling ancestor that every year harvest beer was being offered to the spirits on the father's mother's side, not to the Sekhobo side. The lineage head's father's mother had been a 'wife' and close relative of the queen, a connection which the Sekhobo family tended to stress socially and which was reflected also in their religion (they had a cow dedicated to and representing her).

The Lobedu lineage, in fact, does not operate as a group to the exclusion of other kin except in informal consultations on matters of marriage or litigation; and the lineage does not emerge in everyday activities as a clearly marked unit. A *mokhobo* such as the above is one of two or three rare occasions when the lineage comes together and in every one of these cases both sons and daughters and their children are invited to be present.

Lobedu homesteads vary in size and composition from a typical minimum of a married man with his mother, wife and children to a group of half-brothers, their mothers, wives, children and grandchildren, still living together after the death of the father. Very often other relatives, such as a widowed sister and her children, a maternal relative or an affine of the head are to be found living in the homestead. But these are the least stable elements and tend to move away in a short time. Though small units continuously hive off, and there is a good deal of change in the small homesteads of more recent immigrants or where a migrant labourer husband has never returned, the Lobedu homestead is on the whole, especially in the case of the chief son and his descendants, a remarkably stable unit. Over a period of thirty years most of the larger homesteads known to me have remained in the same place or been rebuilt a few hundred yards from the old site after the death of their head.

Economy of the Lobedu and their attitude to property

The economy of the Lobedu is a subsistence one based mainly on agriculture and stock-raising supplemented by migrant labour in European areas. Land for cultivation is allotted to individuals by the district head. Once allocated, fields are inherited in the male line and cannot be taken away so long as they are in effective use. Only if a man moves away from the district or is chased out as a witch can he and his family lose their right to their lands. It is usual for people to 'beg' fields also in areas other than that in which they are living, partly to take advantage of diverse climatic conditions, partly because of land shortage; but their right to these is not as strong as to fields in their home district. Land shortage has not yet reached serious proportions owing to the fact that since the 1920's the tribe has been buying up sparsely populated Crown lands to the north. Grazing and the right to collect wood, thatching grass, wild fruits and plants for economic use are free to all, though herd-boys jealously guard good pastures in their own areas to which they feel they have first right.

Livestock takes the form chiefly of cattle and goats; fowls, still forbidden at the Capital, were introduced by the Tsonga; donkeys and pigs are a European innovation, the former being popular among Christians for use in ploughing and transport, the latter being kept largely by women for exchange purposes. Though of considerable economic importance cattle play little part in the diet of the people, being used mainly for ritual purposes and as bride-price. They move in a chain of marriage exchanges from one family to another, creating and maintaining social links and knitting together in preferred marriage the descendants of brothers and sisters. It was calculated in 1939 that bride-price accounted for 95 per cent of all transfers of cattle in the Lobedu tribe.[1] Cattle coming in as bride-price are not supposed to be used for any other purpose than marriage for, unlike the Zulu who kept large herds, constantly replenished in the old days by raids against neighbours, most Lobedu families do not possess cattle except for short periods of time.

Lobedu ideas of property and their attitude to its possession and accumulation are rather different from ours. The correct use of cattle in Lobedu eyes lies not in accumulation but in their investment in 'building a house', i.e., setting up a new social and economic unit of a wife and children. Surplus crops, similarly, are not accumulated but are generally consumed in a succession of after-harvest beer parties in honour of kin and affines which adds considerably to one's prestige. This, so often cited as evidence of wastefulness and lack of foresight is, in the absence of any really reliable termite- or pest-proof form of storage (which makes accumulation risky), a means of insur-

[1] Krige, J. D., 1939, p. 396.

ance against future want by building up relations of friendship and goodwill with kin and neighbours whom you can call upon for assistance in time of need. Nor does property, as in Western society, command the services of others to any appreciable extent. The core of helpers in a work-party are there primarily because of ties of kinship and neighbourhood; the beer that is served may be enjoyed by any passer-by who wishes to join in. Traditionally, then, property is of value to the Lobedu only in so far as it can be consumed or meets an immediate need on the one hand or, on the other, is used for creating and maintaining social relationships. This is changing now under conditions of culture contact but the change is still largely confined to Christians.

There is not a great deal of exchange and what there is takes the form most frequently of gift exchange[1]. Property in the form of a gift is a tangible sign of a social relationship. A new bride speaks to no one in her new homestead until given a small gift in token of her new social relationship to the giver and the same holds for a newly-initiated boy or girl. Ties with one's maternal kin and with affines are also kept alive by gifts and gift-exchange. It is significant that agnatic ties are the only ones that do not require continuous gift-exchange. Yet even here a service rendered seldom goes unrewarded. Property and human relationships are, then, closely interlinked. That it is not possible always to separate economic and social relationship among the Lobedu is shown by the following examples. Just after the 1895 rinderpest Khidima, a royal relative, went to the queen, who is traditionally responsible for giving succour to orphans and the needy, to ask for money to buy mealies. She gave him some. A few years later he sent a messenger to her to say he 'had a baby daughter'. The queen accepted the gift and when the girl reached puberty presented her with a *thari* goat according to custom. Cattle followed and the girl, Myakwane, was duly 'married' by the queen. This was the beginning of a permanent bride-giving-bride-receiving relationship, for in 1950 the queen sent a messenger to the widow of Myakwane's brother who had used his sister's cattle, to ask for her daughter in marriage. '*Ge loda dikhomo tja ka. Ge nyaga mosadi a de a nthsidela*—I am following the tracks of my cattle.

[1] Krige, E. J., 1941.

I want a wife to come and stamp for me', said the queen. The girl was married by the queen and shortly after was given to the son of another 'wife' (*motanoni*) of the queen with whom she is now living at the Capital.

Sometimes the transaction takes on more of an economic character, a man pledging his daughter in order to receive economic help. Thus Jim's father in a period of starvation took his ten-year-old daughter to a man at Malemacha and said, 'I am starving and poor. Give me money. I have a girl, a *ledolo*'. Money was given to him and later when the girl was sent in marriage, cattle were handed over in the usual way. More commonly this technique was used when a man had no sister whose cattle he might use to marry with. He then went to a maternal or affinal relative or to a friend or even a stranger who had cattle, saying: '*Ge no khuru*—I have a knee', in reference to his procreative powers, thus pledging himself to send an as yet unborn daughter in marriage. Today such transactions have become infrequent since money can so easily be obtained by migrant labour or a loan can be repaid in money without having to pledge a daughter.

The cattle or other property (marriage hoes were used in the old days)[1] establish tangible obligations between the two families which can be upheld at law even though the contract is fulfilled only in the next generation or later. Moreover the bond is permanent: other marriages will follow the first from generation to generation in a manner that will be described below. The use of women in property transactions of this kind which is not considered to be derogatory by the Lobedu is all the more remarkable in the light of the very high position of, and the power wielded by, women in Lobedu social life.

Some Aspects of Marriage

It will be necessary before discussing the domestic cycle to examine briefly the nature of Lobedu marriage; for not only does marriage establish strong economic and social relation-

---

[1] These hoes were too large and heavy for tilling the soil and were merely kept in a hut. The chief councillor of the queen, a man of about eighty years old, still remembers the use of marriage hoes in a few cases in his boyhood. Six hoes or eight head of cattle passed in marriage at that time.

ships between the families involved but upon it rests the whole character of the domestic group. Payment of bride-price transfers the reproductive powers of the woman to the husband's agnatic group. The husband has genetricial as well as uxorial rights. Genetricial rights apply not only to any children born after the marriage whoever their biological father might be, but also in retrospect, so that any child born before marriage automatically becomes the child of whoever pays the bride-price, with full rights of succession and inheritance from its sociological father. There is thus, in contrast to other tribes such as the Zulu, no way in which a Lobedu man can obtain the right to his biological child other than by marrying its mother. Emphasis on sociological as opposed to biological fatherhood among the Lobedu is very strong and this is an important factor in Lobedu social structure. The rights of a father to a child involve control over it; the right to the bride-price of a daughter (subject to the right of her brother to marry with his sister's cattle and of her mother to the services of the woman married with her daughter's bride-price); and corresponding to his right to his daughter's bride-price the duty to help his son to marry. A father may and often does marry an additional wife with his daughter's bride-price. A father also has the right to be cared for in his old age by his sons.

The levirate is practised, the junior levirate being more common than the senior levirate. The brother raises seed to the deceased and takes over the responsibility of a father and husband though the children he begets are counted as belonging to his deceased brother. Frequently the heir, eldest son of the chief 'house' inherits a young wife of his father. In this case, similarly, the children born of the union are looked upon as the deceased's, i.e., as brothers and sisters of the heir, not his children. The sororate also is practised in all its forms, sororal polygyny being very common. Where a sister is sent to 'awaken the house (*ho dsosa ndo*)' of a barren or deceased wife full bride-price is due for her although, since bride-price is never an absolutely fixed amount, less may be asked for than in the first marriage.

The marriage of a woman transfers to her husband's group the right to her labour. Initially it is the husband's mother even more than the husband himself that benefits, as we shall see. But the fruits of her labour go to swell the property only of that unit of the lineage which constitutes the wife's own 'house', the independence and rights of which must be respected even by the husband.

Bride-price generally consists of some five to eight head of cattle, a number of goats and money (to the extent of at least £5). Today people sometimes pay a sum of money instead of cattle— £40 in a recent marriage. This represents eight head of cattle, bride-price cattle having been regarded as equivalent to £5 each, irrespectively of market prices, for the past fifty years at least. The amount given is, however, never a fixed one as the passing of bride-price initiates a continuous relationship of gift exchange between the two families concerned and the marriage puts the bridegroom under a lifelong obligation to extend economic help to his wife's people. '*Monoalo a o fede*—bride-price is never completed', it is said. When the wife's people have to pay a fine, if they need cattle or goats for the marriage of a son, they will approach their *tsetse* (or *muduhulu*)—son-in-law. The man who has provided a wife has given something 'bigger than cattle' and is in this sense in a superior position. On the other hand the son-in-law (*muduhulu*) or wife-receiver is accorded great honour by his wife's people and once a year at least receives a gift of beer and grain. The relationship is one of reciprocity and the son-in-law must for his part also show respect for his wife's people. He must ever be ready to grant their requests and may never refuse. There is no evidence for Leach's suggestion that the Lobedu have a 'kind of Kachin structure in reverse' with a 'strong tendency for the wife-receiving group to rank the higher'.[1] In endogamous unions in the Lobedu royal group both husband and wife may be members of the same lineage. Lobedu society is, moreover, not a stratified society though the royal lineage enjoys great prestige.

Fully to understand Lobedu marriage one must approach it also from the point of view of the woman. Usually a uterine brother marries a wife with the cattle that have accrued from his sister's marriage. This sometimes happens in other tribes too. But where the Lobedu situation seems to be distinctive is that every woman whose marriage-cattle have been used to

[1] Leach, 1951.

provide a bride, whether for a brother or other relative or even a stranger, has a moral right to a daughter-in-law from the 'house' established by her cattle. Even though it was her husband who provided the cattle and it is usually he who is said to be 'following the tracks of his cattle' when such a girl is obtained for his son, the wife's right to the services of the girl are such that even if the husband himself, instead of the son, were to marry this girl (which quite often is the case, i.e., wife's brother's daughter marriage) this bride would be attached to her house and would cook for her as though she were the mother-in-law.

So strong is a woman's moral right to her cattle-linked brother's daughter to come and cook for her in her old age that even if she has no son she can, especially if her husband is dead, 'marry' the girl herself, using a daughter's bride-price. The Lobedu themselves phrase it as marriage of a woman to a woman. In reality it is in this case the marriage of a girl to a fictitious son of the woman who is said to be marrying her. Such a bride is called *noeji* (daughter-in-law) by the woman, who is 'grandmother', to any children born to the girl. The children take the surname of the husband of the woman just as though her son had married the girl. A woman who practises as a doctor and earns money can marry a girl with her own cattle. Here too the children (whether by an allocated man or born 'in the bush') take the lineage name of the husband of the woman who 'married' their mother. They are of his lineage but belong essentially to the 'house' (*mosha*) of the woman who married their mother.

A woman may also 'marry' a girl on behalf of her own lineage —for a deceased or non-existent brother. This is done where an heir is needed or where a brother has died before marrying the girl who was 'born for' or engaged to him as in the case of Thepize in Figure 1.

It is the source of the cattle that pass which determines the lineage to which the children belong in woman-marriage. Should the cattle come from the 'house' of a married woman the children belong to the husband's lineage; if they come from the family of procreation of the woman the children take her father's surname. The queen and women who rule districts on behalf of a deceased or non-existent brother are called 'husband'

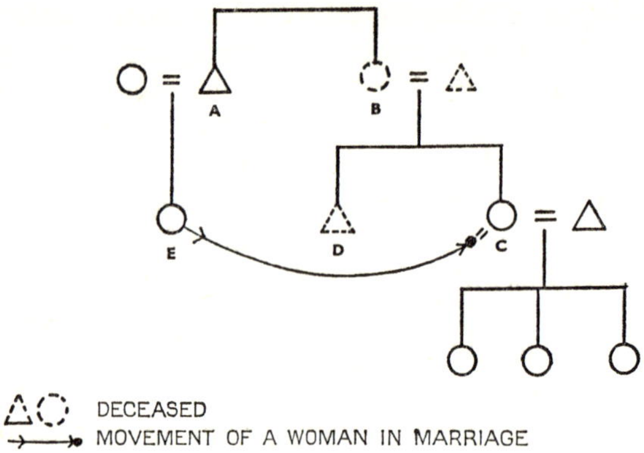

△ ○ DECEASED
→● MOVEMENT OF A WOMAN IN MARRIAGE

FIG. 1. Case illustrating 'marriage' of a woman to a woman.

Thepize's father (A) was the cattle-linked, uterine brother of (B) the mother of Mandike (C), a married woman with children. Mandike's brother (D), whose parents were dead, had been engaged to Thepize (E), his mother's brother's daughter, and cattle had already passed when he, too, died. So Thepize's father (A) took his daughter (E) to Mandike (C), and said: 'Take Thepize and "stay" with her'. So, as it was phrased, Mandike 'married' Thepize (*o mo bekile*), who came to live in Mandike's husband's village. Mandike (C) called Thepize (E) not '*noeji*' (daughter-in-law) but '*mohadibo*' (sister-in-law); E's children called C '*rakhadi*' (father's sister) and took her father's surname.

(*monna wa ka*) by their 'wives' *batanoni* when they marry on behalf of their own lineage and *papa* (father) by the children of these wives, just as though they were men. In ritual matters, however, they act as women.

Preferential marriage with the mother's brother's daughter appears in the Lobedu context almost to follow from relationships established by the cattle that pass and the rights of the sister to a daughter-in-law from whoever has used her marriage cattle. Yet it is not always from the identical 'house' that was established by the cattle that a daughter is sent in marriage, nor necessarily by the same brother as used the cattle. Maseriba's bride-price was used by her brother Andrew. Thirty years later (1961) when she went to ask for a girl to 'come and stamp for her' (she is a widow and has no sons) it was the daughter of Batamedi, her other uterine brother, that was offered. When asked about this the reply was not as I expected it to be, that Andrew's daughters were attending school and would be averse to such a marriage but 'we just gave Kewele to Maseriba because she is *khadi* (i.e., sister in a ritual sense) and "to knit together the family" (*ho ruka leloko*)'. This desire to keep alive the links between brother and sister and to maintain and renew marriage links with women of the lineage from one generation to another is very strong. The marriage of a woman at her father's sister's (i.e., mother's brother's daughter marriage) is called '*ho dsosa moloko*'—to awaken or renew relationship.

There are several variations of mother's brother's daughter marriage that arise from or are bound up with obligations connected with cattle that have passed. If in the case of cattle-linked brother and sister (D and C in Figure 2a), the latter has a daughter but no son who could marry her brother's daughter, she might, rather than break the link with her brother and allow her husband to use the cattle to create new links with strangers, nevertheless, with the agreement and consent of her husband, hand over her daughter E's bride-price to her brother D so that he can marry a second wife and establish a 'house' from which her daughter E may claim a woman later to marry her son and to 'come and cook for her'. Here marriage (of F to G) is with the mother's mother's brother's daughter. When such girl is actually married bride-price will again pass. If, in such a marriage, the woman were to run away or if there were a divorce, both bride-prices could be claimed, as we saw in the 1930's. Today, however, probably as a result of European administrative policy, only one bride-price is paid back, though it is commonly known that both used to be returned.

Besides marriage with the mother's mother's brother's daughter, other variations of mother's brother's daughter marriage are found, such as marriage with the mother's brother's son's daughter (one generation below), with the father's mother's brother's daughter or even with a father's mother's brother's son's daughter.

The fact that in the above example of marriage with the mother's mother's brother's daughter two lots of bride-price are handed over yet only one bride is received, indicates that the economic aspect is not paramount; it is the permanent link between descendants of brother and sister that is valued. In cases where a man has received cattle on the 'security' of a small girl, to all appearances a predominantly economic transaction, the creditor also hands over cattle a second time when the girl comes over to be married. This is puzzling. When asked about it the Lobedu usually quote the proverb '*mobula ndo oa nywala*—the opener or establisher of a "house" pays marriage cattle', i.e., every girl commands bride-price. The explanation possibly lies in regarding the passing of property in the case of wife No. 2 of D in Figure 2a and also the first handing over of property in an economic transaction on the security of a girl as the creation of a cattle-link similar to handing over to a brother the bride-price of his sister to acquire

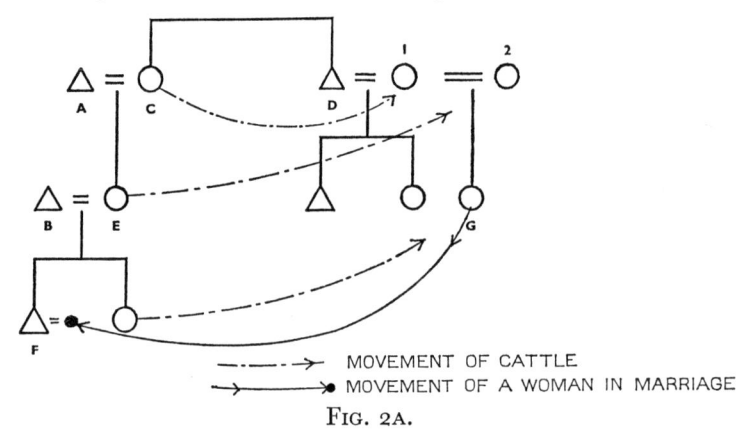

```
                                    -·-→   MOVEMENT OF CATTLE
                                    →——→•  MOVEMENT OF A WOMAN IN MARRIAGE
                                    FIG. 2A.
```

a wife. The subsequent transactions are then on a par with ordinary preferential marriage between the children of cattle-linked brother and sister.

If, in contrast to the case illustrated in Figure 2a where the cattle-linked sister has no son to marry her brother's daughter, it is the brother who has no daughter to give in marriage to his sister's son then sometimes, as in a recent case, the preferred marriage takes place in the next generation. Here (see Figure 2b) the daughter (G) of the son of C's cattle-linked half-brother (D) married the son (F) of the son of the cattle-linked sister (C). In this case E had a brother to use her cattle and there was no need for her cattle to be sent to the mother's brother to establish a new 'house' or 'open a gate', as it is sometimes phrased.

FIG. 2B.

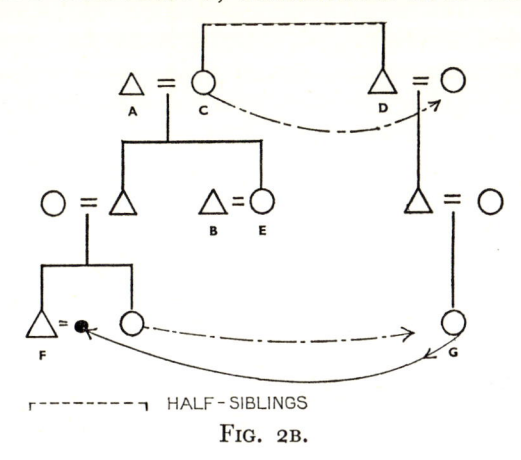

Once a marriage has taken place, even where originating in an economic arrangement, the relationship is self-perpetuating as is shown in Sedena's case. Sedena's elder brother (A in Figure 3) used the bride-price of their only sister; so when Makeakati, his daughter (C), was born this elder brother said to Sedena (B), 'There are your cattle', indicating his baby daughter. When the girl was eight years old and her father already dead, Sedena (B) took her to Mogodo (D), a relative (a classificatory 'sister's son', descendant of his father's half-brother), and, indicating that she was his *ledolo*, asked for cattle to marry a wife. He was given cattle which he used to marry Marita (E). In due course when Makeakati (C) grew up she was sent to marry Mogodo (D), who gave five head of cattle as bride-price (five to eight is the usual amount). Many years later Marita's only daughter, Mojaji (F), followed her 'sister'

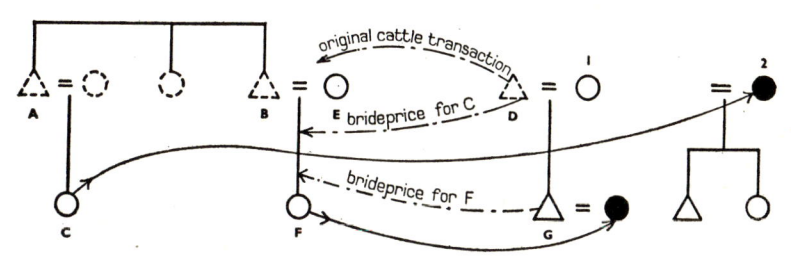

FIG. 3. Preferential marriages arising out of an economic arrangement.

and married Nakampe (G), Mogodo's son by another wife. Makeakati's (C's) 'house' had first claim on the daughter of the man (her father's brother) who had used her cattle, but as her son was a Christian the girl was given to the son of a different 'house'.

Once a link has been created by a marriage a bride-giving-bride-receiving relationship follows, which tends to be reinforced not only by one but by numerous subsequent marriages. Thus, A married a girl from lineage B. Both his sons and his grandson followed in his footsteps (see Figure 4).

The same tendency is present in Lobedu polygyny where the sororate is very popular. Most Lobedu who are not Christians have more than one wife. But it will almost always be found

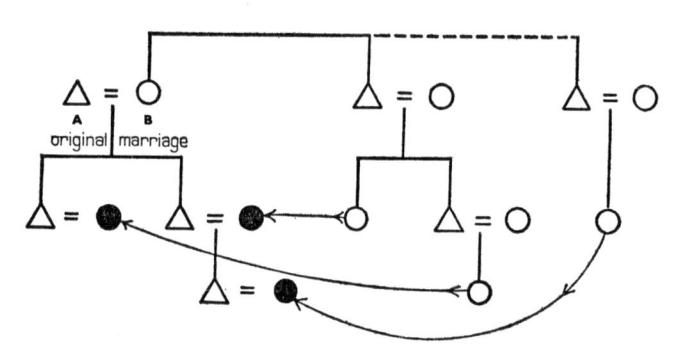

FIG. 4. Reinforcement down the generations of a marriage link between two lineages.

that at least one is a sister or younger relative of one of the other wives. Thus M, a chief councillor, married seven wives: (1) his mother's uterine brother's daughter; (2) his mother's half-brother's daughter; (3) his mother's half-brother's daughter's son's daughter; (4) a non-relative; (5) a non-relative; (6) his mother's brother's son's daughter (brother's daughter to No. 2 and therefore a wife's brother's daughter); (7) a sister to (1) by the same father but a different mother.

S, a man in his thirties, has three wives: (1) his mother's mother's brother's daughter; (2) a non-relative and (3) the uterine sister of his first wife.

Old K had five wives: (1) his mother's uterine brother's

daughter; (2) his father's mother's brother's daughter; (3) a distant relative of his mother's; (4) his mother's fellow-wife's brother's daughter; (5) a sister to his first wife by the same father but a different mother.

Divorce

The use of a woman's bride-price by her brother, and the interest which his cattle-linked sister has in maintaining this 'house' in which her son will find a wife, made divorce difficult in the old days. Today, however, partly owing to migrant labour, divorce is more common and girls, especially in the case of arranged marriages with old men or cross-cousins, quite frequently run away to a lover either before or after the marriage knowing that they cannot any longer be forced to return. A return of the bride-price is not always insisted upon, as in the case of A who chased away his childless wife for being a thief. Her brother had used the cattle so A was satisfied to accept the arrangement that the brother should give his daughter in marriage to A's son by another wife. When there are complicated cattle claims a husband, especially if he is already old, may find it wiser not to press for a divorce if a wife absconds. P's third wife, who had been procured with the bride-price of the daughter of his first wife ran home with her three children and began to lead a promiscuous life during which a fourth child was born. Beyond trying to persuade her people to make her return, P did nothing. The children, two girls and two boys, were his and his first wife had a claim on the bride-price of one of the girls. Eventually, when the two daughters were married, P secured their bride-price; the two sons earned their own marriage-cattle by working; and when P died, the eldest son of that 'house' was called to come and receive his share of the inheritance.

The rule in Lobedu divorce was, in the old days, that the husband's family should receive back the full bride-price plus all increase, irrespective of where the blame lay, in accordance with the saying, *'mosila mobe o boya le noto ea hwe*—even the bad workman (husband) returns with his tools'. The children went with their mother to her people and when she remarried, the new husband had a right to all of them. With European administration came the introduction of the Pedi idea that a man has a claim to both the cattle and the children in the case of malicious desertion. Old men in the 1930's called this a white man's law; today people are claiming it as a Lobedu custom. Only two of the oldest men at court were able to tell me in 1962 what had been common knowledge in 1936. The present custom is for the husband on receiving back the bride-price to return some of it (one beast for each child or sometimes two for a girl) for the rearing of the younger children that remain temporarily with their mother. A father's hold over such children is in practice tenuous though the court will always uphold his claims.

The issues in divorce are rarely simple. The simplest case I came across was one in which a man became insane. His wife left with her children to live with her brother who returned the bride-price. Usually, however, there are endless complications and cases continue for months, even years. If, for example, a man chases his wife and children away and the wife wants to return, he may in the end lose both the children and the bride-price despite the proverb quoted above.

The Domestic Group and the Importance of the 'House'

We have discussed the role of property in establishing and maintaining marriage relationships and links between families. Control over material resources also plays an important part in the structure of the polygynous domestic group with its economically independent 'houses' so characteristic of the Lobedu.

As head of the family the husband has full control over all family resources. Yet each wife forms with her children a unit of production and consumption, the independence of which as against other 'houses' has to be respected even by the husband, whose control thus becomes limited the moment he marries a second wife. This is why a Christian woman among the Lobedu never has the economic independence that a woman in a polygynous household has. There are safeguards against the infringement of the principle of the independence of the 'house', as we shall see.

Though women do most of the cultivation, the Lobedu

husband is expected to play his part in producing food for his family. Every married man, therefore, has a field of his own which he cultivates with the help of his wives. The produce of this field is used for any beer- or work-parties that the man may wish to give and is a kind of bank upon which his wives may draw when they run short. If, however, a man helps one wife from his personal stores he must give all his wives an equal amount irrespective of their needs. When he first marries, the husband works with his wife in their common field. On marrying a second wife he acquires a field of his own (in addition to the one for his new wife) which his wives take it in turn to weed. It is said that if he had no field of his own but were merely to help each wife in turn to cultivate her field there would be endless trouble in maintaining equality between them. One of them for instance might say, 'How is it that when you come and work in my field you just sit but when you go to the field of the mother of So and So even the shade doesn't tempt you!'

A father is responsible for helping his sons to marry. But since a man seldom possesses cattle other than those already involved in bride-price exchange and a son uses the cattle of his sister, boys in a 'house' in which there are no girls often have to go out and work or with the help and advice of their father acquire bride-price in other ways. In the old days an orphan usually hired out his services to carry salt or iron ore from far countries in order in this way to acquire marriage hoes or cattle. Expenses in goats and money over and above the cattle given in marriage are met by the boy himself with the help of his father. A father should see to it that his son is provided with a field when he marries but in practice it is very often the mother who concerns herself with this problem. The father has jural control over his sons and is responsible for their debts.

The wives in a polygynous household differ in status. The chief wife is the daughter of the mother's brother—the cattle-linked or any uterine mother's brother or mother's half-brother. She will bear the heir and future head of the village. Where there has been no marriage with the mother's brother's daughter it is the first wife, the one married with his father's cattle that is chief wife. A chief wife exercises no control over other wives. When the mother's brother's daughter is one of the younger wives in a polygynous household she may be completely overshadowed by the first wife. The eldest son of the first wife occupies a position of importance in the family. He is said to stand in the shoes (literally 'footprints') of his father and after the latter's death has a right to be *suma'd*, i.e., given a portion of any animal killed by any of his brothers long after they have dispersed and live in separate homesteads. There are instances, especially in the case of district heads and where the chief house has no male heir, in which the eldest son of the first wife married tries to usurp the position. But though he may appear for a time to be succeeding as seemed to be the case in more than one instance in the 1930's when first we went into the field, I have not come across any cases in which he has succeeded in the long run.

Each wife has her own fields which it is her duty to cultivate for the needs of her 'house'. On her death her sons have first right to inherit her fields unless their father wants to use them himself or arrange for their cultivation to provide food for the younger children; but they may not be used for the benefit of any other 'house'. A daughter may be given her deceased mother's field to cultivate while she is still in her parental home, but she cannot inherit it. A wife is expected to feed herself, her children, her husband and her mother-in-law from her fields. Each time she cooks she sends food to her husband and to his mother. What is left must be returned to her 'house' unless the husband himself gives it to the herd-boys or other children as a group. In the case of special dishes eaten in-between meals, such as cakes of sesamum or ground peanuts, a little will be sent to each of the other women of the homestead with whom the wife is on good terms. In a large homestead this may be confined to the wives of one man. Beer brought to any one 'house' is usually drunk by all in the village and neighbourhood.

In addition to having her own granaries and cooking utensils every wife has a right to raise livestock. She may keep chickens; she may acquire goats by the exchange of her produce; she may get pigs by feeding other people's pigs in return for a pigling. She may even acquire cattle if she is a doctor. In contrast to the Zulu, where the 'house' like that of the Lobedu is also an economic unit, the Lobedu wife enjoys considerable economic freedom in the disposal of her property. Though she should act in consultation with her husband in the disposal of livestock or large amounts of surplus crops she will often, especially if on bad terms with her husband, act on her own. All these activities, it should however be remembered, are for the advancement of her 'house', which belongs to the husband's lineage. These goods can neither accrue to nor be used by the wife's own relatives. If, for example, she leaves her husband or is divorced she cannot take any of the produce of her fields with her. On the other hand the husband could use such crops or livestock only for the advancement or to feed the children of that 'house,' not for other 'houses'. The only goods a woman may take with her on divorce are cattle or other livestock earned by practising as a doctor because in this case, it is said, she has spirits guiding her which are of her own, not her husband's family.

The Lobedu husband does not in the manner of the Nguni allocate cattle to the 'house' of each wife (milk plays little or no part in the diet). It is said, however, that even if a cow were to be allocated to a house for milking purposes it would not belong to that 'house'. Cattle that come in from the marriage of a daughter are the property of her mother's 'house' and should be used for acquiring a wife for a son of that house. If the son is young and the husband wishes to use his daughter's cattle for a wife for himself, such wife would have to cook for the woman of that house from which the cattle came in the manner of a daughter-in-law. In theory a husband has the right to decide how the cattle of any 'house' are to be used. But he rarely in practice acts against the wishes of the wife. Her right over any woman acquired by the cattle of her daughter gives her great power and makes it difficult for her husband to marry a wife with them himself against her wishes. The bride might run away or her people refuse to let her marry if they hear that the woman the bride will have to 'stamp for' opposes the marriage. That is why so often cattle are handed to the wife's brother in the manner described above.

It is said, '*mosha ha o le yo mongwe*—houses do not eat one another', i.e., the property of one house cannot be used for the advancement of another. Hence bride-price of the girl of one house should not be used by the son of another house. If this is done (as it sometimes is if one wife has only daughters and another only sons) this immediately establishes a new relationship between half-brother and sister who now become cattle-linked; and the girl whose cattle were used has the right to 'follow the tracks of her cattle' to ask for a daughter-in-law from that 'house'.

A 'house' is never wholly dependent in economic matters on the husband and his lineage. It has other possible sources to exploit. Thus a married woman may, and often does, get fields from her own people to cultivate. The difference between these fields and those given by her husband's people is that the latter are hers as a right and are inherited by her sons; the former she obtains through the goodwill of her blood-kin and on her death they revert back to them unless the children are still young and the fields are needed to feed them. Similarly, though it is the father's duty and responsibility to help his sons to marry and though uterine brothers always help one another, a man who has a married sister very often turns to her husband or to the sister's son for help with cattle to marry a wife. There is a difference, however, between help given by a uterine brother and that given by a relative on the mother's side or an affine—a brother does not expect to be repaid but help from other categories of relative becomes converted into a marriage bond or has to be repaid. The close bond between uterine brothers is indicated in the saying 'uterine brothers share even the head of a locust'.

Each 'house' is distinguished, then, from that of other wives of the husband by its cattle-links and obligations to the wife's side of the family (and later the daughters' husbands' families) and by dependence on ancestors on the mother's (i.e., wife's) side in addition to those on the father's side.

In the case of preferential marriage, too, the 'house' is all-important. Here, in contrast to marriage with strangers where the boy's family initiates negotiations, the first approach is usually made by the girl's people who bring the matter in the first instance to their sister, the woman of the 'house' concerned. Thus, for example, when Dumedi obtained cattle from the marriage of his eldest daughter by his first wife (a mother's brother's daughter) her people approached his mother suggesting that as the first wife was not strong they should send her uterine sister as a little 'follower' to help her. Finding that her son was agreeable she reported the matter to his eldest half-brother, head of the homestead, who discussed the matter with his brothers.

The ultimate guarantor of the interests and economic independence of the 'house' is the cattle-linked sister with whose bride-price the wife was obtained. As we have seen, she occupies a very special position in the 'house' built by her cattle. Even before her brother's bridal party arrives at his homestead with the new bride she is taken to his married sister's homestead where a goat is slaughtered for her in recognition of their special relationship. When the sister visits her old home she will 'put down her things' and make herself at home in the hut of this wife of her brother. She is the first to be called to beer there; she must be invited to all activities such as work-parties held by the 'house'; all sickness is reported to her; she is called in to discuss the marriage of all sons and daughters of that 'house'. She or her eldest uterine sister is the one who magically protects a new homestead by drawing a medicated branch in a magical circle around it. If her father and mother are dead she sees to it that her brother treats his wife properly. He cannot chase her away or divorce her unless his sister believes his action to be justifiable; and she may, and very often does, take her brother's wife to live with her in her husband's village if he ill-treats her. She has an interest in this 'house' for here her son will find a wife. When her brother dies it is she and her sisters who will distribute the inheritance. The sanction for her control is a religious one: if she is 'dissatisfied in her heart' this may 'stir up the ancestors' and cause a child of her brother to be ill—a very powerful weapon.

Development of a House

Let us consider the growth and development of a house for it is only by a very gradual process that a house reaches full stature. The marriage of every woman marks the birth of a new unit which may become in time an independent homestead though it does not always do so. This is possible at the earliest only when the eldest son has married a wife and often, if at all, only after the death of both the father and his heir, the eldest brother who succeeded him as head of the homestead. Full independence is not an ideal that is striven for.

In its early stages the new unit or incipient 'house' is still dependent on the bridegroom's natal house (house of orientation). The new bride works for her mother-in-law. She has no fields of her own to begin with, no utensils, nor a hearth and very often not even a sleeping hut of her own, the young couple using the mother-in-law's sleeping hut while she sleeps in her kitchen hut. The bride cooks on her husband's mother's hearth, works with her husband in a field allocated to them and helps her mother-in-law in hers. The husband will, if he has not done so before bringing his bride home, build her a new hut after the marriage at any time convenient to him. Simeon made sun-dried bricks himself, paid one pound to have the walls built, had a work-party for the framework of the roof and did the thatching himself. A man's father may help him but usually a young man uses his own money earned by previous migrant labour.

A woman cooks for her mother-in-law until a new bride, either of her husband's brother or of her husband arrives when she may be given her own pots. When Simeon's second wife arrived both wives cooked together for the mother-in-law for a while. Then when they began to disagree one (the younger one in this case because she was unrelated) was given her own pots to cook separately. Being given her own hearth is an important thing in a woman's married life marked by a little ceremony and a visit home to announce her new status. Even when she has her own hearth, however, she must continue to provide food for her parents-in-law. Children are thus an insurance against old age and it is the duty and responsibility of a son, more particularly the youngest son, to care for his mother in her old age. The father may have young wives to care for him when his elder sons are married.

Even after his marriage a man remains under the jural control of, and subordinate to, his father. Only after his father's death is he free to choose whether to remain in the village under the heir or to hive off. Sometimes, though rarely, a married son does, however, quarrel with his father and move away. Mostly such a quarrel involves the mother rather than the son and the whole house hives off, the son taking his mother with him.

The birth of the first child is an important step in the development of a house. The Lobedu child is born in a homestead in which there are at least three generations represented—that of the grandmother, that of the parents, including usually also the father's brothers and unmarried sisters and that of his own contemporaries. The first child is tended largely by the father's mother while the mother goes about the hard work of stamping, working in the fields, fetching firewood if there are no young sisters of the husband to help, and cooking.

The husband's mother is an essential part of the household and has a dominating influence. She controls and advises her son, especially in regard to his relations with his wife and the needs of his children, and he usually defers to her knowledge and experience. Long after her sons are married and even when they have grandchildren the unit is known as her *mosha* (house). It would seem that a unit of husband, wife and child would hardly be viable in a subsistence economy based predominantly on the agricultural activities of the women. Even the smallest Lobedu homestead includes the husband's mother. It is only when there are several adolescent children or the cash earnings of the husband enable a wife to buy the staple food instead of relying wholly upon what she grows herself that smaller units can survive. Even then they generally live near, and attach themselves to, some relative.

Once children are born, the wife's brother (mother's brother to the children) begins to play a part in forging links between them and the relatives on the mother's side. He will give gifts to the sister's son (*muduhulu*) who often goes to stay for a while with his mother's people; and in his turn the sister's son whenever he returns from migrant labour will be expected to give a gift to his mother's brother. Sometimes he also helps a mother's brother with cattle to marry. As the size of a man's family increases more fields may be needed to feed the children and very often these are obtained by the wife from her own people.

The marriage of the first daughter brings about the first acquisition by the developing house of a large amount of property in bride-price and ensures, even in the absence of sons, the continuation of the house. As important is the fact that the man has now a son-in-law, whom he can approach for economic help whenever he is in need. His wife, too, if she needs anything can brew beer to take as *khirola* for her son-in-law, or crack open *morula* nuts and take them as a gift, in return for which he will give her money or whatever he can. *Khirola* may be taken even to the uterine brother of a son-in-law for he also is a *muduhulu*. A man looks more and more to his affines for economic help as his father ages and his brothers become involved in their own commitments. To the wife the marriage of her daughter is also very important for a different reason. This makes it possible for her to have a daughter-in-law. For on the marriage of her son a woman stops cooking and in addition has the help of her daughter-in-law in her garden work. If she has no son she can in the last resort always use the bride-price to 'marry' a girl herself who will relieve her of the most heavy and onerous household and agricultural work.

With the marriage of his sons there is a gradual handing over of the reins to the younger generation which is completed by the man's death, when the eldest son of his chief wife takes over his position and responsibilities. This is the point at which the house achieves its final independence economically (though not ritually).

It is interesting to note that Lobedu do not, like the Zulu, identify a lineage segment by its female foundress.

Death and Inheritance

On the death of a wife her husband must administer the affairs of her 'house' to its best advantage. If the children have any complaints they may, if their grandparents are dead, make them to the father's cattle-linked sister or to his eldest uterine sister who has considerable influence as 'priestess' of the family. If the father marries a woman with the cattle of the daughter of such a 'house' such wife will be attached to this house and the sons of the house could use the marriage cattle of the daughters of this woman to obtain wives.

When a married woman dies leaving very young children they are generally sent either to the mother's mother or to her sister to be reared. M's son and son's wife died in close succession leaving very young children. Shortly after, when his own wife also died, he sent the children to her sister to be reared and gave her his deceased's wife's fields to cultivate to provide food for the children. When they are big they will be brought back with a gift of beer and their father will give a thanking gift of an ox or money for the rearing of the children.

The utensils of a deceased wife remain in her hut to be used by her children or son's wives; and her eldest son has the right to inherit her fields. Until twenty years ago when it was still the custom for a mother to receive a cow and calf on the marriage of her daughter (if a virgin) in recognition of having reared her, this portion of the bride-price was the special inheritance of the youngest son with whom she generally lived until her death.

When the father of a polygynous family or the head of a homestead dies there is, owing to the property arrangements characteristic of the Lobedu and their attitude to its possession, never a great deal of heritable property. The property of each house is inherited by the eldest son of that house. The heir to the position of head of the homestead is the eldest son of the chief wife. Only he or the uterine brothers of his father are responsible for his father's debts—not the sons of other houses. It is generally stated in discussions that any cattle or goods acquired by the father as his personal possessions should be inherited by the chief son and heir. In practice it is more common to divide out such property among all the sons and daughters.

When Ramalepe, a rain doctor, died about three years ago all his cattle and goods were divided equally among his sons. His rain medicines and his field went to his chief wife's son; his mealies (from his own field) were equally divided between his wives and his uterine sisters. When Philip's father died there was no sister of his father still living so Philip went to the queen and asked her what to do. She told him to call his sisters and to divide out the property in consultation with them. He then called his sisters (eldest and other daughters of his father) and showed them the property—thirty-six goats. They agreed on dividing the goats as follows: the deceased's two elder daughters by his first wife were given ten goats each; Philip, a son by the second wife, received eight; Mutzere, sister's son to deceased, was given one goat to kill and eat at his home; one goat was given to the son of deceased's youngest wife who had deserted him; two goats were killed for the widow of the deceased's eldest son by his first wife when she came from Johannesburg to pay a visit of condolence. Deceased's field was a *leshupe*, a site of their previous village, and as is the custom with such a field, was divided between his wives. His mealies were equally divided between all his wives, his own daughters who were present at the ceremony also receiving some. In the case of Mathekha, all his cattle were given by the *khadi* (his sister) to his eldest son by his chief wife, a man who was a prominent councillor of the queen. It was understood they would be used for helping his brothers and half-brothers to marry. The old man's blankets and money were divided among all his children, the elder ones receiving £1 10s. 0d., the smaller ones only 10s.

The wives of a deceased man if they are still of childbearing age are allocated to his brothers or, in the case of a very young wife, sometimes to the chief son and heir. It is his responsibility to hold the family together after the death of his father. The division of the property is made on the day of purification from mourning (*khitshila*) about a year after the death when all the relatives have gathered together. The person responsible for the division of the inheritance in property and wives is the eldest uterine sister of the deceased who acts in consultation with her sisters, especially the cattle-linked sister of the deceased. If there is no uterine sister the deceased's eldest daughter takes her place. She will act in consultation with her father's brother if one is still alive. In allocating wives some consideration is generally given to the wishes of the parties concerned.

When the heir is a minor, a brother of the deceased, usually the one who inherits the mother of the heir, may be chosen to act as regent. But he must be careful to act only in consultation with the *khadi*. In many instances in the case of the death of a district head when the *khadi* (sister of deceased) is old or a widow and free to leave her husband's homestead she may herself come to rule in her brother's village. When M. died, the son of his chief wife was still a child so his uterine sister, a widow, came to rule, while the younger half-brother of the deceased returned from another area where he had been living to set up his village near by in order to raise seed to his half-brother by the chief wife and help his half-sister by conducting the court cases. Later, when the heir came of age, a new homestead was built. When Mabulana died in the 1940's his daughter, a married woman who does not live in the area was made official district head. Her mother's brother came specially from the Capital to live in the area and help her by conducting cases.

The mother's brother is considered to be eminently suitable as adviser to a ruler. The queen, too, traditionally has a mother's brother as chief councillor. A mother's brother has no claim to succession yet is deeply interested in the welfare of his sister's child. He will see to it that the sister's child gets his rights. The position of the son of the *khadi* who is acting as regent is somewhat different. There is a Lobedu proverb saying '*Bya thoga monye bo dula muduhulu*—where a master is lacking there sits the nephew'. And it is true that the son of a woman regent is often ruler in all but name. In the 1930's there were two blatant cases in which the rightful heirs of district heads who had long reached man's estate seemed in danger of permanently being ousted. In both cases in the long run when the *khadi* died the rightful heir was installed, in one of the cases on the expressed dying wish of the *khadi*. Right seems to prevail in the long run.

The Homestead Through Time

Basically a homestead consists of a group of 'houses' belonging to the wives of the head or of the head and his half-brothers. Other relatives may attach themselves to it but the core remains the group of agnates.

Many of the smaller homesteads that have all the appearance of being independent are found upon investigation to be portion (a 'house') of a neighbouring homestead, which has become separated in space but still considers itself part and acknowledges the authority and control of the senior homestead near by. The most obvious case of this arises where, owing to quarrels between co-wives, a husband has placed one of the wives in a homestead of her own and visits her there. If a wife has a married son then in the event of serious quarrels there is more likely to be a hiving off, the son moving to a different area with his mother and siblings.

In Figure 5 a very small homestead is shown. Here the

woman, K, has, during her husband's prolonged absence in a labour centre, moved away from her fellow wives into another district in order to be near her married daughter. She lives in a small homestead with her married son, who is absent doing migrant labour, and her other children. In contrast to this is the homestead of a neighbour of hers who has five wives and

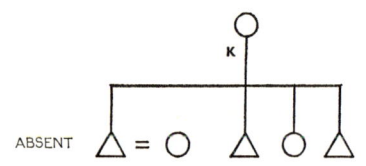

FIG. 5. Composition of a very small homestead.

whose ten brothers together with their wives and children still live with him in the homestead—a total of sixty-eight inmates (twenty-nine adults, thirty-nine children). Of these three married and two unmarried men are away doing migrant labour.

The domestic group indicated in Figure 6 originally lived in one homestead.

On A's death his chief son, B, inherited his youngest wife (No. 3) who as yet had no children. They all moved out of the old homestead, the sons (B and D) of A's two elder wives

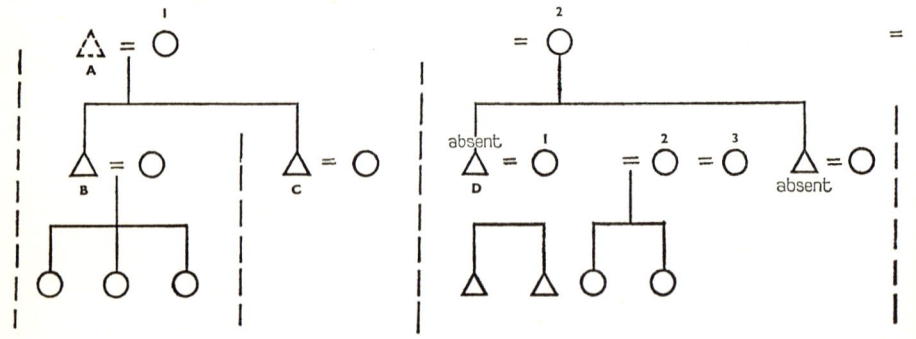

FIG. 6. Segmentation of a homestead on 'house' lines.

building separate homesteads next to one another, where I found them in 1938. The women in the homestead of D considered themselves part of the homestead of A and in the absence of their menfolk at labour centres, reported everything that took place to B. Later C moved away from his uterine brother B and in 1961 there were three separate homesteads.

The cleavage in a homestead then is on 'house' lines, though uterine brothers living together after the death of their father also eventually separate. The break may be the result of an accusation of witchcraft or there may be an amicable separation as in the case described above. Reasons for separating vary: Batamedi moved away from his uterine brother, a district headman, to satisfy political ambitions—he hoped to be made headman of an area to which his family had an ancient claim; Poke, a married man, left the homestead of his brother with his mother and siblings for health reasons, suspecting that someone in the homestead might be bewitching him and hoping that a change would improve his condition. After many years in a different district, he returned to live in the original homestead. Sons do not move away before the death of their father unless there has been a quarrel in which their mothers are involved, or unless they become Christians and marry Christian girls. Even the death of the father does not necessarily bring about the separation of his sons; brothers and half-brothers may live together for years. As they marry more wives the size of the families increases, the homestead becomes more congested, the likelihood of quarrels greater and gradually the 'houses' move asunder. If half-brothers and brothers have not separated before, then the final break-up of the old homestead will come with the death of the eldest brother. For it is rare for a man to live under a young heir of the generation below him. Close religious and social ties, however, persist long after separation. Half-brothers continue to 'inherit' each other's wives and there may be a good deal of co-operation in work-parties and much consultation in family affairs. Lobedu homesteads are stable over long periods and there is a great value attached to remaining together.

Preferential Marriage down the Generations

The development of the 'houses' in a homestead, leading to the gradual segmentation of the domestic group and separation of its males is counter-balanced by a 'knitting' together of the men with their sisters who have married out and a strengthening of their ties with their maternal kin by means of preferential marriage supported by cattle links. This process is illustrated in Figure 9.

The proportion of mother's brother's daughter marriages in its various forms to the total number of marriages among two generations of members of a large lineage which was analysed in detail (counting the marriage of each woman in a polygynous union as a separate marriage) was 34 per cent, of which 91 per cent were marriages with the mother's uterine brother and its derivations. If married men were to be considered, the proportion would be higher, 63 per cent of the married men having contracted at least one mother's brother's daughter marriage; 80 per cent of these were (or were based on) marriage with the mother's uterine brother's daughter. This tallies with a random sample of 100 cases taken in 1936 in the royal area (excluding the Capital itself) in which 67 per cent of the married men were found to have married a mother's brother's daughter. But the situation had materially altered by 1962 when a similar sample of 243 cases in the same area showed mother's brother's daughter marriages to have decreased from 67 per cent to 34 per cent. Of these 94 per cent were with the mother's uterine brother or his descendants, which indicates that despite strong forces making for change and increased opportunities for contacts with strangers of the opposite sex which have greatly diminished marriage with distant maternal kin, the values attached to 'knitting' together close relatives are still strong. The most potent forces at work for breaking down preferential marriage are Christianity, which condemns it and school education which by inculcating Western values makes preferential marriage unthinkable to any school child today however short a period he has spent at school.

That men consciously use marriage to keep alive family relationships and that they are deeply concerned about these alliances, can be seen from the case of Modidi (M) in Figure 7.

M's homestead abutted on that of V, whose half-sister K he had married (see Figure 7). When they were both old. M took his granddaughter L, (his son by V's half-sister K having died years before) to his friend V saying, 'I see we are in danger of

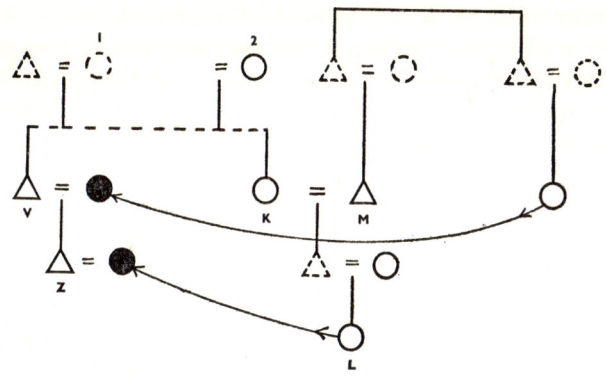

FIG. 7. An arranged marriage (Z to L) to 'knit together' the families of two affines.

growing apart (separating). Here is my son's daughter. Let us knit together the family (*ruka leloko*) else soon we shall be lost to one another'. So Z, the son of V, married L, M's granddaughter. It is interesting to note that while M had married V's half-sister, V had also married a 'sister' of M (M's father's brother's daughter), a case of 'brother-sister' exchange which is very rare among the Lobedu. Z was thus marrying his mother's 'brother's' son's daughter, who was at the same time also his father's half-sister's son's daughter.

Marriage from generation to generation with the uterine brother's daughter has important consequences for ancestor worship. It leads to a merging of ancestors on the father's and mother's sides so that they become *moloko o motee*—one lineage, as the Lobedu phrase it, with identical ancestors in at least two of the four grandparents' families. If a diviner diagnoses an illness as due to someone in a man's father's mother's lineage (which in the case of two generations of mother's brother's daughter marriages will be the same as the mother's father's lineage), then a man's mother, or even his wife, could officiate in a beer-offering in his homestead to the ancestors concerned. The Lobedu call upon and give offerings on different occasions to all four grandparents and other deceased members of their lineages. It is interesting to note that the mother's mother who never becomes by virtue of preferential marriage an ancestor common to both sides of the family and might thus be in danger of being left out, makes herself very much felt in practice. She is thought to be so deeply attached to her daughter's children that she is always troubling them—wanting them to be named after her, to be given her beads to wear, to have a dedicated goat or shrine set up. One therefore sometimes finds three or four shrines in a homestead.

The Local Group

The local group reflects the balance that is achieved among the Lobedu between agnates on the one hand, and on the other, relatives on the mother's side and affines (one and the same thing depending on the generation from which they are viewed).

A random group of thirteen homesteads forming a neighbourhood, is shown in Figure 8. They are closely linked by agnatic,

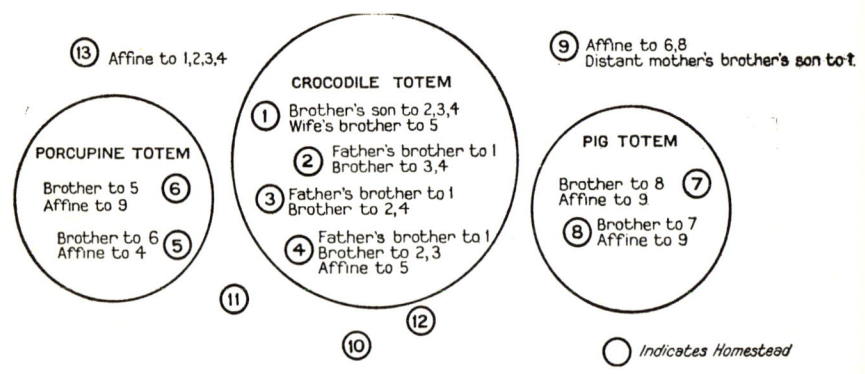

FIG. 8. Agnatic, cognatic and affinal ties in a neighbourhood.

cognatic and affinal ties and share in many economic, ritual and recreational activities.

These homesteads fall into three main clusters of agnates belonging to the Crocodile, Porcupine and Pig totems near which are two homesteads No. 9 and No. 13, which have affinal and cognatic links with these clusters, and three unrelated homesteads, Nos. 10, 11 and 12, the last-named being foreigners, Tsonga, who had little to do with the rest.

The Crocodile cluster (homesteads 1, 2, 3 and 4) had originally been a single homestead which had broken up on the death of the father, head of the district. Other close agnates lived a little further off, not shown on the diagram. This cluster

LOBEDU PROPERTY, MARRIAGE AND FAMILY

was related to all except homesteads 10, 11 and 12: a sister of the head of homestead 1 was married in No. 13; a son in No. 4 of this cluster had married a Porcupine woman in No. 5; they had a distant mother's brother's son in No. 9 and they were related in the same way to two wives in the Pig group.

The Porcupine brothers for their part had a sister married in homestead 4 (Crocodile) and a daughter-in-law from No. 9. They therefore had affinal bonds also with two wives in the Pig group, sisters of this daughter-in-law.

The Pig group had married women from No. 9 and therefore had links also with No. 9's cross-cousins in the Crocodile cluster and with No. 9's affines, the Porcupines.

The manner in which kin of various kinds co-operate with each other and with neighbours could be seen very clearly when Enoch, head of homestead No. 9 had to meet a gift-exchange obligation involving the sending of beer to the head of a neighbouring district. The beer, made from mealies from Enoch's own fields was brewed by his mother and by his sister from homestead No. 8. When it was ready, a messenger was sent to notify (*rapa*) all their relatives (*moloko*). Calabashes for carrying the beer were borrowed from the neighbourhood and early in the afternoon a collection of women and a few men foregathered in the courtyard of Enoch's mother. There were ten calabashes and one petrol tin of beer, six baskets of Kaffir-corn and three half-filled enamel basins of grain into which the calabashes of beer were put for carrying. The grain was contributed by kin—by the cross-cousin in homestead No. 1; by the husbands (*baduhulu*) of the two sisters in homesteads Nos. 6 and 8; by two father's sister's daughters living outside the area and by a sister of the 'wife' of his mother, also outside the area, all of whom were present for the occasion. Women from the whole neighbourhood turned out to carry the beer. After the eldest sister of Enoch had poured a little beer on the ground with a prayer for luck on the journey and had drawn a magic circle round the mouth of each calabash with a charm, the party set out with ululations of joy and much talking and noise. Kin of all kinds and neighbours all contributed to the success of the enterprise and all took part in the feasting at their destination where the beer was consumed and a beast slaughtered for their entertainment.

Conclusion

Emerging clearly from this study is the fundamental role of property in maintaining the distinctive features of Lobedu social structure. The scarcity of cattle among the Lobedu and the fact that they play little part in subsistence, coupled with an attitude to property which makes its accumulation of little interest and in which economic aspects of property are not always clearly distinguished from the social relationships it creates and maintains—all these factors make for a social system in which the main function of cattle is their use as bride-price and in which women can be used in quasi-economic transactions without their status being in any way depressed thereby.

The independence of the 'house', a basic feature of the Lobedu lineage, likewise rests upon property, a husband being subject to strong sanctions to respect the economic independence of each house as against other similar units. Both husband and wife have an interest in the development of the 'house' as an entity. From the point of view of the husband each house, besides increasing his following and adding to his prestige, also adds to the number and strength of his relations with affines upon whom he can count for economic help and as friends and allies. '*Ba djealane ke ba khonane*—people who marry one another are people who agree', it is said when a man has the support of his affines. To the wife her 'house' is a means of personal fulfilment and advancement. She has considerable say over the property of her 'house'; everything she does for its advancement is for the benefit of her own sons, its heirs; the bride-price of her daughters ensures an old age free from arduous toil, while the marriage of her sons brings in addition the prestige and control that a mother has in the households of her sons and their wives. The 'house' is the most important unit in the structure of the husband's lineage yet at the same time has strong economic and social links with the wife's family.

An important principle in the social structure is preferential marriage between the son of a sister and the daughter of her uterine brother who has used her bride-price. This form of marriage and the moral right of a sister to a daughter-in-law from the 'house' established by her marriage cattle are on the one hand a means of binding the women of the lineage, even after their marriage, by strong links to their father's family and on the other of maintaining from generation to generation the bonds with the maternal kin created by the marriage of the parents.

A woman has a dual role in the social structure. On the one hand by establishing a 'house' in her husband's lineage, she is the means whereby his lineage is perpetuated and its numbers increased; for even after the death of her husband his brothers will raise seed to his name and in the absence of sons she can herself ensure the continuation of her husband's lineage by marrying a woman on behalf of a fictitious son. On the other hand a woman remains important to her own lineage: if she is the eldest child of her 'house' she will officiate at all important religious offerings (if her brother is older he may officiate but she will always be called to collaborate with him); when she dies her name and those of her sisters will be included among the names of ancestors called upon in prayer; she divides out the inheritance on the death of her uterine brother; she guards the interests of the children of her cattle-linked brother's 'house' whence she will obtain a daughter-in-law; upon her falls the responsibility in the absence of her parents of providing an heir in her mother's 'house' (of her father's lineage) should there be no son; and she may even act in the place of her deceased father as ruler over a district until the heir is of age or until one can be raised.

The maintenance of links with married sisters and its complement marriage with the mother's uterine brother's daughter, by means of which one's links with one's wife's (or mother's) family are perpetuated, are supreme values in Lobedu society. That is why a wife who has no son has little difficulty in persuading her husband to hand over her daughter's bride-price to her brother rather than create links with a strange family. It is possible thereby to 'build a house' (or 'make a gate') at her brother's home from which her daughter's son will obtain a wife. This may at first sight appear to be very like the transfer of rights from mother to daughter but this is not the case. It is made possible by the transfer of cattle belonging to the daughter's husband and is bound up with the great desire to maintain links between the descendants of brother and sister. The right of a woman to 'someone to stamp for her' from the 'house' created by her bride-price also enables the father of a woman who has no uterine brother to control to some extent, by the placement of his daughter's cattle, the marriage of her sons. Her husband 'follows the tracks of his cattle' to find a wife for his son but it is her father who determines where these 'tracks' will lead to.

There are thus to be found in Lobedu social structure a neat balance between the various kinds of kin; a combination of patrilineal principles with strong matrilineal bonds; a merging of ancestors on the father's and mother's side of the family; and an equality in the importance of paternal and maternal kin which is seen on all social and ritual occasions and is reflected also in the composition of local groups.

LOBEDU PROPERTY, MARRIAGE AND FAMILY
APPENDIX I

THE manner in which many of the characteristics of Lobedu marriage arrangements operate in practice is illustrated in the case of the lineage segment of A and his descendants set out in Figure 9. The arrows in the diagram all represent the passage of women in preferential marriage from their parental home to that of their husband: single arrows indicate women of the mother's brother's family (i.e., the Mabulanas) who have married into A's lineage (Matsui); double arrows indicate the departure of women of A's lineage to marry at their father's sister's. The following are points to be noted:

(a) The tendency for Lobedu polygynists to marry more than one wife from the same family is seen in Figure 9 in A's marriage to his fourth wife who was his second wife's brother's daughter.

(b) The manner in which cross-cousin marriage perpetuates links with the wife's kin down the generations is illustrated by the marriages of A's sons G, H, W and X. G's fourth wife, H's third wife and W's first wife all come from the same lineage, that of their mothers (A's second and fourth wives). A's son X's third wife is also his uterine cross-cousin but it was not practicable to indicate her family of origin also in the diagram.

(c) Besides reinforcing links with the maternal kin, mother's brother's daughter marriage serves also to knit together descendants of a man and his sisters. The bonds between A and his sisters B and C have been kept alive over a span of two generations of their descendants by the marriage of A's daughter D to I (daughter of his sister B) as indicated by the double arrow in Figure 9, and the marriage of A's daughter E to Z (son of J, and grandson of A's sister, C). Similarly G's daughter N by his first wife is married to the son (M) of his sister L (see double arrows), and H's daughter K is married to her father's sister E, widow of Z, a marriage which took place in 1961.

(d) The part played by cattle links in ensuring preferential marriage is also illustrated in the diagram; but it is clear too that children of brother and sister who are *not* cattle-linked often also marry one another. Z married E because of cattle-links two generations above him as is explained below. But when E grew old and needed a 'wife' G had no suitable daughter; so H's daughter K 'married' her. Cattle-links also did not account for the marriage of A's daughter, D, to his sister I, nor of G's daughter N to his sister L's son M. These indicate the tremendous value attached to maintaining links with married sisters. The reasons for the marriage of

E to Z are complicated and indicate how personal and other factors may interfere with the best-laid cattle-linking arrangements. C, the cattle-linked sister of E's father, A, had no son; so C gave the bride-price of her only daughter, J, to her brother A in accordance with procedure described in the text of this essay. All but one of these cattle died shortly after and then A said he did not want the cattle. C then tried to establish a 'house' with her daughter's cattle by handing over the remaining head of cattle to a classificatory brother (her father's half-brother's son). Her husband augmented this head of cattle by others obtained with his earnings from migrant labour. Unfortunately, however, these cattle instead of being used for marriage were 'eaten' (squandered) by her 'brother' and the whole plan came to nothing. Now, because E's father A had used C's cattle to marry his first wife and then had married E's mother with the bride-price of D (a daughter of his marriage to his first wife), therefore A, repenting of his earlier treatment of C and realizing he was indirectly indebted to C (and J) also for his second wife (mother of E), sent his daughter E to 'cook for J' (C's daughter) and marry her son.

(e) An example of the judicious placement of cattle for purposes of promoting marriage alliances between one's own male descendants and the daughters of a friend or relative in a preferred family is to be found in the action of P in Figure 9, who was married to R the daughter of A's half-sister F. After his son's death he gave his daughter S's, bride-price to G (a descendant of his wife's mother's brother) who acquired his third wife T with it. P has thus 'built a house' (that of T) where his son's son Y will find a wife.

(f) Three instances of the marriage of a woman to another woman are to be found in the lineage-segment of A—that of D to I; that of K to E, widow of Z; and that of A's daughter N to the queen. In the first case I wished to raise an heir to her deceased brother, in whose place she was ruling a district; in the second case E had daughters but no son and she wished to have someone to 'cook for' her; in the case of N, her father A as district headman had sent his daughter to be a *motanoni* of the queen.

(g) That the same lineage can be both wife-receiving and wife-giving in respect of the queen is illustrated by the fact that A's father had received in marriage from the queen a wife Q but A had also sent his daughter N to marry the queen.

(h) The incidence of cross-cousin marriage and its variations in two generations of descendants of A (counting only the actual members of his lineage as shown in Figure 9) over a time-span of over sixty years (i.e., from about 1895 to 1962) was 31 per cent (nine out of twenty-nine marriages).

The arrangements in the above lineage segment are by no means unusual. This lineage is that of a district head, but it is representative of numbers of cases that could be chosen from among non-Christian traditionalists who still form the majority of the tribe.

REFERENCES

KRIGE, E. J. and J. D. 1945. *The Realm of a Rain Queen*, London, Oxford University Press.

—— 1950. 'The Lobedu of the Transvaal', in *African Worlds*, ed. D. Forde, London, Oxford University Press.

KRIGE, E. J. 1941. Economics of Exchange in a Primitive Society; *The South African Journal of Economics*, 9, No. 1.

KRIGE, J. D. 1939. 'The significance of Cattle Exchanges in Lobedu Social Structure', *Africa*, 22, No. 4.

LEACH, E. R. 1951. 'The structural Implications of Matrilateral Cross-Cousin Marriage', *Journal of the Royal Anthropological Institute*, Vol. 81.

THE ARUSHA FAMILY

P. H. Gulliver

Introduction

THE Arusha are sedentary agriculturists living on the south-western slopes and peripheral lowlands of Mt. Meru, an extinct volcano 14,979 feet altitude, in northern Tanganyika. In 1957 nearly two-thirds of the population of 63,000 lived on the mountain slopes, the traditional lands of the tribe, where rainfall is good and reliable and volcanic soils are fertile. There, at an average density of more than one thousand people per square mile (Gulliver, 1960), their economy is based on bananas, maize, finger millet and legumes with, increasingly, coffee and onions as cash crops. Beginning in the second quarter of the last century with a small group of immigrant settlers, the Arusha accommodated a rapidly expanding population by a continuous expansion of settlement upwards on the mountain slopes, cutting away at the edge of the forest.

This extension was halted by the establishment of a forest reserve by colonial governments, and in the last three decades the Arusha have turned to the less favourable peripheral lands. There rainfall is poor and unreliable, the dry season is long and hot and soils are less fertile. Population densities average about one hundred and thirty people per square mile and cultivation is limited mainly to maize and beans. Because of the relatively unfavourable conditions of the periphery, many men preferred to remain on the mountain and manage on what land they could obtain there; and in the 1950s the limit of peripheral extension and agricultural settlement was reached so that virtually all men have come to depend either on inheritance of their father's land or on persuading another land holder to give them a tenancy (Gulliver, 1960, 1963a).

The Arusha have been closely associated with the surrounding pastoral Masai during the whole of their history to the extent that they have often been called 'agricultural Masai'. Partly because of this, domestic livestock have always had a significance in social and ritual affairs beyond their numerical and economic importance. Until the last few decades there were probably always few cattle, and in 1958 there was less than one beast per human being.

The significant local group is the 'parish' (*embalbal*), which is an autonomous territorial unit containing its own age-group system which provides its political machinery and its internal leaders. Land rights are strongly individualized, and the parish has neither a land-controlling nor a kinship basis. It is essentially a self-administered community.

The Arusha practise a Masai-like age-group system. In simplified terms, this means that within his parish a man is a member of a corporate age group which successively passes through a number of age grades. Each grade establishes certain obligations and privileges and institutionalized attitudes. The two youngest grades of junior and senior *murran* ('young men') cover periods when the members of occupant age groups are regarded as having few responsibilities; they are politico-jural minors taking little part in public or ritual affairs except as servants and labourers, and they spend a good deal of time in hedonistic pursuits. The grade of junior elder is one in which men undertake executive responsibility in politico-jural matters, as well as the period in which they finally settle down as households and farmers; they are now mature men, fully self-responsible. Senior elders give up public executive tasks, but they participate in public affairs as the experienced men, versed in law, custom and precedent, and also in the approved diplomatic skills essential to the solution of Arusha disputes and conflict. Finally, in the grade of retired elders, members of an age group abandon almost all participation in public affairs, and they are thought to have largely fulfilled their lives and potentialities. The whole system provides a set of successive statuses and roles which are of great importance, penetrating even into relationships within the family.

THE ARUSHA FAMILY

An Arusha is a member of two effective patrilineages: the inner lineage, based on the father or grandfather of the senior living generation of men, is a closely co-operating, small group of agnates but without residential unity; and the maximal lineage, the exogamous unit based on the grandfather or great-grandfather who was an original settler on the mountain slopes. Each maximal lineage (or specifically, its members who are of elder status) selects a 'counsellor' or spokesman, who is himself an elder. He acts as a focus of affairs and proceedings affecting members of the lineage: he arbitrates in intra-lineage conflicts and participates as a judicial agent in *ad hoc* moots convened to discuss and settle disputes between members of different maximal lineages. The counsellors of each of the four Arusha patri-clans often associate together in their judicial capacities, and they deal especially with matters concerning inheritance, land, blood-wealth, marriage and children. Counsellors in the lineage-clan system administer a second political and judicial system, autonomous of that provided by the age-group system operating within the individual local community.

For some sixty years a centralized polity has been superimposed on the indigenous political system. At first each of the two sub-tribes had its own chief, but since 1948 there has been a single chief, popularly elected. People have come to accept the chiefship and centralized administration: but these have come to operate at a different level, mainly concerning different interests, from that of the persisting indigenous system based on the parish age groups and the lineage.[1]

Outline of the Developmental Cycle

>Every man has his own homestead (*engang*) and he lives there with his own people—his wives and children—one family (*engang*). Each wife with her children has her own field and her cattle. Then the children grow up and become young men, and later they marry and have wives and children. These young men leave their father's homestead and go and cut new fields in the forest; and they make their homesteads there and live there with their wives and children. They have fields and the father gives each

[1] A full account of the Arusha age group, patrilineal and modern local government systems, and of the interlocking system of social control, is given in Gulliver, 1963b.

some cattle. The youngest son stays at the father's homestead in order to help the old people; he has fields there and cultivates. But all the sons are only children and the father is great (powerful) and has strength (authority) even over those who live at a distance. There is only one family (*engang*). But when the father dies, then the sons who are big (mature) take their own fields and cattle and they inherit. The inheritance is discussed and settled and each man has his own and lives in his own homestead and cultivates, and the wives and children with him. But these men remain together—one lineage (*engang*)—because they remember. They remember their father. They all must beg the (dead) father at his grave-shrine and they must help one another.

Translation of text by an Arusha informant.

This text gives a simple account of the process of development continuously in operation in the family which leads through the natural succession of the generations to the emergence of new families and new lineages. It is quoted here for that purpose, and also to show that the Arusha have a clear, generalized conception of the recurrent pattern which they accept as normal and inevitable. It is, in fact, a reasonable first approximation to actual occurrences.

The essentials of this developmental sequence are straightforward and of a kind that has been described in some detail for a number of other African societies. There are three main phases: the period of the nuclear family, the period of the compound family, and the period of inheritance and post-inheritance following the father's death and the dissolution of his family. We begin with the nuclear family when, by at least early middle age, a man with his wife or wives and children occupy a discrete homestead which (except in the most lately settled peripheral lowlands) is usually clearly bounded by fencing, hedge and trees. The man is head of the homestead and family (both called *engang*) in his role of husband and father, but also as the legitimate, individual owner of an 'estate' of land and livestock which provides the economic resources of the group. The land is his either by outright inheritance from his father at the latter's death or by right of pioneering unoccupied land which is confirmed at the time of inheritance. Livestock (cattle, goats and sheep) are similarly inherited and are augmented by legitimate acquisition in such transactions as bride-wealth, judicial compensation or purchase. Economically the land is the more important both for subsistence and to produce crops for the market; nevertheless livestock are quite essential for a multitude of social and ritual transactions, and a high premium is put on their milk supply. Within a nuclear family—monogamous or polygynous alike—a wife and her children comprise a separate sub-unit identified physically and verbally by the separate house (*engaji*) which they occupy. The husband and family head is not a member of such a house and this is manifested outwardly by his occupation of a separate and smaller dwelling (*oltombo*). To each wife the husband allocates a portion of his estate, both land and animals, and this provides at once the means of subsistence for the house and also the assignment of direct responsibility for the management and exploitation of the estate. Where there is more than one wife, allocations are equal but they are revisable in the light of relative, differential needs. The family head retains an unallocated reserve of his estate which, although tended by all members of the family, remains unrestrictedly at his use and disposal. Nowadays cash crops are mainly, often entirely, grown on unallocated land so that the family head retains full control of the main non-subsistence production and income of the group. He also makes use of the unallocated reserve to augment earlier allocations as new needs arise and as his personal inclinations influence him.

The phase of the nuclear family is marked, as the Arusha conceive it, by the residential unity of the group of a man, his wives and young children under the single control of that man as owner of the estate.

The second phase begins with the marriage of a son, for this introduces a new kind of sub-unit and changes the relationship between father and son. A bride comes to live in the homestead of her husband's father, in the house of her husband's mother where her first child is born. Within a year or two the son must provide his wife with a house of her own by creating a new homestead separate from that of his father. He may move right off his father's land either to pioneer a new farm in unoccupied land, or to take a tenancy on another man's land; or he may remain on his father's farm, but still he must shift out of his father's homestead. Ideally, only the youngest son of each wife remains on the parental farm, in a separate homestead, and eventually inheriting there in ultimogeniture, while all his older brothers acquire land elsewhere. It was probably never as simple as that, but in any case unused land is nowhere available any longer in the Arusha country: older sons now claim rights in their father's land and remain to establish their homesteads there. A son remaining on the family land takes a part of his mother's allocated fields, augmented by such additional allocation as his father can be persuaded to make from the unallocated reserve. Livestock are similarly acquired.

In any event, however, a married son becomes residentially and economically semi-autonomous both of his mother's house and of his father. The total family becomes a more articulated group—a compound family. The Arusha use the same word, *engang*, as for a nuclear family and homestead. This usage indicates that, despite a new order of segmentation and residential dispersion, the family as a group retains its unity under the persisting authority of its founder and head who remains the owner of the estate on which it depends and who retains full ritual and jural competence and responsibility for all its members. Land and livestock obtained by a son and his wife are said to be allocations only, and not outright transfers of property rights; they are said to be capable of revision as the family head sees fit and disposal of them is impossible without his full permission. The compound family perpetuates the jural unity of the earlier nuclear family: married sons, no less than their junior brothers, are jural minors who must be represented by their father. He is ultimately responsible for their actions, and they all share a corporate obligation for each other which residential dispersion and economic autonomy cannot deny. Contractual obligations by married sons can be undertaken only with the father's consent, and obligations incurred may be properly charged by an outsider against the father and through him against the whole compound family. The reason for this, say the Arusha, lies partly in the facts of kinship *per se* and in sons' respect for their father; but specifically it results from the father's lifelong retention of his ownership rights in the estate. Continued control of the estate affords continued control over his sons dependent on that estate.

This control is reinforced by unavoidable ritual necessities.

THE ARUSHA FAMILY

A man with a living father cannot possess his own ancestral shrine for such a shrine can only be established at the father's grave, or a symbolic replica of it. The ancestors can only be approached through the deceased father, the most powerful and active ancestor. While the father is alive, therefore, he undertakes all ritual in the ancestral cult on behalf of his whole family—nuclear or compound alike—directing it primarily at his own dead father. Sons of whatever age and status are completely dependent on their living father's ritual monopoly. And although it is logically possible for other kinds of ritual (i.e. non-ancestral) to be performed by a married son, nevertheless it seldom is because there is danger that it may be inefficacious, that outsiders may be unwilling to accept it as adequate, and that the living father may actively resent the implication of independence.

Thus the original family tends to become increasingly articulated internally and decentralized, but it retains an essential unity under the enduring authority of its head. The principal component parts are the heteronomous nuclear families of married sons, and the residual nuclear family of the head in his original homestead.

Only at the death of their father do sons take their share of the estate, each obtaining his own allodium by inheritance. The pattern of inheritance should follow precisely the already established pattern of allocations made by the father before his death. Ideally, the unallocated reserve should have disappeared, or at least the dispositions of its parts should have been determined and reliable witnesses have been informed (e.g., the father's brothers, the lineage counsellor). After post-mortuary observances a formal assembly is held, composed of the deceased's sons and other members of his inner lineage, and usually (inevitably if difficulties are foreseen) the lineage counsellor. At this time, in addition to the settlement and affirmation of inheritance, all outside claims against the estate must be stated and responsibility determined (e.g. outstanding bride-wealth) for thereafter the former unitary estate is irretrievably broken up and claims against it are no longer tenable.

The sons of the dead man at this point become autonomous heads of their own nuclear families and each possesses his own estate. They enter into a new relationship with each other within the new minimal lineage. Each acquires the jural self-responsibility and independence which attaches to the ownership of an estate; each establishes his own ancestral shrine ('the father's grave') where with full competence he can perform ritual pertinent to his own nuclear family. The image of the father remains strong, not only in the ancestral cult, but in the conceptualization of the persisting continuity of the former single estate despite its new diversity of ownership by the several heirs. This idealized continuity serves as a symbol of the integrity of the new lineage which has come to replace the old, defunct compound family. Although each successor nuclear family is internally autonomous, close co-operation persists between the family heads in ritual, jural and, to a lesser extent, economic affairs.

In the preceding account an attempt has been made to give a skeleton description of the developmental process as the Arusha themselves conceive it. It is now intended to examine in detail four key features which are especially crucial to its operation. These do not, of course, exhaust the factors which are relevant to the process, but within the limits of this essay it is not possible to attempt an exhaustive treatment. These features are: the residential unity and integrity of the nuclear family, and the position of dependents who are not members of it; the nature of the authority of the head of a compound family; the inheritance process and the attainment of autonomy by sons after their father's death; and, finally, the nature of relations between those sons in the context of the effective inner lineage. These features are naturally interrelated, each affecting the others, but for purposes of exposition it is possible to examine each separately, beginning, again, with the initial point of an autonomous nuclear family.

The Nuclear Family

The residential unity of the nuclear family within the confines of its homestead is regarded by Arusha as a practical necessity as well as an ideal. In a sample of 315 families in three mountain parishes, no case was discovered where members of a nuclear family resident on the family land were not at the same time

THE ARUSHA FAMILY

living within a single homestead. This is at once both a symbol and a demonstration of the unity of such families and of the authority of their heads. In the same sample, however, there were forty-eight cases where a wife, with or without her children, was resident elsewhere, away from the family land, as a result of marital estrangement. Among these, reliable informants suggested that twenty-one cases were purely temporary separations as indicated by the fact that, despite the absence of several months or more, the wife had made no attempt to build a new house or consistently to cultivate elsewhere, and her house and fields were still held available for her by her husband. In the other twenty-seven cases estrangement appeared to be more nearly permanent, although without divorce. This means that, for the sample, a maximum of 15 per cent and perhaps as few as 9 per cent of the nuclear families were residentially divided.

Where separation had occurred as a permanent feature, the wife was living and cultivating on a piece of land obtained from a kinsman (see below) and there she maintained a separate establishment, domestically and economically independent of the rest of the family and its head. About one quarter of these cases concerned childless wives; and of the rest rather more than half had left their children with the husband where they were cared for by a co-wife or their father's mother, and all or most of their mother's allocated land and animals was retained for their subsistence. Disruption here was minimal. In the remaining cases—about one third of the total number—the separated wife was accompanied by her children, and thus a whole sub-unit was in part cut off from the family. It is still considered to be an integral part of the family, although it is no longer dependent on the family estate for subsistence. In particular the family head retains both jural and ritual responsibility and privilege over such a sub-unit. For example, no case was discovered where the family head failed to be the prime actor in his daughter's marriage or to obtain the usual premarital and bride-wealth payments although the girl lived apart with her mother. Only a subsistence payment of a calf can be claimed by the man who has accommodated the wife and daughter. In one case, not believed to be unusual, the father was held responsible and had to pay compensation for injuries caused by his son in a fight, although the young man was living away with his mother. Only a father can intercede with the ancestors on behalf of his children, and most often on behalf of the wife also, wherever they live. Nevertheless in this minority of cases of a separated wife and her house an equivocal situation emerges since they are no longer dependent on the family estate yet they cannot become fully independent.

In the same 315 families, only six contained a wife and her children resident on another, geographically separate portion of land which was part of the family estate. At least one reason for this is that only about one man in ten held such additional land—and in earlier generations far fewer; but even when it does occur, it is still not generally associated with a residential division of the nuclear family.

This residential segregation of a nuclear family is likewise strongly emphasized by the Arusha because it is a practical and public mark of the achieved autonomy of its head with his estate. To share a homestead with another man and his family would, say people, indicate that neither were fully autonomous estate-holders, and it would be a degrading situation for both of them. In fact it never occurs among men whose father is dead, and only infrequently among married men whose father is still alive. Neither do extra-familial dependants frequently live within the family homestead. Young, unmarried sisters of the family head (their father being dead) may live with his wife until their marriage, but they make no claim on the estate other than temporary subsistence although they are a ritual and jural responsibility. They leave no claim behind them when they marry. Similarly, unmarried brothers may be residents but then, at least after boyhood, the homestead is principally a convenient *pied-à-terre* and much of their time, including nights, is spent elsewhere in the company of age-mates. Seldom do they have a house of their own (seven cases in the 315 families) and they contribute little or nothing to the labour force.

Extra-familial dependants live in their own houses outside the homestead fence. Obligations to assist and accommodate certain kin, almost invariably women and their children, may not be avoidable, and such people make claims on the estate of the family—but without affecting its residential integrity. Here we are not concerned with a 'tenant' proper—an adult man and his family—who obtains the long-term loan of a portion of the land on which he establishes a separate homestead in which his nuclear family is sociologically quite distinct from that of the landowner. The land held in tenancy is for a long period (often permanently in fact) virtually detached from the family estate, and it is used and cultivated as a quite separate unit.

With few exceptions, even when inter-personal relations are poor, a widowed mother lives as a dependant of her youngest son or, pending his maturity, of the son or other man acting as guardian to him. In only three cases in the sample families was the mother's house within her son's homestead, and even then it was situated in a fenced enclosure off to one side. In the other cases the mother had her own house outside the homestead. She retained a portion of her original allocation from her husband, or had acquired a similar piece in substitute; she maintained a marked degree of economic autonomy which, except in chronic infirmity, did little to affect the labour supply or economic organization of her son's family. As this physical and economic separation indicates, the mother is not a member of any of the nuclear families of her sons. After the dissolution of the old family the matri-centred house is of little importance, except that full-brothers retain prior residual rights in each other's estates in the event of death without heirs. The significant point here is that each son inherits his share of the dead father's estate and there is no notion of any fraternal corporation. Structurally the mother is a residuum of the preceding family. Affectively she is most closely linked with her youngest son, who accepts primary ritual and jural responsibility for her. Eventually with her death she leaves no claims behind her.

For the moment we shall not be concerned with the class of dependants comprising widows and children of deceased brothers and other close agnates of the family head. It is more convenient to treat these important dependants in the context of the inheritance process (see below, pp. 218 ff.).

Other dependants were, in the sample families, invariably married kinswomen who were either widows or separated from their husbands, with or without children. As before, cases are ignored where estrangement from a husband appeared to be purely temporary so that the women were merely lodgers. Fifty-five nuclear families (18 per cent) had permanent dependants: forty-two full-sisters of the family head, six half-sisters, five paternal female cousins and two wife's sisters. Each woman had her own house on her host's land and she cultivated there on a portion which he had allocated to her. Always, however, the attached house was sited outside the family homestead and often it was bounded by its own fence or hedge. It remained a separate domestic group and hosts emphasized this. The dependent woman usually cultivated on her own and did not necessarily participate in the co-operative domestic economy of her host's family, although in some cases she enjoyed an informal and mutually useful friendship with a wife of her host on a neighbourly basis. Such claims as she was able to make were regarded as privileges rather than rights. Her host usually assisted her in the building and repair of her house; he often, but not invariably, assisted in the heavier cultivation work; and he undertook to support her in minor things normally the responsibility of the husband, e.g., in petty disputes, non-ancestral ritual, domestic protection, etc. Although these privileges tend to harden into established rights, nevertheless essentially such dependants are not integrated into the domestic routines and the social organization of the host's own family. At no time does the host accept major responsibility of a ritual or jural nature on behalf of his dependants which in any case he would not acknowledge by virtue of the close kinship tie. Ritually he is unable to enlarge his competence: his performance in the ancestral cult on behalf of an extra-familial dependant would be ineffective, if not positively dangerous. Jurally, his responsibility invariably ceases at the limit of his own nuclear family, or, in an extended sense, it is confined to his own lineage. A dependant kinswoman by marriage, and her children by payment of bride-wealth, are the wards of another man and another lineage whose interests and obligations cannot be denied because of residential separation (cf. the cases cited at pages 205–6).

Permitted claims against the host's estate—even though they may harden into effective rights—are either erased completely on the death of the dependent woman, or they are converted into a new and separate tenancy in favour of her son for whom, thereafter, the host accepts little or no responsibility. A case in point occurred in one of the sample families.

The elder, married full-sister of Moravu had lived on his land for some fifteen years. Her eldest son had married and had prevailed on Moravu to allocate him a portion of land on which to build his homestead and to cultivate. In 1957, when Moravu's own son married, the sister and her married son together occupied almost as much land as Moravu's own monogamous nuclear family. At that time, Moravu attempted unsuccessfully to engineer the return of his sister to her husband's homestead several miles away—the husband being anxious to have her back, and to reinforce his control of his daughters' marriages and bride-wealth. By tacit consent Moravu had earlier permitted his sister's son to plant coffee bushes on part of the allocated land; now he saw no way of being able to afford to pay the compensation for those bushes legally required before regaining the land to his own control and use. In effect, therefore, the sister's son had a strong claim on the portion of land concerned, for although he might have been evicted from that part which contained no coffee, Moravu was unwilling to take this drastic step. The sister was ageing and her two other children were daughters, both betrothed and soon to marry. Moravu accepted no greater responsibility towards his sister's son than any mother's brother should: merely there was an additional domestic group—a heteronomous unit of a quite different compound family based elsewhere—which it seemed would in due course become an autonomous nuclear family in its own right. The sister's son became, that is, an independent tenant of Moravu but not a member of Moravu's family. Formerly such a sister's son would most likely have left the land altogether and pioneered a new farm elsewhere in virgin land; nowadays that is impossible. But the net result is only a reduction—probably a permanent one—of the land of Moravu, i.e. of the economic resources available to the family. This may of course, affect the development of that family by increasing the pressure on its resources, but quite clearly a specific distinction was maintained between Moravu's family (just then on the verge of becoming a compound family) and the nuclear family of his sister's son.

To put this conclusion in another and more generalized way: a dependent kinswoman and her children do not become part of the host's family nor does the host extend his authority and responsibilities, except temporarily and marginally, over the attached group. It remains a separate domestic unit, and in the course of its own development it can become autonomous of the host in a way in which the family of a married son of the host cannot.

Thus, on the one hand, non-members of the nuclear family can obtain some access to the family's economic resources (to land but not to livestock) so that in those cases the estate is not monopolized by the owner and his own wife and children. Almost all Arusha find it impossible to refuse assistance to a near kinswoman who persistently seeks it, unless land is most critically scarce; and, as some men pointed out, the generosity arising out of obligations and sentiments of kinship may be more limiting on a man and his control of his estate than his responsibility towards his own nuclear family. It is easier, these men said, to modify the allocations of arable land to a wife than to a dependent kinswoman, precisely because the latter is not a member of the family. On the other hand, such dependants cannot become a permanent responsibility of the host nor integrated members of his family. The integrity and separateness of a nuclear family persists. Finally, it must be remembered that probably less than one family in five is in any case affected by such dependants.

The Father's Authority in the Compound Family

The Arusha lay great emphasis on the strong, persisting authority of the father, as head of the compound family, over those sons who are married and occupying their separate but heteronomous homesteads. In economic, ritual and jural affairs, say Arusha ubiquitously, the father's authority remains supreme. Married sons cannot own land and livestock but are merely allocated portions which are revocable; and, it is asserted, they take legitimate possession only by inheritance *after* the father's death. Thus, in this view, the nuclear family becomes a more complex (i.e., a compound) family, but it remains fundamentally a single unit under a single authority.

This authority, as we have seen, stems from the fact, firstly, that the father is the owner of a single estate which affords him the monopoly of economic control and jural responsibility; and secondly, that sons of a living father have no ritual competence in the ancestral cult.

It may be remarked at this point that this emphasis on the authority of one person over another is not found elsewhere in this society. The Arusha are markedly egalitarian in their social relationships and resentful of imperious demand, though amenable to diplomatic influence and reciprocal obligations. There are a number of roles of influence and leadership—in particular, lineage counsellors and age-group spokesmen—but overbearing individuals even in these roles are invariably checked by hostile reactions and obdurance. Even lineage counsellors who have ultimate power of force, both physical and supernatural, very seldom resort to them and their use is regarded as a sign of failure.

The question arises, then, how far the authority of the father is in reality maintained and exercised over his married son; or, in the context of this essay, how far the operational integrity of the compound family persists under his unifying control up to the time of the father's death.

A married son has at least autonomy in his day-to-day management of his own homestead and his allocated farm. In subsistence he with his family is self-sufficient, and the cash crops and other produce are disposable with little or no paternal interference. Having been allocated a portion, a married son is expected by the father to be self-supporting even when he remains on his father's farm. Formerly, and until the early 1950s, when elder sons left their father's land and pioneered a new farm at a distance, the degree of economic autonomy was rather greater. The Arusha are equivocal concerning the locus of control over pioneered land: some assert that the pioneer-son lays an automatic right to it by his act of first occupancy, but others say that such land becomes part of his father's estate. On the whole, sons take the former view and fathers the latter. It is true that the son's right to his pioneered land is formally endorsed at post-mortuary, inheritance discussions, just as are formerly allocated portions of the father's own farm. On the other hand, when active dispute arises—usually when another brother, at the father's instigation, seeks a share—traditional-style moots and modern courts alike have been careful to avoid rigorous definition of legitimacy. They affirm the pioneer-son's prime privilege of occupation and give chief attention to exhortation and suasion. The latter stresses the moral obligation between brothers and of a son towards his father, and it is directed at gaining the son's agreement to accommodate his brother and to honour his father. Now although this judicial technique is not uncommon, in other kinds of disputes it follows from enunciated legitimate rights and obligations concerning the matter in conflict, for these provide a basis from which to seek mutual agreement by negotiation. Concerning pioneer land this is not the case, but rather the rights and obligations appealed to are of a generalized nature, not specifically defining particulars. Further, neither moots nor courts are willing to enforce their moral strictures, and in consequence some sons acquiesce to paternal and fraternal pressures and some refuse, albeit uneasily. This represents, it can be argued, a feature in which reality and the ideal diverge in a delicate matter. What is significant is that a father cannot obtain a definitive affirmation of his alleged right and authority when the matter is put to a judicial test. He may well be able to gain something like his claims by non-judicial pressures against the obstinate son as a result of bargaining and of threats to withhold other benefits, but experience shows that he cannot depend on this.

In the case of a married son who holds a tenancy on another man's land, the father's authority is even weaker, for a tenancy is a personal arrangement between land holder and tenant. In both these cases, then, a serious breach exists in the allegedly indisputable authority of a father. These cases occur, moreover, where the son is resident at some distance from his father, and where therefore economic, land-holding autonomy is coupled often with life in a different local community where it is more difficult for the father, however authoritarian, continuously to interfere.

Opportunities for pioneering have been decreasing for a generation, or rather the desirability of it has decreased since the only possibilities have been in the unfavourable, disliked peripheral lowlands. Increasingly, therefore, married sons have sought to remain on the father's land;[1] this has strengthened the father's authority not only over the land they use but also over his sons' activities now close at hand. Elderly fathers insist on their superordinate power and they may threaten a married son with revocation of an allocation for alleged unfilial behaviour. Adult sons—even those approaching middle age—seldom remonstrate and seemingly acquiesce; and yet the reality is otherwise.

No case was discovered where a married son had suffered the revocation of part or whole of the land allocated to him by his father, except where he himself had agreed to it for approved reasons, e.g., to accommodate a younger brother recently married. Whether or not father-son relations are amicable—and clearly there are well-founded sources of tension and conflict—a son is evidently able to retain his portion of land. Resolute retention may well deny additional allocations at a later time, or other disabilities. In recent years this has meant that sons have sometimes succeeded in putting the land to uses disapproved by the father, e.g., concentrating on coffee rather than food crops, or using a grazing paddock for arable purposes.

Disputes over land between father and son seldom go outside the inner lineage (i.e., the smallest effective patrilineage). My impression is that a father seeks a means of expressing righteous indignation as much as he hopes to gain assertion of his authority. The close agnates of the father (brothers, paternal cousins) invariably incline to an acceptance of the *fait accompli* and cautiously recommend the father accordingly, although they morally condemn the unfilial conduct of the son. Much is made of the paternal duty of magnanimity, and of his superiority over the son which permits forbearance; at the same time the father is assured of the retention of his ultimate rights and authority although in truth these are partly being denied him simultaneously.

All this applies to usufructuary rights in the land, and it does not vitiate a father's ability to refuse to make an initial allocation to a newly married son. A son can scarcely be denied

[1] But each son has his own physically separate homestead. I came across only one case of a married son and his wife residing permanently in his father's homestead.

access to a portion of his mother's allocated fields, but one in paternal disfavour may be denied a part of the unallocated reserve. Rights of transfer (sale, gift, loan, pledge, exchange) of land allocated to a son remain strictly in the father's hands. Courts and moots have shown a readiness to nullify illicit transfers made without his witnessed approval, and few men are willing to hazard attempts to deal secretly with a son whose father is alive; rights here are strongly reinforced by Arusha detestation of secret dealings. Concerning livestock, however, which are economically less valuable than land, rights of transfer are generally tacitly allowed to sons. Transactions in small stock are commonplace, but even concerning cattle there is not the emotional involvement which pertains to land, for land is a *sine qua non* of Arusha life. Many fathers incline to the view that if a son mismanages his livestock the misfortune is the son's own; livestock are more easily replaceable, and moreover fathers find it easier to retain animals in their unallocated reserve than to hold land, and to release them as a proper need arises (e.g., a bride-wealth instalment, a fine, a ritual need).

The other two sources of paternal authority in the compound family are ritual and jural in nature. Especially concerning the ancestral cult, sons are dependent on their father in matters believed vitally to affect the whole of the well-being of the living, for it is impossible for a married son to possess his own ancestral shrine ('the father's grave') or to make supplications to the dead. On the other hand, a father finds it difficult to use his ritual monopoly to bolster his authority in mundane affairs. Whilst fathers are aware of this potentiality, nevertheless the right and power of ritual performance carry with them obligations and responsibilities. If, for example, a son or his child becomes ill because of the divined displeasure of one or more ancestors, it is impossible for the father to refuse to conduct ritual intercession because of the son's filial disobedience in some other matter. The refusal might be tantamount to homicide if the illness is serious enough; but in any case it would be an evil act and an insult to the ancestors, and the father must employ his power on behalf of members of his family. However there is no need to deny the influence in the father's favour arising out of his ritual monopoly. A son feels gratitude, both for the opportunity to obtain release of emotional tension and worry, and for the treatment of the misfortune itself. If a father cannot refuse his ritual obligations, he can exhibit his superiority and he can be prompt or dilatory in performance. He may take the opportunity to remind both the son and the ancestors of unfilial conduct in other matters, so that at least ideal, moral standards are reiterated. Paternal pre-eminence is, in general, emphasized in the ancestral cult which is, indeed, a supernatural reflection of it. In addition the unity of the total compound family is promoted and actively demonstrated, for all adult members (including wives) should participate in each performance for proper efficacy. Absentees draw not only the reprobation of the living but the wrath and possible vengeance of the dead. In practice an ancestral ceremony is a prime occasion for the gathering of the dispersed group and its purposeful co-operation.

The ritual authority of a father is primarily an expression of generalized values and norms, but a consideration of his jural authority brings us back to his position as owner of the estate. Not only is the father responsible for the actions of each member of the family, but that group is a unit of collective responsibility. A married son, say the Arusha, like a wife or child is a minor, and disputes should not be formally considered in the absence of the father, the head of the family. Moots and courts adopt the ideal viewpoint: if a fine or compensation is due, it is levied on the father and not directly on the son who is the immediate cause of it; and if compensation is allowed for some injury to a son, his father is the proper claimant.

Whilst the father is an active elder (of either junior or senior status—cf. page 198) and whilst therefore his sons are in the grades of young men or *murran*, this ideal view is most effectively practised; but it seems that it is more a result of their inferior age-status and inexperience than it is of subordination to their father as such. Magistrates, and even more the traditional-type counsellors and spokesmen, are not willing to permit a young man to present his own case: they demand that he be represented by a man of elder status—invariably the father if alive. When sons attain elderhood (becoming junior elders in their age group) their father automatically becomes a retired elder. In that status he should give up participation in politico-jural affairs in favour of the younger and active elders (Gulliver,

1963b). His sons, as elders, have now proper competence to engage in those affairs, and indeed they have an obligation to do so. In practice, of course, the change-over is less simple than that: there is a gradual relinquishment of active participation by the older men and a gradual, complementary accession by the younger men. But without here going into detail, it is fair to say that all sons do gradually achieve an acknowledged jural competence as their fathers progressively retire from participation. A son of elder status becomes able, therefore, to manage his own case as plaintiff or defendant, and he acquires the skill to do so effectively. It would be highly derogatory in Arusha to suggest that an elder, whether or not his father is alive, is not responsible and liable for his actions and the adjudicated results of them. To this extent, then, a father in his later years cannot maintain absolute jural prerogatives over his elder sons. Conditioned both by physical old age and culturally imposed retirement, fathers become increasingly inclined to cede authority to them.

Nevertheless, and especially in more important matters, an old father cannot merely be ignored. If a son requires material assistance beyond his immediate means to meet juridical necessities, the father must be consulted if he is not quite senile. The material and jural support of others is most effectively obtained through the father's intervention—whether other members of the compound family, or members of the inner lineage—for he acts as the focus of activity. Judicial assemblies insist on the father's formal acceptance, as a minimum, of whatever final judgement or agreement is reached. Frequently a good deal of trouble is taken to accommodate the moot or court to the attendance of the elderly father whose son is involved in a dispute—even when the old man does little more than sit passively and give his formal acquiescence to his son's actions and commitments there. The father's authority over his sons is thus not only enunciated in form but much of its reality is retained; and as the father remains vitally involved, so too is the whole compound family for other sons cannot evade the responsibilities of membership of it.

An older man, whose father is alive, may be able to negotiate his own contractual arrangements with other men—e.g., marriage and bride-wealth, or a loan—but few men are willing to conclude such an agreement without the witnessed concurrence of the living father of the other party. This arises partly as a matter of respect and propriety; but more importantly because the arrangement, in case of later dispute, might be seriously weakened otherwise. A contractual agreement cannot usually be wholly invalidated in this way, but it can certainly be rendered much less satisfactory. In the case of a transaction in land, however, the demonstrated non-approval of the father may nullify the whole matter. Thus again, an adult son remains in this way dependent on his father.

In conclusion, the authority of a father over his married sons is, in some respects, considerably less than the Arusha ideal admits, and this means in effect that the persisting unity of the compound family as a co-operative, collectively responsible, property-using group is also less. The points at which this is so have been indicated. It is necessary, however, to note also the points where paternal authority is sustained—in original allocations of land and livestock, over rights of transfer of land, over the unallocated reserve and its eventual disposition, and in more important jural matters. And additionally, the father's monopoly of competence in ancestral ritual at least emphasizes his superior status, and the necessity of collaboration reiterates in a practical way the unity of the compound family despite its residential dispersion in economically autonomous units. Although, therefore, the unity of the compound family is less than Arusha tend to claim, nevertheless mature (i.e., married) sons and their nuclear families are unable to gain the independence which is possible in some African societies.

Inheritance and the Developmental Cycle

For the Arusha, the proper culmination of the compound family occurs when, at the father's death, the whole of his estate has already been apportioned in allocations by him among his sons, each of whom now inherits outright and becomes the head of his own fully autonomous, nuclear family. This does sometimes happen—and it brings much general approbation—but it requires that all the sons are already married and enjoying usufructuary rights over their allocated portions, and that what little remains as an unallocated reserve has been expressly designated to one or another of them. Post-mortuary inheritance discussion is then a formality, and all that remains to be settled is the assessment of any outstanding debts against the total estate before its final dissolution. This in effect means that the father must have lived to a comparatively great age and that he has, before his death, surrendered the bulk of his estate to his sons and become content to acquiesce in more or less passive retirement, even to a considerable dependence on them.

As far as can be determined (mainly by reference to age-group chronology) only a minority of men live much beyond the age of seventy years, and a very few beyond eighty years. Especially if they are polygynous, men may produce children in their fifties, so that at death they leave immature sons. Many men die earlier and leave a number or even all of their sons immature and thus unable to take up their inheritance and to achieve immediately the ideal autonomy. Some arrangement is then required for their guardianship.

In any event a formal trustee ('heir of the family') is appointed by the deceased's inner lineage, and he should be the nearest surviving agnate. But where immature sons are left after their father's death, two types of development are possible, both involving their becoming wards of a guardian. If one or more sons are already mature, they may assume active guardianship over their younger siblings and the widows. In this case the former residual nuclear family of the dead father may perhaps continue under the protection and supervision of one of the mature sons; or the young children and their mothers may go to live in the homestead of such a son, or become dispersed among the homesteads of several of them. In these cases the formal trustee's obligations are limited. He is appealed to only if conflict occurs over the final dispositions of inheritance when the younger sons come to marry, to seek their shares of the old estate and to achieve their autonomy. In practice the trustee then usually leaves the dispute to be settled by the whole of the inner lineage with the help of the (maximal) lineage counsellor and, sometimes, more distant agnates also as conciliators. Fraternal disputes can be both bitter and protracted, particularly in recent decades when, with land shortage, a new dependence on inheritance has emerged as the principal means of obtaining land. In addition the trustee is usually expected to give formal approval to the major transactions of his wards and to participate in their ritual affairs.

An alternative development is that immature children and widows come directly under the protection of the trustee or another agnate of the deceased's generation. This inevitably occurs when no mature sons survive the father, but it may also be the arrangement for some or all of the immature children even when elder, married brothers do exist. By virtue of his generational superiority, on which the Arusha set a high premium, the trustee has first claim to become pro-husband to the widows; and other brothers or paternal cousins of the deceased may lay similar claims. A widow often prefers her husband's brother rather than the son of a co-wife because she prefers an older man with his established homestead and domestic régime. Her children follow her in her choice.

In either case the ideally simple developmental pattern may be considerably complicated, if not altogether distorted. Firstly, because sons remain who are not able to take up their inheritance and must become wards of some mature man *in loco parentis*; and secondly, because at least temporarily, and often more nearly permanently, an elder brother or senior agnate obtains control of part of an estate which is not his own and authority over the people attached to it. It may be, of course, that this state of affairs is transitory and of little or no lasting significance—the young sons mature within a few years and are able to take up their inheritance at that time without much difficulty. This is merely a short postponement of the simple development. The real complications occur where immature sons are but children and where widows have many years of child-bearing potentiality remaining. In such cases the estate of the guardian (whoever he may be) and the whole or part of the deceased's estate tend to be compounded, and the authority and responsibility of the guardian extends beyond the limits of his own family (nuclear or compound).

The guardian may maintain two homesteads—his own and that of the deceased; but if his responsibility is foreseen as protracted, he most usually consolidates them and the two estates in order to administer the whole as a single unit, even where the two farms are not contiguous. The establishment of a single homestead is a matter of practical convenience, but also it is for the Arusha symbolic of the establishment of a single family under the guardian's authority. The significance of the single, separate homestead has already been discussed (pp. 204ff.). Strictly speaking, declare Arusha, he should not do this for the estate of an autonomous man should never lose its identity by absorption into any other estate: nor should the due portion heritable by the son of the dead man be absorbed, however close the agnatic tie between the guardian and the deceased. Similarly the guardian should be only pro-father and pro-husband to the children and their widowed mother respectively: he should not become a full social substitute for the dead man, but merely assume temporary responsibility for them pending the sons' maturity. In practice, however, and gradually over the years, a guardian can succeed in gaining virtually complete *de facto* control over both the estate and the widow and children. It is unlikely that knowledge of the deceased's estate can be entirely erased by absorption, for old field boundaries and the progeny of livestock are remembered. Nevertheless by his actions, premeditated or not, a guardian may so effectively inter-link the two estates that their later separation becomes practically impossible. He may take advantage of his position to allocate part of the deceased's estate to his own wife or sons so that they come to establish some claim in it. He may dispose of animals of his wards or use his own animals in their interests, and so initiate a complex debt pattern. He may put encumbrances on the wards' land by planting his own trees, bananas or coffee bushes, or by putting buildings, hedges or water channels on it, so that the true heirs later on are unable to gain legitimate access to it without first paying rather heavy compensation for these improvements. It is not unknown for a guardian to sell a field of the wards' estate or to encumber it with a pledge or tenant for his own advantage. Where the two estates are contiguous, the whole pattern of field boundaries, banana groves and grazing paddocks may be so transformed that reversion to the initial condition is made virtually impossible. Almost all Arusha have a fund of stories concerning the alleged chicanery of guardians and, cautiously executed, there is indeed little to prevent it. The inner lineage as such has no direct responsibility for supervising the actions of the guardian, though individual members may sometimes move to check the worst abuses. But a guardian generally takes a righteously indignant stand on his status and responsibility and on what he claims to be the practical good husbandry of his actions. Arusha are not inclined to endanger their relations with a near agnate through intervention on behalf of widows, children and property which do not pertain to their own autonomous family and estate.

These stories concerning guardians tend to be exaggerated, however, for naked self-interest is not entirely rampant among them. At least sometimes it is clearly most economical to work the two estates as a single unit. For example, the planting of coffee bushes or trees, or the amalgamation of arable fields for easier ploughing, may well be agriculturally sensible, despite the encumbrances which they establish. The wards may benefit from the good husbandry of their guardian even while he too benefits.

For good reason or not, the net effect tends to be that the estate (both land and livestock) of the guardian and of the wards gradually emerge under a single control as a single estate in which the two parts are inextricably intermingled. Because of this the wards become inextricably members of the guardian's own family, and the immature sons of the deceased become in effect the sons of the guardian. They are no longer able to obtain their due inheritance, except at his agreement and his allocation. In practice the allocation of land and livestock may not be confined to the deceased's own estate, while the guardian's own sons may likewise obtain allocations which are not confined to their father's estate. The end result need not necessarily be to the obvious disadvantage of either side, and in fact both may gain some advantage.

One further aspect may be noted: there is a tendency among wards, once they have married and obtained allocation from the mixed estate, to assume a markedly greater autonomy of their 'father' (i.e., their guardian) than his own sons can. Mature wards may not feel the sentiments of attachment to their guardian, and they may resent real or believed injustices towards them by him. More importantly, they are able to assert a ritual independence of him by the establishment of their real father's grave-shrine, and to claim a high degree of jural autonomy. That full separation does not inevitably occur at this period (no statistical assessment is possible) gives an indication of the strength of accumulated ties which have developed during the immaturity of the wards and the advantages which remain to them by their acknowledgement of their guardian's continued superiority. Integration of wards into their guardian's family seems to be more complete where the wards are of a generation genealogically junior to that of the guardian, rather than of the same generation. However, case data indicate that this is not inevitably the case. An elder brother may be up to thirty years older than his immature half-brothers who are his wards, and he then acts in substantially the same way and for the same reasons as a guardian of a senior generation who is a classificatory father. Indeed in the age-group status categories such an elder brother has the equivalent of that seniority. In any case particular personalities and inter-personal relations can affect the ultimate issue.

This kind of process, of course, affects the development not only of the deceased's family and estate and that of the wards as they mature, but also it affects that of the guardian's family and estate. In the one case the ideal pattern of the dissolution of the deceased's estate is halted and diverted; and in the other, the guardian's own family is augmented by outside recruitment so that its simple integrity is spoiled. The composition of the guardian's family does not follow the ideal pattern: dependants are added to it, as well as additional property, who tend to become fully incorporated into it. These are of quite a different order from those extra-familial dependants considered earlier (see pp. 207–10) who live outside the homestead and who can exercise only limited claims of restricted duration. Some Arusha families, then, are recruited by wardship as well as by marriage and the procreation of children; similarly some estates derive not only from inheritance, pioneering and legitimate transactions with outsiders (e.g., purchase, bride-wealth, etc.). Conversely, some autonomous families and their estates lose their identity by absorption into other units. Inevitably bound up with this, the guardian gains both ritual and jural authority which go beyond the limits of his own simple family, and through him both his sons and his wards participate in a wider, single

THE ARUSHA FAMILY

unit of domestic organization and collective jural responsibility.

It has not been possible to make an adequate quantitative assessment of this kind of 'unorthodox' development because of the difficulty of establishing satisfactory categories: that is, fairly rapid survey techniques did not permit the ready determination of the precise relationship between a guardian and his simple family and his wards. There were too many cases where absorption appeared to be in process of occurring, although clearly there were some where it had been virtually completed and some where it seemed unlikely to happen at all. Nevertheless among the 315 sample nuclear families, there were seventy-one cases (23 per cent) where the homestead contained wards of the family head; and among 186 compound families, fifty-one (28 per cent) contained wards, married or unmarried, who in general acknowledged essentially the same relationship to the family head as did his own sons. This illustrates one side of the picture. The other side, concerning men who have been members of a second family before gaining eventual autonomy, may be illustrated from a smaller number of more intimately known cases in which about one third of autonomous family heads had known that experience. This 'unorthodox' developmental cycle affects, then, a minority of Arusha men and their families; but it is a substantial minority which makes the process more than merely a minor, aberrant pattern in this society.

This means that there is not a single developmental cycle for all Arusha men and their families. Only a minority of cases occur in which the ideal cycle is completely fulfilled, but in a large number of other cases immature sons experience only a brief period of wardship before proceeding to marriage, inheritance and full autonomy. These two kinds of cases account for well over half of all occurrences. The remaining cases comprise two kinds of families: those containing additions of wards of the same generation as the family head, and those containing wards of a junior generation. It must be emphasized, finally, that the nature of the developmental cycle which occurs in any particular case results primarily from the effective control over property which can be gained in the circumstances at the time of the death of an estate owner.

P. H. GULLIVER

Autonomous Brothers and the Inner Lineage

This essay is concerned with the processes and roles operating in the development of Arusha families, and therefore it has only a limited concern with the nature of relations between mature brothers who, their father being dead, are heads of their own autonomous families and possessors of their separate estates. Nevertheless some mention of these relations is called for: partly because of the further light thrown on the autonomy of the family and its head, partly because they are directly connected with and arise out of the conditions of earlier common membership of a single family, and partly because the Arusha speak of their smallest operative lineage as a direct (though different) descendant of a defunct family.

After inheritance and the assumption of autonomy, brothers establish a new order of relationships with one another on an egalitarian basis. No longer are they subject to a single, over-riding authority, however restrictedly that may have been exercised; nor are their joint interests in or accepted responsibilities for one another any longer the product of common subordination as minors. In gaining autonomy they do not reject altogether their mutual interests and co-operative potentialities, or their sentiments born of fraternity. Indeed the influence of the father persists among them so that they sometimes speak of themselves as the joint owners of his estate—though never forgetting its new, irrevocable division among them—and they may refer to themselves and are referred to by others as *engang* (i.e., homestead, or family, or lineage) of their dead father. Although each man has his own ancestral shrine, and much importance is placed on this as an active symbol of autonomy, yet each man makes his prime supplications to the same ancestor—the father. And for the efficacy of performance as well as in fear of ancestral retribution for non-co-operation, brothers participate in each other's rituals.

Thus, say the people, the old family does not die but it is transformed into a new unit. They agree, however, that this is not strictly true for they also say that the new unit is primarily comprised of the brothers themselves alone, each acting as head of his own nuclear family. In describing the membership of a particular lineage Arusha give the names only of the autonomous family heads. Structurally it might be paraphrased that families as corporate entities are not related directly, but are linked only through their heads who alone engage in supra-familial relations and activities. Sons of living fathers cannot participate in these, or at least only in so far as they are able to usurp their father's authority. This group of brothers can be called a 'minimal lineage', with the dead father as its founder.

It may be noted briefly here that within this group, fraternal relations are but slightly affected by former house affiliations in the old family. That is, there is little differentiation between full-brothers and half-brothers (cf. p. 207). Unstructured sub-units which may emerge are as likely to be based on approximate coevality as on maternal origin in this society which is so powerfully influenced by age-status considerations. Because both of age differences and frictions stimulated by competition over former house allocations, full-brothers may well not be particularly friendly nor is there a strong idea that they should be.

Despite the marked tendency for newly autonomous brothers to discover a working unity and co-operation out of past association and present need, the minimal lineage seldom emerges immediately, and sometimes never at all, as an operating, corporate group. Instead the men become members of the already existing inner lineage of which their father had been a member up to the time of his death, and of which his surviving brothers, and maybe his paternal cousins, are still members. This is the group of near agnates which was hitherto most closely associated with the father. It supervises post-mortuary inheritance and selects both the formal trustee (see page 218) and the 'lineage heir' ('heir of the calf') whose acceptance of a calf from the deceased's estate on behalf of the lineage formally completes and seals the inheritance agreement. These agnates are those with whom the father co-operated in ancestral and other ritual, in certain jural co-responsibility and in other kinds of mutual assistance. Being of a senior generation to the sons of the dead man they have, of course, a degree of gerontocratic superiority over their autonomous nephews.

Thus, although the smallest patrilineage is usually idealized as a set of autonomous brothers, it does not generally emerge as such in practice for a particular set at least until they are older men—until, that is, their father's brothers are all dead and it has been possible gradually to disassociate themselves from intimate connections with their father's brother's sons. If a set of brothers is small (i.e., only one or two men) it will be most practicable and beneficial to retain close working ties with those paternal cousins; or a vigorous and influential man may retain the adherence of his cousins even in a more numerous group. Thus the *effective* lineage—which descriptively I call the 'inner lineage'—may be simply a set of elderly brothers (i.e., the lineage based on their father); or that group may be augmented by the autonomous sons of those brothers who have died; or the lineage may be a group of paternal cousins comprising all or some of the grandsons of the founder. To some extent these three main forms (and there are variant types also) of the inner lineage represent three successive phases in the developmental cycle of a lineage; but in practice it is not so simple as that. For example, a single set of brothers may never break away from their contemporary sets of paternal cousins to form an effective lineage stemming from their own father. Conversely, such a set might break away from their father's brothers and their paternal cousins precipitately to achieve their independent lineage.

This is not the place to examine the processes of Arusha lineage evolution: it is desired merely to indicate that the embryo minimal lineage—the newly autonomous sons of a dead father—does not usually become an effective corporate group immediately, and sometimes never at all. Although the image of the father remains strong and the tendency is to the establishment of a lineage with him in focal position, yet other and practical necessities defer this and tend to determine when if ever it occurs. Newly autonomous men seek and reciprocate assistance, sympathy and general support and they acknowledge a degree of mutual jural responsibility within a rather wider category of agnates; and although primarily concerned with ritual directed towards their own father, they participate with agnates concerned with a different father. Although autonomous brothers claim the right to consultation and approval where one of them desires to transfer permanently or temporarily rights in a portion of his inherited estate to an outsider, they may admit other near agnates to participate in the matter. This fraternal right is said to result directly from the former unity of the several estates now held by the brothers, yet paternal cousins may share that right. Outright sale of land by a member may be vetoed by the inner lineage. If sale is compelled by imperative need for money or animals, lineage members should rally to contribute the means required to remove the necessity for the sale; and if the sale is merely to gain profit, then lineage members have the first opportunity to buy the land themselves.

On the other hand, no case was discovered among the Arusha where a set of brothers had split up. Whatever the genealogical structure of and relations in the effective inner lineage, all of a set of brothers are members of it. Although, therefore, the minimal lineage may not emerge as a corporate group, it never loses its potentiality to do so. To this extent at least the notion of the persistence of a family after the dissolution of its single estate and unifying authority is valid.[1]

Conclusion

Explicitly and otherwise, a distinction has been repeatedly drawn between on the one hand the verbal descriptions by Arusha themselves of their family system and the developmental processes concerned in it (briefly exemplified in the text at page 199), and on the other hand the reality of social roles and relationships in that system. It seems most useful to regard the people's verbal accounts primarily as embodying the main values and attitudes they hold, rather than as descriptions of actual events; and in particular cases the Arusha are ready to acknowledge the inadequacy of their generalized versions. We may, therefore, fairly call these accounts idealized descriptions and we may identify the chief values as follows: (a) the persisting authority of the father over his sons right up to the time of his death, and thus the persisting unity of the group of people subordinate to him—the family in one form or the other; (b) the autonomous control of an estate of land and livestock which a man obtains at his father's death and which gives him his authority over his family dependent on it; (c) the jural unity of the family under its head as a single group

[1] A fuller account of the inner lineage is given in Gulliver, 1963b, chapter 5.

of collective responsibility; (d) the ritual unity of the family based on the monopolistic competence of its head in the ancestral cult, in which the authority of the father is strongly reflected; (e) the unity, as an association of autonomous men, of a set of brothers after their father's death. These values strongly influence men's expectations and aspirations, and an appreciation of them is essential to an understanding of concrete situations.

Nevertheless it would be an error to take the idealized account at its face value as a description of real events. Probably it never holds true in all particulars in any single case. Even in that minority of cases where a man lives to a comparatively great age, so that all his sons are mature and able to inherit directly on his death, the authority of the living father is rather less, and often a good deal less, than is claimed ideally. This is the first modification which is required as a result of empirical investigation. It is a most important one; in part it is associated with the effective control a married son can obtain over his allocated property, and in part it arises out of extra-familial factors relating to the status system provided by the age-group organization.

The second major modification lies in the fact that although dependent kinsfolk (married kinswomen and their children) cannot invade the integrity of the family homestead nor exercise claims of the same nature as members of the family, certain close agnates (sons of the brother, or own younger brothers, of the head) can become fully incorporated into the family. Again this can be seen to be principally the result of the control of property which passes in effect to a family head in his role as guardian. Because a guardian controls the property, he controls the people associated with it; and because he consolidates his own estate and that of his wards, he consolidates into one the two groups of people. His jural authority and the jural unity of the amalgamated group is derived directly from that situation. The nature of recruitment to a family and the method of obtaining control of property, and thus authority over people, may vary in actual life.

Thirdly, it has been indicated briefly that the minimal lineage—the ideal structural successor to the compound family—does not usually immediately emerge as an effective social group: it is for a longer or shorter period only a potential unit within a larger encompassing lineage of variable genealogical span.

These considerations do not invalidate the value system of the Arusha in so far as that system is considered as a guide to action and expectations rather than as an absolute set of criteria. The divergences do not worry the Arusha, for they are well aware of the practical possibilities; they do not cause a necessary revision of their value system because those values as such are still valid enough, and they still continue to articulate social behaviour in a meaningful way. There is, that is to say, no essential logical fallacy inherent in the divergence of norms and actual practices. Norms are generalized and they are simpler than the real conditions of concrete life. Indeed it may be suggested that they have to be simpler in order to be effective, and they represent a distillation, as it were, of the totality of motivations and requirements in the complexity of human interactions at this level.

REFERENCES

GULLIVER, P. H. 1960. 'The Population of the Arusha Chiefdom; A High-Density Area in East Africa', *Rhodes-Livingstone Journal*, 28, pp. 1–21.

—— 1961. 'Structural Dichotomy and Jural Processes among the Arusha of Northern Tanganyika', *Africa*, 31, 1, pp. 19–35.

—— 1963a. 'The Evolution of Arusha Trade', in *Markets in Africa*, ed. Paul Bohannan and George Dalton, Evanston, Northwestern University Press.

—— 1963b. *Social Control in an African Society*, London, Routledge & Kegan Paul (Boston, Mass., Boston University Press).

SONJO LINEAGE STRUCTURE AND PROPERTY

Robert F. Gray

The Homestead

IF a student were to study a Sonjo village by means of visual observation alone and without asking the people any questions, he would be forced to conclude that individual households possess a high degree of economic and social independence. He would find the beehive huts as evenly spaced as the rough terrain of the village permitted. With only a few exceptions, no obvious clustering of houses would reveal the presence of organized groups larger than the occupants of a single house. The exceptions, of which there are three or four in a village, would consist of two or three houses joined or surrounded by a fence and sharing a small courtyard with a common entrance. The observer would later find out that these compound homesteads belonged to polygynous men, but had no other special significance. Not all polygynous families are housed in compounds, and this particular arrangement is regarded as nothing but the personal preference of a few men.

Polygyny is not widely practised by the Sonjo, and only about 12 per cent of married men have more than one wife. The number of men who pay bride-price for a second wife is considerably smaller than this figure indicates, for a substantial proportion of polygynous wives are acquired through inheritance of the widow of a dead brother. Therefore, in this paper I shall consider the normal Sonjo family to be monogamous. Polygyny resulting from widow inheritance will be dealt with as a special development of monogamy. The remaining cases of polygyny, in which separate bride-price is paid for every wife, involve only a small minority of families, and these will be excluded from the general discussion unless it is otherwise specified.

If our student then went on to investigate the composition of the individual households, he would find married couples, with or without immature children, living in most of the houses. A few small houses would be occupied by elderly widows, and occasionally an old man would be found living alone and supplied with food by near-by relatives. The basic social units for food production and consumption are these households consisting of a single nuclear family. The wife of the house normally tills the family fields, stores the crops in the house, and prepares meals for her husband and children. One other kind of dwelling would be found in each quarter of a village. This would belong to a group of young bachelors of a warrior age-set, who use the house as a dormitory, but who are provided with meals by individual family households, which they visit in turn on different days. At this stage of the investigation the village would almost appear to be an unstructured aggregate of discrete nuclear families: there would be few clues as to the manner in which households are grouped into larger social units.

Clan and Ward

Visual inspection alone, however, would reveal one set of features suggesting that the village was subdivided territorially. Somewhere near the centre of the village would be a large level plaza, and several smaller plazas would be found in different quarters of the village. Let our observer now start asking questions freely, and he will find that the large plaza is reserved for ceremonies of the whole village, while the smaller plazas belong to different wards (*nkaia*) of the village. These wards are not everywhere separated by visible features, although their boundaries are quite definite. In some places a main path or ravine lies between two wards, while in other places the houses of adjacent wards run together. An average ward contains about fifty houses, more or less. Thus the village of Ebwe, with about 160 houses, is divided into three wards, while Soyetu has

300 houses and six wards. Each ward is associated with a different patrilineal clan (*bukolo*), the male members of which have exclusive rights to reside in the ward with their wives and children. These rights are not just rules for regulating the spatial distribution of the people, but are also of economic significance. For all the Sonjo villages are built upon rocky hillsides, and most of the house sites have been produced through laborious excavations; therefore, the rights to their use are strictly reserved for clan members. There is a sound reason for the rather awkward location of the Sonjo villages. In every case the village is situated on a hillside or escarpment adjacent to a level valley which is cultivated under irrigation. Each village is surrounded by a dense thorn hedge as a defensive measure, and thus the settlements are necessarily as compact as the topography allows.

Each ward has an elected leader, usually one of the oldest men, whose principal function is to allot house sites to individuals. He also has authority to adjudicate in minor disputes within the ward. The houses of close agnatic relatives—a father and his adult sons, or a set of brothers—are often adjacent or at least near one another. However, there are numerous exceptions to this, and it is best described as a tendency rather than a rule. The ward leader may assign a vacant lot to any clan member who needs it, and thus over the generations the different family groups have tended to get somewhat separated and mixed together. In some cases a son prefers to move to a different part of the ward from his father or brothers. At present there is plenty of space in all the villages, and from 10 to 20 per cent of the house sites in various wards are now vacant. This is partly explained by the fact that the thorn hedges are no longer needed for protection and have been mostly cut down, so that people are starting to build houses outside the old village perimeter. It also appears that the population has decreased in recent generations for some reason which I cannot explain.

The clans are exogamous groups, but the villages tend to be endogamous, at least with respect to the first marriages of the women. As a result of these rules, the girls of a clan must marry men of different clans of the same village, and must then live in their husbands' wards. The clansmen draw their wives from other wards of the village. Thus there are numerous bonds of kinship and affinity between all the wards of a village. When a woman is divorced, her remarriage is usually to a man of a different village, and this results in some kinship bonds between villages, but fewer in number than those within a village.

These two functions of regulating residence through control of house sites and regulating marriage through rules of exogamy are the only important functions that a clan serves as a unilineal descent group. The ward, however, serves other functions as a local or neighbourhood group. Thus the young people of a ward gather at the ward plaza nearly every fine evening for dancing and singing. This is often carried out as disciplined practice, for there is keen competition between wards for supremacy in singing. The people of a ward tend to share their milk supply in a communal spirit. Although cattle have recently been introduced in small numbers at two of the villages, the Sonjo traditionally kept only goats and sheep. The limited supplies of milk from these animals are allocated primarily for the use of infants and herd-boys. The adults do not normally consume milk themselves or make butter from it until the needs of these children have been satisfied. This principle of communal sharing within a ward does not, however, apply to other kinds of food.

Sonjo clans are not systematically divided and subdivided into descending orders of lineages in the classical manner of the Nuer and Tallensi. The largest constituent subdivisions of a clan having any corporate existence are small lineage groups of two to three generations depth. The people do not customarily trace their genealogies, and indeed it is uncommon for a person to remember his ancestors by name farther back than his grandparents. The small lineage groups thus tend to be discrete and are not aligned with other similar groups to form larger segments on the basis of genealogical relationships. Hereinafter I shall simply refer to these groups as 'lineages', for there is no other unilineal descent group to which the term could possibly be applied. A Sonjo clan, then, can be described as an aggregate of lineages, all of which recognize the same degree of brotherhood because of their presumed common descent as equivalent segments of the same patrilineal clan, but which are not grouped or aligned into larger lineages of intermediate level. The main task of this paper will be to analyze these small lineages and their mode of attachment to the family estate. We have already noted that they have no obvious existence as territorial or co-operative groups, the village appearing superficially to be comprised of independent households or nuclear families. In order to understand the structure of the lineage we must first know more about their social and ecological setting.

The Villages

The six Sonjo villages are located in a dry tract of northern Tanganyika, a short distance west of Lake Natron and not far from the Kenya border. They are scattered over an area some twenty miles in diameter. Several of the villages are close together, while the most remote village is sixteen miles from its nearest neighbour. The people speak a Bantu language; their total population is about 4,500. This general region is used as grazing land by the pastoral Masai, and hostile relations seem to have prevailed between the two tribes. For protection against Masai raids, the Sonjo villages were encircled with dense hedges of thorn and could only be entered through fortified gates. The Sonjo warriors, who successfully defended their villages, were adept in the use of poisoned arrows, for which the Masai seemed to have a healthy respect. The social institutions of the Sonjo were undoubtedly affected by their proximity to the war-like Masai. Thus, the Sonjo were forced to develop an effective military organization for defence, and it was necessary for them to live in compact, fortified settlements.

Sonjo economy is based upon irrigation agriculture and the raising of goats and sheep. Each village has its own separate irrigation system, fed by water from local streams and springs, and therefore the villages are economically independent and, for the most part, self-sufficient. They are also autonomous political units. The major factor in maintaining the cohesion of the whole tribe is a religious cult shared by all the villages. A second factor is intermarriage between villages which creates kinship bonds among all the villages. The political organization of a village is closely related to its irrigation system. Political authority is in the hands of a hereditary council of elders numbering from sixteen to eighteen members at different villages.

The village council derives its political power largely through its control of irrigation water, and this water control is supported by ritual and mythological sanctions.

The irrigation system of each village is operated as a single co-ordinated unit. The various streams and springs constituting the water sources funnel into a single channel at the head of the valley by which the village is located, and from there the water is distributed to the cultivated plots through a network of furrows and small ditches. The unity of the irrigation system is reflected in the social structure, in which the principle of village unity is strongly stressed. The water is divided among individual users by means of a system of primary and secondary rights. A relatively small number of the wealthier men pay tribute in goats and receive primary rights entitling them to the use of irrigation water for a standard six-hour period during every irrigation cycle. The fields of several owners can be irrigated during one of these six-hour periods. The majority of the men obtain secondary irrigation rights by paying fees to individuals possessing primary rights, this payment usually consisting of an agreed amount of honey or grain. The village council as a group receives the goats paid as water tribute, but these goats are not regarded as personal gain for the council members. The tribute goats are all supposed to be sacrificed in communal rituals, and the meat is distributed to the people of the village.

The council members themselves obtain primary rights to irrigation water without being required to pay any tribute, and this is the greatest economic advantage attached to the position. The adult sons of a council member may share in this advantage, but not usually his brothers. I was able to obtain complete data on council memberships and their clan affiliation at two villages. At Kheri the seventeen council memberships are divided among the four clans of the village in the proportions 5, 4, 4, 4, which is as close as possible to equal representation. This, however, has no great political significance, for at Soyetu the six clans are represented on the eighteen member council as follows: 9, 5, 2, 2, 0, 0. Here there is no semblance of equal representation, and yet the councils at the two villages function in the same manner. The Soyetu clans which lack any council members are not regarded as inferior or weak, the reason being that the clans in any case play no significant political role in the village. The political structure of the village is best visualized as a series of unrelated households or small lineages unified by common interests in the irrigation system and ruled by a relatively impartial village government which draws its strength from control of irrigation water and from the sanctions of a religion that is accepted by everyone.[1]

Work

The population of a village is divided, with respect to economic activities, into several categories on the basis of sex and age differences. Within each category, every individual does more or less the same kind of work. I am excluding from this discussion a small endogamous group of specialists who manufacture iron goods and pottery and who constitute a pariah caste. The priesthood will also be omitted from consideration, as they are not relevant to the problem of this paper. There are no other economic specialists in the society. Among the women of a village, the only sharp age distinction is that which separates married from unmarried women. This distinction pertains not so much to the kind of work they do, but rather to the question of whom they are obliged to work for. Older girls before their marriage apply their labour mainly in helping their mothers in the fields, though a betrothed girl is expected to help her future mother-in-law from time to time. After her marriage a woman is occupied with tilling her husband's fields. For the most part she works alone, or with the help of her daughters if she has any. However, at the beginning of the planting season it is customary for groups of women to form work-parties for the hard work of digging up the soil to prepare seed beds. These groups move from field to field until the fields of all the members are prepared. Some women, however, work alone during the whole agricultural cycle. The women work with digging sticks, which is the only implement used in cultivation. After a woman is too old for field-work she usually depends upon her daughters-in-law for food supplies.

The young boys of a village are assigned the task of herding goats. A goat owner divides his goats into two herds. The

[1] A more detailed description of Sonjo society is given in Gray, 1963.

new born animals and their mothers are kept at the village to be tended and milked. At night they are brought into the house, and during the day they are herded in the vicinity of the village. This work is done by very young boys, as the goats are never out of view from the village. The main herds are kept at pasture camps which may be as far as seven miles from the village. There they are herded by older boys, six or seven being the minimum age at which boys are sent to man the goat camps. These boys spend most of their time at the goat camps for the next few years, sleeping in the sturdy shelters into which the goats are brought at night. A man sends his own sons to herd his goats if he has sons of suitable age, which only happens in a minority of families at any one time. Otherwise he arranges with a neighbour's boy of his ward to take charge of the goats. Thus the herding tends to be done communally by the members of a ward, but there is no strict rule about this and sometimes a boy may be sent to herd goats belonging to a different ward. The provisioning of these herd boys, particularly with milk, as was mentioned earlier, tends to be regarded as a joint responsibility of the whole ward. Cooked food is brought out to the camps every day from the village, often by a boy's father, and whenever possible it includes porridge cooked with milk. The number of available boys is not always sufficient to take care of all the goats, and a few girls may be sent out to supplement the herding force. At these camps, however, an older relative comes to spend the night with the girls.

The herding career of a Sonjo boy comes to an abrupt end with his circumcision sometime between the ages of about ten and sixteen. Shortly after circumcision he is initiated into the grade of junior warrior. The initiation ceremony is performed for the whole tribe every seven years, and thus there is a considerable range in the ages of the initiated boys. The warriors are divided into two grades—junior and senior. At the same time that the younger boys are initiated as junior warriors, the former group of junior warriors are promoted to the grade of senior warriors, and the former senior warriors then leave the warrior force and become 'elders'. Thus a young man spends fourteen years altogether as a warrior of the two grades.

This system of warrior age-grades is not very relevant to our immediate problem, and it will only be necessary to state here that the warriors take very little part in the economic life of the village. Traditionally the warriors were not allowed to marry—though they were usually betrothed while still in the warrior grades, or even while uninitiated boys—but this rule is no longer strictly observed. It is becoming more and more common for young men of the warrior grades to leave home for several years to work at whatever occupation they can find. The wages which they earn constitute virtually the sole source from which money enters the tribe. When a man of senior warrior grade returns home after working for money, he is often able to make a substantial contribution to the family property with his accumulated earnings, and some of these young men are permitted to marry. However, their social position then becomes rather ambiguous, for they must leave the traditional life of a warrior without having yet acquired the status of an elder.

The wage money which a young man brings home is turned over to his father, who assumes the same control over it as over other forms of family property. It is used mainly for paying the head tax imposed by the government upon all adult males. Any money left over is usually invested in goats.

After a man has finished his fourteen years of military service he normally marries and establishes his own household, which in most respects is economically self-contained. His main economic interest from then on is with irrigation matters, for irrigation is the principal concern of the married men of the tribe. The fields require flooding about every two weeks during the growing season, and every man must make arrangements to obtain water without fail during each cycle. This requires frequent negotiations over the payment of fees for secondary irrigation rights, or of tribute to the village council in order to obtain primary rights. Several times a year the men of the village turn out *en masse* at the order of the village council to clean and repair the main furrows. The actual irrigation operations are carried out by the men whose fields are being watered at that time. This is the only labour that men regularly contribute to agriculture. Women take no part in irrigation operations. The married men, on the whole, perform relatively little physical labour and regard themselves primarily as supervisors of the economic activities of their wives and children. They frequently visit the pasture camps to inspect their goats, but the actual herding is done by the boys.

Land

The basic law of ownership decrees that a father retain ultimate rights in his property and in that of his descendants as long as he lives. When he dies these rights pass to his descendants. The application of this law has a strong influence on the structure of the lineage, and my procedure in the remainder of this paper will be to analyse various situations involving lineage property rights.

The principal forms of property are land, goats, crops, beehives, and honey. House sites, as we have seen, are controlled by the clan as a group and are not regarded as personal property. The houses themselves are built and used by their owners and are seldom transferred to different owners. Cultivated land, however, is individually owned and is an important item in inheritance and exchange. Land has agricultural value only if it can be irrigated, for the rainfall is too uncertain to attempt to raise crops without supplementary water. This sharply limits the amount of land available and renders it a relatively scarce and highly regarded form of property. The irrigated area is divided into small plots of which an ordinary family requires at least a half-dozen for its subsistence needs. The individual plots are bounded by irrigation ditches and they are also marked with cornerstones, as the ditches tend to meander from time to time. It is regarded as a very serious offence to move a cornerstone except by agreement with the owners of the adjoining plots.

The land needs of different lineages fluctuate as new generations come to maturity and later split up to form new lineages. In order to adjust to these changing needs, the Sonjo allow land to be transferred from owner to owner, but only under certain specified conditions. Land transfers have more the character of a lease than an outright sale. Land is always paid for with goats. The two men concerned in the transaction come to an agreement as to the amount of the payment. During my visit, this sum ranged from five to fifteen goats for a plot of land, depending on the quality of the plot and the relative scarcity of land at the time. Payment may be made in full at the time of the transfer, or in instalments if that is the agreement. The original owner, however, retains an option to buy back the land (if we regard the transaction as a sale) whenever he needs it for exactly the same price that he received for it; or, stated another way, he may terminate the lease whenever he wishes upon refund of the payment. If payment is by instalments he need only refund the amount already paid to him. This option lasts for the lifetime of the original owner, but is not inherited; when he dies, the new owner then acquires unchallenged title to the land, though he must pay any remaining instalments to the heirs of the dead man. This system of leases and recovery options applies only to land transfers and not to any other form of property exchange.

In order to see how the system operates, let us start with a land owner who has a wife and small children. His land needs at that early stage in his career are minimal, and if he owns land in excess of his needs, he may very likely lease it to other men who require additional land. Another factor limiting the amount of land that it is feasible to keep is the labour available to the owner. In a monogamous family there will be only one woman to work the land for a long period of time, though the labour force will be gradually strengthened as her daughters grow up. The sons have no need for land of their own until they have passed through the warrior age-grades, and while serving as warriors their food is supplied by the whole community rather than their own family. As the time for his son's marriage approaches, the father may start to recover land that he has leased to other men, and he may also acquire additional land through purchase or lease at that time. His own household needs also diminish during this period as he now has fewer children to feed, or perhaps none at all. When the eldest son finally marries and establishes a household of his own, he immediately needs land for his wife to cultivate, and this must be provided by his father, for he has no other means of obtaining land.

As younger sons marry, their father provides them in turn with plots of land, and if there are many sons it may be necessary for him to expend a sizeable proportion of his goat herd in exchange for additional land. The father may also withdraw land from one son and allot it to another if this should be necessary for the maximum welfare of the group. It happens not infrequently that two brothers, or even three, belong to the same age-set and become 'elders' at the same time, for the age spread of an age-set is about seven years. The order of marriage for brothers always follows their age order, and the time space between marriages of age-mate brothers will be determined by the economic resources of the family with respect to land or the ability to obtain it through lease. It may be necessary for the younger of the age-mates to remain a bachelor for several years until his father can provide him with the necessary cultivation plots. In the meanwhile he occupies a kind of transitional social position which might be described as that of a post-graduate warrior. In poorer families the sons often start married life with an absolute minimum of land; such men strive to accumulate goats through their own efforts with which to obtain more land. The father, however, retains ultimate control over the land and other property of his sons no matter how they obtain it.

It might be well to raise the question here as to what forces compel a Sonjo father to sacrifice part of his own resources in order to provide land for his married sons. I cannot satisfactorily answer the question but will comment on it. It is not wholly satisfactory to say that the sons have *rights* to this land and that the father has an *obligation* to provide it, for there are no specific sanctions supporting the rights of the sons; there is no legal procedure to which they can have recourse for securing their claims. A father has the ultimate right of cursing a son and denying him any of the family property. I have no case history of such an affair, but was assured that it happens. Informants assumed that a father would have just cause for taking such drastic action, and failed to give a definite answer to the hypothetical question of whether a father could arbitrarily and unjustly expel a son from the lineage. The plight of a disinherited son is extremely grave, because there is no occupation for a Sonjo man except farming, and for that he requires land which can only be provided by his father. I was told that he would have to go to a different village and seek to be adopted by an older man who had no son. Failing in that, he would offer his services to the Masai and become assimilated to their society.

The problem has different aspects which tend to counterbalance one another. From one viewpoint we see adult men competing for goods and resources, which results in opposition and tensions between them. In some societies these oppositions are particularly prominent, though it may be that some observers overemphasize the father–son tensions through assuming that they must exist in any case as a derivation from a situation of rivalry and tension arising during the son's infancy which they suppose to be universal in human societies; this assumption may lead to neglect of other family processes. These tensions certainly exist in Sonjo families, but they are countered by other tendencies. Thus the members of a Sonjo nuclear family normally take their meals together in their own house, whereas in many village societies of Africa men eat apart from women and children. A young boy receives much of his training and instruction from his father, and relations between them are often companionable. During his many years in the warrior age-grades a boy has very little intimate contact with any members of his family. His father periodically supplies him with a goat or two, but these are consumed communally by the whole age-set and are not regarded as the personal property of the son. After the son marries, the father must share his land with him, and may also have to part with goats and other property in order to lease more land, and he may feel resentment at this. Normally, however, he anticipates and prepares for this economic crisis in advance; this is accepted as the normal course of events, and there is no alternative use for property so attractive that it would tempt a father to withhold from a son the necessary resources for starting a household.

Polygyny, as was explained earlier, is the exception rather than the rule; it is practised only by a few wealthy men, and no man would think of taking a second wife if it meant denying his son the land he needed. The most important incentive for insuring conformity with expectation in this regard is the need for support in old age. The possession of property alone will not provide a man with satisfactory subsistence in his old age, for there is no general market at which food may be regularly obtained in exchange for other goods. The only way for a man to assure himself of comfort and security in his old age is to help his sons establish thriving households of their own. The sons are then obliged to provide food for their aged parents, and since the father still retains control of the lineage property, he has the means of compelling this aid.

Other Forms of Property

The principal Sonjo crops are sorghum, millet, pigeon peas, beans, and sweet potatoes. Sweet potatoes are consumed within a short time after being dug up, but the grain crops are stored for as long as a year, or until the next crop is harvested. In general, each household stores and consumes its own crop, but there is a certain amount of sharing among the members of a lineage. Newly-married couples may need help for a year or two until their own domestic economy is efficiently organized. The lineage head directs this distribution, and if need be he exercises control over the food crops as well as other forms of property. Food production seldom exceeds consumption needs to any great extent, but any surpluses that are accumulated may be exchanged for other goods, usually with the motive of increasing the family holdings in goats. Grain is not used for making beer, but only for food. The wives normally manage the food stores, but the ownership resides with the men of the lineage. In case of divorce, the food supplies remain in the house with the husband; the wife takes none of it with her when she leaves.

Goats occupy a crucial position in the economy of a Sonjo village. They represent an important source of subsistence goods—meat, milk, and skins—and they can be exchanged in suitable circumstances for almost any other kind of goods. Goats are not generally slaughtered for meat except on ceremonial occasions, but these are numerous. Meat obtained from communal sacrifices is distributed through the village without regard for kinship or lineage distinctions. At non-religious ceremonies, such as village festivals, betrothals, or weddings, goats may be privately slaughtered, but the meat is often distributed beyond the kinship group to neighbours. Meat is not regarded as an item of economic exchange since most of it is provided through redistribution of the meat of animals collected by the village council as water tribute or fines, and sacrificed on behalf of the whole village. Milk also (as was explained earlier) is distributed communally, but usually within a ward.

Because of the fact that the subsistence goods derived from goats tend to be distributed on a communal basis rather than being consumed exclusively by the owner, the personal possession of goats does not have the same meaning as cultivated plots. A young married man has no immediate need for goats and no means of taking care of them until his own sons are old enough for herding duties. He is then allotted a portion of the family herd by his father, and when his brothers reach this stage in life they too are given shares of goats. These particular goats are earmarked, figuratively speaking, to be inherited by those sons when the lineage head dies, and for the sons the most important thing is the anticipation of this inheritance. In the meanwhile they are entrusted with herding the goats and are entitled to use the milk, but they cannot dispose of any of the goats through slaughter or exchange without their father's permission. An elderly father who has no young son to stay at his goat camp may divide up his entire herd among his married sons, keeping only a few female animals at his house for their milk. When he requires goats to use as water tribute or for exchange purposes he demands them from his sons. He may alter the distribution of goats among his sons any time he wishes. In short, he retains essential control over the goats of his lineage even though they are in possession of his sons.

Beehives constitute another form of property that is highly regarded. The manufacture of a good beehive entails considerable labour. First a hardwood tree is felled in the forest and the trunk is cut with an axe into proper lengths. These logs are then split and hollowed out with an adze. The heavy beehives must be transported to a suitable location and hoisted high in a tree. A good beehive is very durable and may be exchanged for several goats, though an inferior one made of soft wood has a much lower exchange equivalence. Sonjo men try to accumulate as many hives as possible, either by making them or acquiring them in exchange for goats or other goods. Some men have as many as one hundred beehives, while every man has at least ten. The work of placing beehives in trees and gathering the honey is a difficult and dangerous occupation and is generally done by the younger adults. Therefore a father usually divides his hives among his sons soon after they are married, and thereafter he is freed from the hazardous work of tending them.

Beehives are not prized because of their intrinsic value but because they provide the means of obtaining honey, which is the basic ingredient in the only fermented drink used by the Sonjo—a kind of hydromel or honey beer. A little honey is eaten as a sweet, mostly by women and children, but the great bulk of it is used for making beer. Now the Sonjo law governing beer making is simple and explicit: no man is allowed to make beer while his father is still alive. This law automatically gives the lineage head a monopoly on beer making, and it also gives him control over the consumption of beer. All the honey his sons collect from their beehives must be turned over to him. He may use this honey for acquiring more goats if they are needed, for there is always a demand for honey. The prevailing exchange rate during my field-work was about three gallons of honey for a goat, and by this means a man may acquire quite a few goats in a season when his hives are fruitful, but at the cost of depriving himself of the pleasure of drinking beer. Otherwise he uses the honey for making beer, and wealthy men may part with some of their goats to purchase additional honey. Beer is used as an oblation on various ritual occasions, but mostly it is drunk for pleasure. It adds to a man's prestige and general popularity to be able to offer beer to his friends. Young married men are not entirely prohibited from drinking, but they depend on the generosity of their elders for their supplies of beer and are expected to show moderation. Heavy drinking is a prerogative of older men, and the older a man is the more he can drink with propriety.

Thus we find that the Sonjo lineage is sharply structured in terms of property rights. The lineage is unified in its attachment to the family estate comprising all major forms of property. The lineage head retains ultimate control of the estate as long as he lives, while his descendants are granted limited rights to the use of the property, the circumstances in which these rights are exercised differing for the different forms of property. The descendants also have valid expectations of inheriting full control of a fair share of the property when the lineage head dies. These property-based relationships, however, involve relatively little overt interaction or co-operation among the members of a lineage, so that a student would hardly be able to discern the existence of the lineage group just through visual observation of village activities over a limited period of time.

Women and Children

Sonjo marriage involves the payment of a comparatively high bride-price; in 1955 the amount ranged from sixty to 300 goats. The bride-price is paid at the time of betrothal, and it must be paid in full within two months of the agreement, never in instalments. After payment, the bride-price is never refunded, even though the woman should die or prove to be an unsatisfactory wife.[1] For a Sonjo family of ordinary means, the payment of bride-price strains the resources of the group more than any other event in its economic history. Fortunately the bride-price payment does not as a rule coincide with the need to provide a newly-married son with plots of land; the betrothal usually takes place much earlier than marriage, so that the two economic crises can be dealt with separately.

Because of the early age of betrothal, it is common for the grandfather of the betrothed boy to be still living when the bride-price must be collected for payment. In that case, he has control of all the live stock of the lineage and directs the manner in which it will be collected. About half the bride-price goats are taken from those in the possession of the boy's father, if the family resources are that extensive; the rest are taken from the boy's uncles and from the residual herd of his grandfather, the lineage head. If the grandfather is dead, the uncles are still obliged to contribute to their nephew's bride-price needs, and this is the most important economic obligation existing among a set of brothers whose father is dead. In return, the uncles receive a share of the bride-price that is paid to their brother for his daughter. Since girls are betrothed younger than boys, the incoming bride-price for daughters is usually already in hand and may be used in paying bride-price for sons' wives. If

[1] For a fuller account of Sonjo marriage customs and bride-price, see Gray, 1960.

every father had exactly the same number of daughters as sons, the receipts and payments of bride-price would tend to balance. However, the sex ratio of offspring is often unequal: where daughters predominate there is no difficulty in producing bride-price for sons, but where sons predominate it may be necessary to part with other property, such as land or beehives, in order to collect enough goats for bride-price.

Divorce is always followed immediately by the remarriage of the divorced wife, and the new husband pays bride-price directly to the first husband. Sometimes two men exchange wives, but usually the second husband pays with goats for the divorced wife. If there are children they remain with their mother and are adopted by her new husband, but he must pay an additional four goats for each child. Such children are assimilated to the lineage and clan of their stepfather. This is only one of several methods of adoption. A widow sometimes returns to her natal homestead, and her children are then adopted by her father or a brother. Every man wants to have at least one son to inherit his property and look after him in old age. If he has no son of his own and no other means of obtaining one, he may adopt an unrelated boy of a poor family, sometimes when the boy is quite old. There is no discrimination against adopted sons in matters of property rights. The Sonjo do not stress the biological bond in the father–son relationship. A man has the rights of a father in all children belonging to his wife, regardless of who their genitor was, and also in any children he may adopt. On the other hand, he must fulfil the obligations of a father towards his children.

Inheritance and Succession

We have already seen how the property of a lineage is divided by the lineage head among his sons as they marry wives. Although their rights to this property are not absolute, the sons normally expect to permanently retain the property allotted to them, except for that which they may be required to surrender for general lineage needs. The sons are not given equal shares, but the eldest son receives more than his brothers. One of the sons, quite often the youngest, is usually appointed by the father before his death for the task of burying him, and with this honour the appointed son receives an extra share of goats. When the lineage head dies, his married sons become full owners of the property already in their possession, and the residual property of the father is divided among them, with the eldest son receiving the largest share and the others sharing more or less equally. With this realignment of property rights, the original lineage goes out of existence as a group of men attached to a single estate. It is transformed into a set of new lineages, with a son of the dead man occupying the apex of each lineage. The normal Sonjo lineage is a living lineage in the sense that not only the descendants but also the apical member is living; when he dies, the hierarchical form of the lineage is dissolved but reappears, often in multiple form, a generation lower down. The brothers who had previously been joint members of a lineage group, bound together by mutual interests in the lineage property and by common dependence upon their father, now become heads of independent lineages. Their grandchildren may not even know that they were brothers, as the genealogical knowledge of a Sonjo seldom extends beyond his grandparents. There is no need for wider knowledge, for only in exceptional circumstances would there exist economic rights or obligations between an individual and his grandfather's brothers.

The only special social position of any economic significance in ordinary Sonjo clans is that of membership in the village council. There are two possible candidates for succession to this position. The eldest son, if he is a mature adult, automatically succeeds his father provided no other arrangements had been previously made. The successor is installed as a council member in an initiation ceremony performed within a week or two after the death of his father. He is required to pay an initiation fee equivalent to seven goats. At that time the next youngest brother has the option of contributing one goat towards the initiation fee, and with that act he establishes his right to succeed to the position in place of the new member's eldest son. When a council member dies and his sons are not yet married, he is then succeeded by a brother. The position must be filled immediately and cannot be left empty while a son grows up, for the council is not allowed to meet and transact business unless all positions of membership are filled.

After he is once installed a member has a permanent hold on the position and is succeeded by his own heir: the position does not revert to the line of a previous incumbent. The economic advantages of the position are largely confined to the immediate lineage of the member and do not extend to the lineages of his brothers.

In return for the bride-price which his lineage pays, a man obtains certain exclusive rights in his wife—rights to her children, her labour in the fields and home, and sexual access to her. These rights may be exercised by her husband or transferred to another man in exchange for property. Thus a wife is dealt with in some ways as a form of property, but with this important difference: that the lineage head has no control over his sons' wives and cannot dispose of them against their husbands' wishes. If a husband sells his wife to another man, the transaction is his personal affair; he keeps the bride-price for himself, because this is his means of obtaining a new wife. If a husband dies, his right in his wife are usually inherited by a brother, not, as with other forms of property, by a son. The reason for this is that a son could not take his own mother as a wife.

The character of the rights in a wife alter with time, and the actual arrangements for the disposal of a widow depend on this variable factor. If the widow is still young, most of the rights in her are transferred to the heir; he may live with her as a wife or divorce her and accept bride-price from another man. In the latter case, the bride-price is fixed at exactly thirty goats, which may be only a fraction of the bride-price that would be paid if she were not a widow. The explanation for this is a mystical belief of the Sonjo that when a widow dies her ghost will rejoin the ghost of her dead first husband in the spirit world. The second man who marries her has full rights in her as a wife in this world, but will lose possession of her ghost in the spirit world. Thus it is relatively unprofitable to divorce a brother's widow, and one effect of this myth and the associated rule of bride-price may be to encourage an heir to retain the widow so that her children will remain within the line of descent of their father and grandfather.

If the dead husband has no brothers who are capable of inheriting the widow and taking her as a wife, she may return with her children to the home of her father or a brother, where the children are adopted into the lineage of these men. The actual procedure which is followed in these cases may depend upon the relative wealth and resources of the two groups, and also upon the desire for children of the different men concerned. Where the father dies leaving considerable property, his widow and surviving children are very likely to stay with his lineage so that the children may inherit his property in due time. On the other hand, if the dead man leaves little property, then if the widow's brother wants to adopt the children, they will probably be attached to his lineage. If there is an adult married son at the time of the father's death, he may temporarily act as head of the family until his brothers grow up. In such a case, the rights in the widow as a wife are regarded as having expired, and she lives as a dependent at the homestead of her adult son.

Allomorphic Forms of the Lineage

I have now presented in outline the basic rules governing authority and property rights among patrilineal relatives, and have described some of the situations in which these rules are applied. These property rights do not remain constant but from time to time undergo change and realignment. The composition of a lineage is altered with the occurrence of births and deaths. Marriages of sons result in major redistributions of property rights within the lineage. In short, the structure of a lineage is constantly being transformed in response to the shifting pattern of events in time. Any portrayal of a Sonjo lineage, unless it is to be very superficial, must take into account the time dimension of its existence, for the property-based relations revealing its structure at any given time can only be understood by reference to antecedent events and anticipations of future events.

In studying the lineages as structures in time, we find that different lineages are constituted of different patterns of occurrences. The rules and principles of lineage structure I take to be constant, but operating through different sequences of events and economic circumstances they produce different constellations of roles and relationships within the lineage.

These can be called allomorphic forms of the lineage structure. Of the different variations which are possible, I shall discuss five which appear to be the most basic. For each of these allomorphic forms I attempt to illustrate the crucial stages in the lineage process with a series of geometric models. In each case I arbitrarily choose a starting point for describing one of the recurrent patterns which any lineage may follow at certain times and under certain circumstances. These are segments which for analytical purposes are cut out from what is actually a continuous process.

One lineage situation which will not be specifically analysed is that of a man who has no heir. This may occur—though rarely, because of the ease of adoption—but is regarded as an abnormality by the Sonjo; such a man would have a disagreeable time in old age, as he would have no sons or grandsons to provide for his subsistence needs. In my simplified lineage models, no distinction is made between natural sons, stepsons, or adopted sons. These distinctions make little difference to the lineage structure, because sons of all kinds are dealt with economically in the same way. Polygynous families are not specifically dealt with in these models. They would add some minor variations in form, but in most respects a father treats the sons of different wives alike.

In the lineage diagrams that follow, an outline triangle represents a living male. A solid triangle stands for a male who dies before the next phase in the lineage process. A broken-line triangle indicates the position of a person who remains of structural significance in the lineage after his death. The different allomorphic forms are given descriptive titles and designated by capital letters (A to E). The phases in each lineage process are numbered, but phases bearing the same number in different lineages are not necessarily comparable.

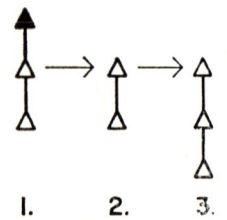

Fig. A. Single line lineage.

SONJO LINEAGE STRUCTURE AND PROPERTY

A. Single-line lineage

It is common practice in constructing generalized patrilineal kinship diagrams to draw in two sons for each father. For most purposes this is a useful device, and I make use of it in the remaining diagrams. Demographically, however, it is unrealistic, for it implies that the population of the group doubles itself every generation, assuming an equal sex ratio, and it is doubtful if this actually occurs in any native African society. At any rate, single son families are not uncommon among the Sonjo, and if this is repeated in two generations we get the situation illustrated in the diagram. The lineage property passes undivided from generation to generation. A single-line lineage is vulnerable in one respect: it becomes extinct if any member fails to have a son. I think this seldom happens among the Sonjo, because a man lacking a natural son attempts to adopt a son or obtain a stepson through marrying a woman with a son.

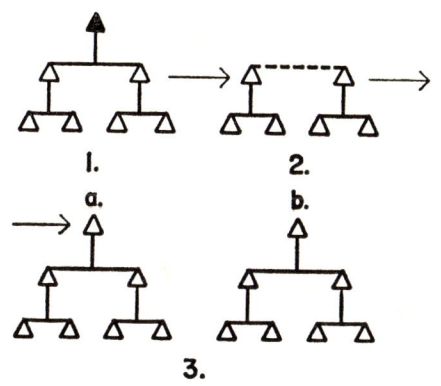

Fig. B. Bifurcating lineage.

B. Bifurcating lineage

In this structure, each lineage member has two sons so that the lineage is constantly bifurcating. If any male member has more than two sons, the process of perpetuating the lineage remains basically the same, so that this diagram serves adequately for several subtypes. In the general account of property arrangements given earlier in the paper, I have assumed this form of the lineage to be normal because it most clearly exemplifies the basic rules. In phase 1, the lineage head is still living, while his sons have established households of their own as evidenced by the fact that they have sons. They are already in possession of most of the property which they will ultimately inherit, but have not yet gained full control of it. When the lineage head dies, each son then acquires full control of his share of the lineage property. In phase 2, the brothers are connected in the diagram with a broken line, indicating a potentially active relationship between the two lineages. If bride-price for their sons' fiancées had not been paid before the old lineage head died, the brothers must help one another to meet this expense. Furthermore, if one of the brothers should die in this phase, the surviving brother would enter into special relations with his nephews, the dead man's surviving sons. (This situation will be dealt with in the next allomorphic form.) When the brothers acquire grandsons, as in phase 3, there is no longer any property-based bond between them, and they are now heads of fully independent lineages. Should either one of them die, his sons are in position to take control of the property and carry on the lineage. This form of the lineage is cyclical in character; the cycle ends with the identical structural group it started with.

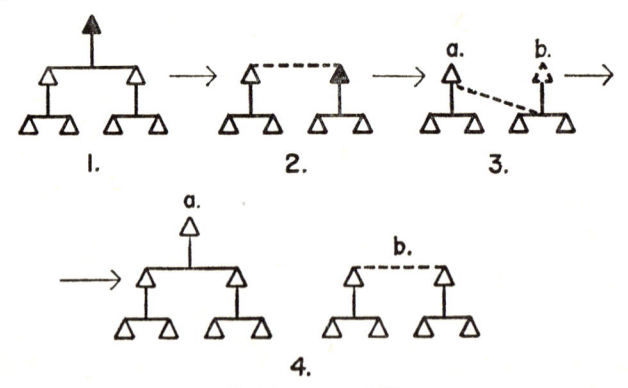

FIG. C. Truncated lineage.

C. *Truncated lineage*

The first phase of this lineage is the same as in the previous situation (form B), but in phase 2, one of the brothers dies.

SONJO LINEAGE STRUCTURE AND PROPERTY

The important point to note here is that each of the two brothers, having established a household of his own before the death of the lineage head, had come into full control of his own share of the property. This property division remains unaltered when one of the brothers dies so long as he has heirs who in time will be capable of inheriting this property. If this estate amounts to very much, in all probability the widow will continue to till her husband's fields. She may live as the wife of her brother-in-law (the dead man's brother), or she may live alone with her children. In the case of a poor family with a small estate, it may be advantageous for the widow and her children, and also for her brother-in-law, if she is divorced and married to another man in more affluent circumstances. In this case, the young sons forfeit their claim to their father's property, but they will acquire the rights of sons in their stepfather's property. In the diagram it is assumed that the widow and her sons remain at their own homestead.

In phase 2, the relationship between the two brothers, which was only a potential relationship in the previous example, becomes active with the death of one of the brothers. The surviving brother assumes some aspects of the role of father to his dead brother's sons. This is indicated by the broken line between them in phase 3. He does not, however, have the full powers of a lineage head with respect to the property rights of his nephews. The property of the original lineage had already been divided between the two brothers and this division stands unchanged so long as heirs remain in both lineages. The two nephews, being still immature, are unable to exercise their rights in their dead father's property, and these rights are in this phase only potential. The control of this property still resides, so to speak, with their dead father, and I have indicated this by drawing him as a broken-line triangle in phase 3, lineage *b*. As a living group this lineage lacks a head; for that reason I have named this type of structure a *truncated lineage*. It could also be called an *immature lineage*. In his partial role as father, the surviving brother acts as trustee for the property of the truncated lineage. He administers it and allocates the property for use up to the time his nephews establish households; then he must turn it over to them. This is one of the few situations in which a dead person retains a position of significance in the social structure.

More commonly a man disappears from the structure after his death in the sense that thereafter there is no occasion to refer to him for the purpose of determining property rights. This is one reason that the Sonjo pay so little attention to genealogies.

When the two brothers of the immature lineage are in position to receive their inheritance, through marrying and establishing their own households, the bond between the two lineages (*a* and *b*) disappears. Three new lineages then appear: lineage *a* becomes completely autonomous, while the two brothers of lineage *b* remain related to one another with a potential bond. Their situation is now that of phase 2 in the bifurcating lineage (form B).

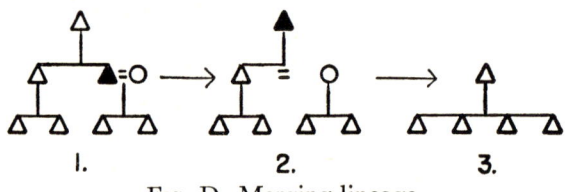

FIG. D. Merging lineage.

D. Merging lineage

The structural process that I call a *merging lineage* is precipitated, as in the case of the truncated lineage, by a crucial death. Again the death concerns one of the sons of the lineage head— a man who has established a household and has immature sons of his own. His death, however, takes place before that of his father, the lineage head, and this order of deaths gives to the subsequent development of the lineage a different form. Although the dead man had already been allotted a share of the lineage property for his subsistence use, the ultimate control of this property resided with the lineage head, who was still alive at his son's death. A Sonjo lineage is most clearly delineated in terms of the transfer of property from father to sons in lineal descent down through the generations. What is actually transferred from father to son is full control of the property. Partial rights in property, or potential control of it, cannot be so transferred, and this was all that the dead man possessed. His limited rights are not transferred to his sons. In such a situation the lineage head redistributes the rights in this property to heirs who are able to exercise the rights—in the lineage diagrammed in form D, to the surviving brother.

Phase 2 of the diagram shows the intermediate process. The surviving brother inherits his dead brother's widow, and assumes the role of father in relation to the surviving sons. At this point he is not yet a lineage head himself. The actual household arrangements may be little altered, with the widow living on in her house together with her children, and continuing to cultivate all or some of the plots of land she had previously cultivated. However, when the lineage head dies, his sole surviving son inherits full control of all the lineage property, and all members of the lineage then come under him as their head. The sons of his dead brother are now fully assimilated to his lineage, and there will be no further distinction, with respect to property rights, between them and his own sons. This is indicated in phase 3 of the diagram. The two potentially diverging branches of the original lineage are now merged as a single lineage group, hence the term *merging* for this lineage form.

This particular process can perhaps be better understood if we recall that immature children remain attached to their mother, and thus belong to the lineage of her legal husband. In accordance with this rule, the surviving brother in the situation under discussion obtains his brother's children by virtue of inheriting their mother. Or, to state it another way, the sons obtain rights in the lineage property because their mother is a wife of a lineage member. This latter interpretation offers the advantage of accounting for the situation in which the surviving brother divorces the widow and accepts bride-price from another man instead of taking her for his wife. In that case the children go with their mother, break their ties with the lineage of their birth, and become members of their stepfather's lineage.

E. Dead-head lineage

The last form of the lineage to be considered here differs from the others in that the lineage is asymmetrical in phase 1. The lineage head has two sons, but only one of them is married and head of a household; the other son is still immature and does

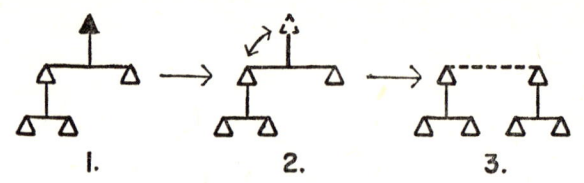

FIG. E. Dead-head lineage.

not yet require the use of any lineage property. He has potential rights to a share of this property, just like his brother, but unlike the latter he is not now exercising partial rights in it. When the lineage head dies, his eldest son takes charge of all the lineage property and administers it up to the time his younger brother marries; the latter then claims his share of the property.

This situation could be interpreted, as it often is in ethnographic accounts, by saying the older brother succeeds his father as head of the lineage, and this would be a fairly accurate description of the lineage during the interim in which the younger son (or sons) remained immature with respect to property needs and rights. I think a more adequate interpretation is that indicated in diagram E. Although the lineage head is dead, he retains his position in the social structure because the circumstances of his sons are such that the lineage property cannot be decisively and finally divided; it must be administered as a single unit for the time being, just as it would be if the lineage head were still living. The older brother now has two roles to play. He is head of his own independent lineage, and he also has to undertake certain duties attached to the position of his dead father, this position being indicated in phase 2 of the diagram by a broken-line triangle. This form can be called a *dead-head lineage*, because the position of lineage head still exists although the real lineage head is dead.

Thus the elder son does not really succeed to his father's position as lineage head, for he loses all control of his brother's property when the latter establishes a household; whereas a real lineage head retains control of all lineage property throughout his whole life. In phase 3, the two brothers are on an equal footing with respect to property rights, each head of an independent lineage, but they still have mutual responsibilities, as indicated by the broken line between them.

Conclusion

In this paper I have focused on a small component unit of Sonjo society—the patrilineal lineage—and have attempted to demonstrate the basic structure of this unit by analysing its mode of attachment to the family estate. In this concluding section I shall inquire as to whether any broader structural principles are exemplified in these property-based lineage groups, and then consider briefly the relation of the patrilineages to the total society.

Radcliffe-Brown, in a study of kinship systems in societies with unilineal descent groups,[1] formulated several 'structural principles' which are utilized in these societies. Two of these principles are relevant in the interpretation of the Sonjo lineage, namely, the principles of the unity of the sibling group and the unity of the lineage group. Sonjo kinship terms give evidence of the unity of the sibling group, since children apply the term 'father' to their own father and all his brothers as well, suggesting that these male siblings are regarded as a unified group. The unity of the lineage group, however, is not apparent in the kinship terminology, for the Sonjo kinship system is not of the Omaha type in which this principle is stressed.[2] When we consider property arrangements, the principle of lineage unity is seen to predominate, and sibling unity then appears mainly as a derivative principle. The property of a lineage is essentially a unified estate, which is tentatively divided among the lineage members, but which is redistributed from time to time as the composition and structure of the lineage change. The economic unity of the lineage is particularly clear when viewed from outside the lineage, for in the economic exchange system of a Sonjo village the social units concerned in the exchange of goods are lineages, represented in the exchange transactions by their lineage heads. In an economic context, the unity of the sibling group is seen clearly only among brothers whose father is still living. Their unity results from the fact that they are all members of the same lineage, and are united in common dependence upon their father.

[1] Radcliffe-Brown, 1952, pp. 49-89.

[2] For an analysis of the Omaha system of kinship terminology, see Radcliffe-Brown, 1952, pp. 70-75.

The interdependence of brothers who are not members of the same lineage group is of a tenuous and temporary kind. Two such instances were discussed. When the head of an immature lineage dies (as in allomorphic form C, phase 2) his brother temporarily takes over his role as property administrator. His duties are essentially those of a trustee; when the dead man's sons establish their own household they gain full control of their property and the trusteeship ends. The other case concerned the relations between adult and immature brothers whose father was dead (allomorphic form E, phase 2). This situation is best interpreted by considering that the original lineage is temporarily reconstituted with an adult brother taking the role of his dead father. This role comes to an end as soon as the immature brother becomes economically adult. Thus, while there is unity among Sonjo brothers, this unity is not so much the manifestation of a primary principle as the indirect result of the principle of lineage unity.

Another structural principle which is responsible in large measure for the distinctive form of the Sonjo lineage—one which Radcliffe-Brown did not specifically mention so far as I know—is that of the pre-eminence of the father with respect to property rights in the family. This might be called the principle of *economic gerontocracy*, since it is always the oldest man in a lineage who possesses control of the property, and therefore authority. One of the effects of this principle is in limiting the size of the lineage group. All major forms of property are owned and utilized within the lineage. The only important economic resource not controlled by the lineage is irrigation water, which can hardly be considered a form of property. Water is dealt with in some respects as a public utility with ultimate ownership vested in the political community as a whole. The village council controls and distributes the water, and individuals obtain limited rights to the use of water through paying fees or tribute which funnel upwards to the village council; this group, representing the village government, accepts the tribute on behalf of the whole village. Property, however, is dealt with largely inside the lineage group, all of whose members (including the apical member) must be living; this limits the size of the group to three generations except in rare instances. One reason for the absence of any larger lineage groupings or clan segments is that larger groups of this kind would have no economic functions in the present organization of the society. The small size of the Sonjo lineage may explain the fact that the society does not use the Omaha type kinship terminology, for that system is usually applied where the lineage groups are of wider span.

Like most African societies, the Sonjo practise a cult of ancestral spirits. This, however, constitutes but a minor element in the ritual life of the society, being overshadowed by a cult which is centred upon a tribal god. An adult normally sacrifices only to his own dead father; once a year he makes a libation of beer on the ancestor's grave. Ritual recognition is occasionally given to a more remote ancestor, sometimes a matrilateral ancestor, when there is reason of a mystical nature to believe that the ancestral spirit desires a libation. The important point is that the ancestral rites are normally carried out in the individual households and concern only a small group of immediate descendants. The clan as a whole never performs ancestral rites, nor any large subdivision of it. Thus the Sonjo ancestral cult tends to be limited to the lineage group which is primarily defined by property rights.

As was explained early in the paper, a Sonjo village is divided into wards, each occupied by a patrilineal clan, which is an exogamous unit and has the further function of controlling residence within the ward. The clan has no other significant functions. Nearly all political power and authority is concentrated in the village council, which is essentially independent of the clans. The basic economic activities of production and consumption of subsistence goods are carried out in separate households, and on superficial observation the ward appears to be composed as an aggregate of these individual households. As we have seen, however, there is one intermediate grouping —the lineage, comprised of several such households attached to a single estate—which, although it is not normally a co-operative unit of production and consumption, is the only group concerned in the control and transfer of property. The lineage is also the unit involved in the exchange system of a village.

A unilineal descent group, if it is to be a social unit of any vigour, must certainly have functions of a political and/or economic character. Ritual functions may also serve to give corporate existence to a unilineal group, but I think this is usually secondary to political or economic functions. Among the Sonjo, both political power and the important ritual functions are attached to the village as a whole, and not to any constituent unilineal descent groups. Economic functions, on the other hand, are mainly confined to the households and small lineages. The clans are left with only minimal functions, and these are not, strictly speaking, either political or economic in character. I suggest that the village—the basic Sonjo community—has an unusually pressing need for solidarity and unity because of its irrigation-based ecology and also the ever-present danger of attack by external enemies. The centralization of political power and ritual functions tends to foster this necessary unity. Control of economic resources in a community of this kind might conceivably also be centralized. But if this control is to be delegated to constituent sub-units of the community, it is in the interests of village unity that the smallest possible units, such as the Sonjo lineage, be entrusted with this economic control, thereby minimizing the danger of disruptive competition and discord between groups which are large enough to challenge the authority of the constituted village government.

REFERENCES

GRAY, R. F. 1960. 'Sonjo Bride-Price and the Question of African "Wife Purchase"', *American Anthropologist*, 62, pp. 34–57.
—— 1963. *The Sonjo of Tanganyika*, Oxford University Press.
RADCLIFFE-BROWN, A. R. 1952. *Structure and Function in Primitive Society*, London, Cohen and West. (Glencoe, Illinois, The Free Press).

INDEX

Adultery, 78, 102
Affines, brother-in-law, 137, 139, 145
　father-in-law/son-in-law, 43, 127, 145, 164
　mother-in-law, 128-9, 134, 178, 237
Age-group system, 198, 215, 238-9, 242
Agriculture, 35, 64, 85, 91-92, 118-19, 237, 244
　shifting, 84
Ancestral cult, 26, 37, 41, 50, 53, 67, 157, 158, 187-8, 203, 206, 214-15, 224, 261
　primacy of dead father in, 41, 203, 215
Anthropology, and biology, 10-11
　and history, 9-10
　and psychology, 13
Arusha, 13-16, 197-229
　counsellor, 199, 211
　elders, 198, 215-16
　lineage system, 199, 204, 224-7
　political system, 199
　population, 14, 197

Bachelors' house, 39-40, 232
Barnes, 126
Beehives, 245-6
Betrothal, childhood, 47, 239, 247
Blood-pacts, 124, 147
Bridewealth, 17-19, 28, 39, 40, 43, 44, 46 ff., 64, 68, 70, 78, 97 ff., 126-7, 164, 247
　and economic exchange, 17-18, 30

　economic aspect not paramount, 167
Bride price, *see* Bridewealth
Brothers, relations between, 78, 224-7, 254 ff, 259-60
　see also House
Brother-in-law, *see* Affines
Burling, 18
Bwamba, 24

Cash crops, 35, 45, 46, 47, 64, 118, 133, 201
Cattle, *see* Livestock
Christianity, effects of, 50, 99, 161, 172, 185, 186
Curse, 67, 91, 95, 107, 242

Descent theory, 22 ff.
Divorce, 98, 100, 115, 167, 171-2, 175, 234, 244, 248, 257
Domestic domain, 2, 3
Domestic group, 124 ff.
Durkheim, 6, 13

Elopement, 47-48, 75, 78, 81
Estate, family, 4-7, 200, 220-22, 246, 259
Estate, lineage, 93
Evans-Pritchard, 2, 9, 13, 26
Exogamy, 63, 66, 96, 233

Fallers, 37
Family, definition of, 2-4, 125
　compound, 202, 210-17
　extended, 37, 41, 42, 57 ff, 69, 76-78, 125

263

INDEX

Family, (cont.)
  nuclear, 3, 38, 39, 41, 68–69, 73–76, 101 ff, 125, 150, 200–1, 204–10
  and ecology, 5
Family estate, see Estate, family
Father, authority of, 39 ff, 48, 55, 77–78, 80 ff, 123, 210–17
Fatherhood, sociological, 163, 248
Father-in-law, see Affines
Father-son relations, 40, 46 ff, 52, 55, 67, 77, 104 ff, 123, 127, 131, 141, 144, 178, 210 ff.
Feud, 67
Fishing, 92
Forest reserve, 54, 197
Fortes, 2, 3, 7, 9, 126
  and Evans-Pritchard, 13

Goats, see Livestock
Goody, 2
Guardianship, 57, 72, 76, 218 ff
Gusii, 16, 18, 28, 63–82
  lineage system, 63, 66, 67, 68
  political system, 63
  population, 63, 64
  settlement pattern, 65–66

Half-brothers, 42, 79–80
History and anthropology, 9–10
Homestead, 66–68, 124, 159, 177, 183 ff, 200, 204 ff.
Honey, 246
House, 27, 67, 70–71, 79, 135, 165 ff, 173 ff, 201, 207, 225
Houses, debts between, 70, 77, 176
Hunting, 29, 88, 92, 106
Husband-wife relations, 44, 46, 75–76, 77, 101 ff, 140 ff, 173

Incest, 96, 150
Inheritance, 6, 41, 55, 72, 94, 121, 135 ff, 180 ff, 203, 217 ff, 245, 248–9
Initiation, 69, 238
Irrigation, 26, 235–6, 239, 240, 260

Jie, 1, 28

Joking relationship, 107

Kilindi, see Shambala, royal clan
Kipsigis, 63

Labour migration, 74, 94, 129, 159, 171, 179, 239
Land, allocation to sons, 40, 128, 213, 241
  control over more important than over cattle, 49, 214
  dispersal of lineage holdings of, 54
  fragmentation, 73, 82
  pledges and leases, 49, 60, 92, 123, 132, 240 ff.
  pioneered, 14, 49, 53, 64, 65, 200, 211–12
  and population, 13–16
  rights of wife in, 38–39, 45–46, 68–69, 127, 174, 176
  sales, 25, 49, 51, 60, 64, 92, 123, 132, 227
  shortage, 54, 64, 197
  tenancy, 201, 207, 209, 212
  unallocated reserve, 45, 46, 140, 201
Leach, 8, 9, 12, 126, 164
Levirate, 21, 42, 56 ff, 71, 163
Levy and Fallers, 3
Lineage system, theory of, 22 ff.
Livestock, 64, 118, 160, 198, 237–8, 244
  control over, 16–19, 41, 49, 93, 130–1, 140, 142, 175, 245
Lobedu, 16, 17–18, 28, 155–95
  lineage system, 157–9
  local group, 188 ff.
  political system, 155–6, 182–3
  queen's wives, 156, 161
  totem groups, 157, 188
Lugbara, 12–13
Lunda, 83, 86

Marriage, 96 ff, 121, 122, 162 ff, 193–5
  preferences, 96, 100, 113, 122, 150, 165, 166 ff, 176, 185 ff.

264

INDEX

Marriage, (cont.)
   residence at, 38, 69, 85, 87, 109, 126, 201
   woman to woman, 165, 180
Masai, 63, 65, 198, 235, 243
Mayer, 63, 64, 67
Middleton, 12
Monomotapa, 155
Mother-in-law, see Affines
Mother's brother, 45, 52, 53, 102, 105, 109, 126, 127, 179, 183
Mourning ceremonies, 41
Murdock, 3, 126

Nadel, 8
Ndembu, 12
Nuer, 26

Omaha kinship system, 259
Orphans, 20-22

Pedi, 172
Political system, 36-37, 51
Polygyny, 26-27, 38, 68, 73 ff, 99, 105, 125, 149, 231, 243
   sororal, 99

Raiding, cattle, 74
Radcliffe-Brown, 6, 8, 259
Ritual, see Ancestral cult
   medicines, 87, 90, 97, 123

Shambala, 15, 35-61
   lineage system, 37, 42, 44, 60
   political system, 36-37
   population, 35-36
   royal clan, 51
   villages, 38, 53
Shell money, 29, 93
Slaves, 103
Social structure, theory of, 7 ff.
Son-in-law, see Affines
Sonjo, 14-15, 16, 17, 231-62
   lineage system, 233, 246-7, 249, 251 ff.
   political system, 235-7, 249-50, 261

population, 235
specialist caste, 237
village, 231, 235-7
ward, 232-4
Sororate, 99, 163
Suku, 28-32, 83-116
   elders, 90-91, 94
   matrilineage system, 85, 86 ff, 113
   patrilineages, 31, 106-8, 110-12
   political system, 83, 84, 88, 90, 95
   population, 83
   villages, 84

Taita, 16, 117-53
   elders, 123, 146 ff.
   house-type, 124
   lineage system, 120 ff.
   population, 118
   settlement pattern, 119 ff.
   woman's rights in property, 151 ff
Turkana, 1, 28
Turner, 12

Ultimogeniture, 202
Usambara Mts., 35

Vogt, 10

Wambugwe, 22
Widows, 20-22, 42, 71, 109, 135, 137, 139, 182, 207, 248, 250
Widow-inheritance, 21
Wife, husband's authority over, 44, 46, 250-1
   see also Husband-wife relations
Wine, 92
Winter, 24
Witchcraft, 44, 90, 91, 159
Wives, co-, 75, 76-77, 105-6, 124, 173-4, 183
Work-teams, 128, 161, 237

Yaka, 83-84, 86

Zulu, 155, 163, 174